FLOWERS
IN THE
GUTTER

FLOWERS
IN THE
GUTTER

**THE TRUE STORY OF
THE EDELWEISS PIRATES,
TEENAGERS WHO RESISTED
THE NAZIS**

K. R. GADDY

DUTTON BOOKS

Dutton Books
An imprint of Penguin Random House LLC, New York

Copyright © 2020 by K. R. Gaddy

Visit us online at penguinrandomhouse.com

LIBRARY OF CONGRESS CATALOGING-IN-PUBLICATION DATA IS AVAILABLE

Printed in the United States of America

ISBN 9780525555414

5th Printing

Book design by Kate Renner
Text set in Walbaum MT Std

To Heather Heyer,
and all the young people
who have risked their lives
fighting Fascism

Table of Contents

NOTES ON SOURCES

This is a work of nonfiction, which means everything is true. The dialogue and descriptions of events are taken from the memoirs written by Jean Jülich, Fritz Theilen, and Gertrud Koch (née Kühlem); the Gestapo archives; and oral histories with surviving Edelweiss Pirates and their family members, mostly done in the early 2000s, but some done as early as the 1970s.

Even though this is nonfiction, real truth is hard to come by, especially during times of war and trauma. A memory can be as faulty as the archival records of the Gestapo. For example, Gertrud "Mucki" Koch writes in her memoir and says in interviews that she spent nine months at the Brauweiler prison from the winter of 1942 into 1943, but the Gestapo records say that she was only there for nineteen days. It doesn't mean that she is lying—intentionally or unintentionally. Being in prison is traumatic, and what she went through most certainly left her with post-traumatic stress.

The Gestapo records are also biased. We know that confessions were coerced—either by physically beating prisoners or by psychologically tormenting them with promises of release or threats against family members. The Gestapo had a particular worldview that they were trying to prove with each report, arrest, and interrogation. I tried to verify the memories of people present with the Gestapo record and have indicated where there are discrepancies in the text and in endnotes.

Names of people are rendered as fully and accurately as possible when they first appear in the book. Many of the Pirates and their associates went by nicknames or aliases. Often sources don't include real names or surnames of important figures. If a person is introduced by a first name or a nickname only, it means I was unable to confirm a full name. I also chose to keep misspellings of names as they appear in the original Gestapo documents.

Descriptions of places are taken from the memoirs and from my own visits to the locations that the Pirates mention, from the parks in Cologne to where they hiked, to Ellern, to Simmern, to the EL-DE House, to Brauweiler. All of the translations are my own.

Edelweiss are faithful.
—Motto of the Edelweiss Pirates

✿ ✿ ✿

We weren't academics.
We were from the gutter.
—Jean Jülich

TEEN-AGE LADS TELL OF ANTI-NAZI "PIRATES"

KASSEL, Germany, May 8, 1945 (United Press)

Two 17-year-old German boys, who flirted with death by aiding the Allies, proudly told today of the "Edelweiss pirates"—The only anti-Nazi undercover organization yet found in the Reich.

The Edelweiss gang, a loosely-knit network of teen-age lads, banded together to sabotage the Nazis in every way possible—destroying material and beating up party members. They wore a gaudy five and ten cent store flower pin underneath their left lapel as their only identification.

"We had up to twenty in the band in Kassel, but our strength was unsteady since members were drafted when they got older," said baby-faced Hermann Bannenberg, who has three brothers in the Wehrmacht, one a United States war prisoner.

The Edelweiss organization apparently is an almost leaderless nation-wide gang of boys that took its name from the Alpine flower. Members usually are children of working class parents. In most cases, the "pirates" worked without the knowledge of their families.

Although the group was strongly anti-Nazi, it made no attempt to get in touch with American units.

"We hated the Hitler youths. When they started parading around, giving orders and beating up people, we wanted to show them we weren't taking their orders," said Heinz Johannes, whose father is an American war prisoner and whose brother was killed on the eastern front.

"The Nazis made us work from ten to twelve hours daily and after that we were supposed to work for the party," said Hermann. "We didn't even have time to sleep."

The two "pirates" worked in a munitions plant that used about 500 slave laborers.

PERSONS OF INTEREST

The Edelweiss Club—Cologne

- Gertrud "Mucki" Kühlem, b. June 1, 1924
- Gustav "Jus" Hahn
- "The Mountain Climber"
- "The Guardian"
- Willi "Banjo Willi" Alt
- Käthe "Lolli" Thelen, b. May 31, 1925
- "Ellie"
- Ernst, called "Ätz"
- Eduard "Sepp" Lindner

The Edelweiss Club—Düsseldorf and Wuppertal

- Franz "Hadschi" Nobis and his brother, known as "Ali"
- Charlotte "Pepita" Kreuz
- Gunter "Pico" Goldbeck

The Edelweiss Pirates—Beethoven Park

- Jean "Schang" Jülich, b. April 18, 1929
- Ferdinand "Fän" Steingass, b. November 8, 1928

The Navajos

- Fritz Theilen, b. September 27, 1927
- Hans and Maria

Taku Bunker Pirates

- Fritz Theilen
- Gerhard
- Helmut
- Hermann
- Emil

The Edelweiss Pirates—Ehrenfeld

- Bartholomäus "Barthel" Schink, b. November 27, 1927
- Franz "Bubbes" Rheinberger, b. February 22, 1927
- Günther "Büb" Schwarz, b. August 26, 1928
- Hans "Lang" Balzer, b. January 29, 1928
- Wolfgang Schwarz, b. August 25, 1926
- Gustav Bermel, b. August 11, 1927
- Adolf "Dolfes" Schütz, b. January 3, 1926
- Johann "Little Hans" Müller, b. January 29, 1928
- "Keunz"

The Ehrenfeld Group

- Hans "Bomben-Hans" Steinbrück, b. April 12, 1921
- Cäcilie "Cilly" Serve, b. April 17, 1919
- Auguste "Gustel" Spitzley, b. October 3, 1910
- Peter "Black Peter" Hüppeler, b. January 9, 1913
- Josef "Jupp" Moll, b. July 17, 1903
- Else Salm, b. November 3, 1923
- Roland Lorent, b. March 12, 1920
- Wilhelm Kratz, b. January 6, 1902
- Johann Krausen, b. August 8, 1887
- Heinz " Uncle Hein" Kratina, b. January 15, 1906

Prologue
Late 1942

Gertud Kühlem — aka Mucki

Mucki stepped out of her apartment onto narrow Boisserée Street. On Fridays, she had a standing date with her friends in the *Volksgarten*. Wearing leather loafers that probably needed to be replaced and white socks hanging around her ankles, Mucki made her way toward the park.

The mile between her house and the meeting spot was surrounded by destruction. Some buildings had roofs that looked like they had been removed by giants, others were just walls, or piles of brick and stone. Sides of buildings had black scorch marks streaming up around the windows. Trees with massive trunks had been snapped in half like matchsticks. Mucki was lucky the apartment where she and her mom lived still stood.

As she moved through the city, she knew at any moment a siren could go off, signaling another attack, and she'd have to duck into the nearest air-raid shelter.

In the end, though, her trip was uneventful and when she arrived, the Volksgarten was empty. Before the war, the park would have been filled with people on a late afternoon like this: a mom out walking with her kids, a couple sitting on the bank of the pond whispering to each other, little dogs prancing around on their leashes. None of that happened anymore. The park was all but deserted, and that was how Mucki and her friends liked it.

This time, the Mountain Climber, Banjo Willi, Ätz, and Jus showed up. Sometimes there were more people, sometimes fewer. Usually they talked, hung out, and sang songs—all stuff that would have been typical for *bündische* youth groups in the early 1930s in Germany. Lately, they'd been planning some stuff they didn't want anyone to hear about.

"Listen up, I know what we should do next," said the Mountain Climber. He was skinny, with sinewy arms and legs, and on hikes, he was always the first to the top of a rock, or you'd find him up in a tree somewhere. He was newer to the group, but really committed, and really trustworthy.

"And what have you been thinking about?" Mucki asked.

The Mountain Climber looked around the park to make sure no one was lingering.

"I thought that we could fill a backpack full of flyers, I'd throw it on my back, and make my way to the Cologne Central Station," he said.

He was crazy. They all knew that the main train station in Cologne was crawling with activity. Every day, the military used the trains to ship German soldiers to battle, and to send Jews, leftists, homosexuals, and anyone else they didn't like to a *KZ*—a concentration camp. Every day, supplies and food arrived, along with forced laborers from Poland or occupied territories in the East. The Mountain Climber wanted to take the flyers and make them flutter down like dead leaves in an autumn wind, to show people that there was a resistance.

"That's a way for you to find yourself in a camp," Mucki said. She knew this was not the plan of a person merely intent on surviving the war. She knew well that the punishment for this kind of thing could be jail, possible torture, concentration camps; her father had experienced it.

Ätz agreed with Mucki and added, "I don't want to see my neck in the noose yet. I have a lot to live for." Ätz was tall and scrawny too, and generally slanted his body in a way that made it seem like he didn't really care. But right now, he cared, and he wasn't convinced by the Mountain Climber's plans.

"Do you think I want to play a game with my own life?" the Mountain Climber asked. "Look, we only take calculated risks, and we make the decision together. But at least hear my plan.

"I know the train station. In the middle is the big glass dome, and all around it are ladders for the workers, for when, you know, the electricity isn't right or they have to fix some other problem. I thought that I could climb one of those ladders with the backpack and just let all of the flyers go. Two or three of you keep watch below and I come back down. You'll all be safe. And then we get out of there."

"You realize that's really risky, right?" said Jus, who hadn't said a word yet. Jus and Mucki trusted each other; they'd been friends a long time.

"But what do we have to lose?" Mucki started to change her mind. "Yeah, we could get caught. But we could have also got caught when we graffitied buildings around town. We've done a lot and people haven't noticed. We need something to motivate us and something that reaches more people. I say we go for it."

"Do we have a choice? We're already in it pretty deep." Ätz seemed to change his mind too. "I'm in."

"There can't be a worse fate than Hitler," Banjo Willi said.

"It'll go well," Jus said. Sometimes, he knew exactly what to say. "So far we haven't had any big problems; why would it be any different this time?"

The long August evening had almost come to an end, and dusk started to settle in. They hurried up and made their plan before dark, when they had to be home. They gave themselves two weeks.

Mucki took on the duty of getting the flyers. She made her way to a small street in Pesch, on the northern border of the Cologne city limits.

Jus had introduced them to a man with a small print shop in his basement. He normally printed church newsletters for Catholic congregations in the area. He knew that what they were doing was dangerous. If he got busted with the flyers, he wouldn't get off easy. Creating the material was one of the riskier parts of the operation. He couldn't play dumb like someone just carrying the flyers. So he had one stipulation: no one could know his name. They called him Tom.

"Hello, Mucki," Tom said as she entered the shop. He didn't know her real name either.

Tom printed his church bulletins in a large font so that the older readers in the congregation could easily make out the words. This was perfect for the flyers since no one would dare pick one up for fear of being carried away by the police. Even looking too long at one on the ground could be risky. People would need to be able to read the messages as they walked by.

"The flyers are under the canvas bags," Tom said. "Goodbye." He had said ten words to Mucki and that was all he would say. The less they knew about each other the better. The less Tom knew about the operation the better.

She grabbed the package and put it under the padding of a baby stroller she'd borrowed from a neighbor. She arranged pillows and a blanket inside the blue stroller to make it look like a child was snuggled inside. She gripped the handles as she quickly pushed it down the street.

The big wheels bounced over cobblestones and destroyed sidewalks. Her heart must have been pounding as she pushed the stroller through the outskirts of Cologne. What if someone wants to peek at the sleeping angel? What if someone questions the fact that she was eighteen with a baby? How would she cover? What would she say?

In the end, people around her didn't pay her any attention. They had their own worries. Would another air raid come tonight? Would their rations last until the end of the week? Could they get a new coat for winter? Had their neighbor overheard that private conversation? People in Cologne were known to mind their own business, and since the beginning of the war, that was even more true.

Finally, Mucki made it to a specific pile of rubble in Cologne. To someone who didn't know the city, that's what it looked like: one of the thousands of piles of stones, mortar, wood, and bricks that used to be a home, office, school, or church in the city. This heap had been a Catholic church. The steeple had fallen; the bells had been taken off to be melted down for the war long ago. This was the perfect place to stash the flyers until they needed them.

Mucki looked around to make sure no one had followed her. Quickly, she placed the flyers in a hole and put stones on top. Her job was done. Tomorrow, the Mountain Climber would begin his. He'd be risking his life. They'd all be risking their lives.

The Central Train Station was a magnificent building, almost as grand as the nearby Cologne Cathedral. The main entrance was under a semicircular glass window, probably forty feet in diameter. The glass dome arched just behind that window. This was where the Mountain Climber would ascend. At the busiest time of the evening, he'd drop the flyers.

At 5:00 p.m., they were all there: the Mountain Climber; Mucki; Jus; Ätz; Banjo Willi; and the Guardian, who hadn't been at the park. They gathered near a ladder inside, and the flow of rush-hour traffic moved around them. They had been visiting the train station daily around this time to figure out the layout,

Cologne Central Train Station, 1890.

the best ladder for the Mountain Climber to use, and whether it really was safe.

No one seemed to be paying them any attention. People just moved about as normal.

One of the group winked. That was the sign. Time to start.

The Guardian and Ätz went to two corner positions, Jus made his way to a platform across the tracks from where they had met, and Mucki and Banjo Willi stayed by the ladder, disguised as a couple in love. Willi slipped his hands around Mucki's waist and pressed his nose closer to her neck. Mucki's arms were around Willi's back. Their embrace was code: arms around each other's waists meant "hold." They looked over each other's shoulders and could whisper without looking suspicious.

They looked for men in uniforms, taking in a 360-degree view of the station. Mucki looked over Willi's shoulder and whispered in his ear. Was everyone in place? He looked over her shoulder and whispered back. Were any men in uniforms nearby? They whispered again. This was as clear as it was ever going to be.

The Mountain Climber was keeping an eye on them near the ladder, waiting for the sign to begin. They whispered one last time. Slowly, Mucki raised her arms from Willi's waist up to his shoulders, and he did the same.

This was the sign. Like a cat, the Mountain Climber bounded to the top of the ladder, his long, chestnut-brown hair bouncing as he climbed.

Mucki and Willi scanned the station. No one seemed to have noticed. No expressions changed. No one looked up. No one was screaming about the boy on the ladder. No police. No Gestapo. This was good. With each passing moment, the risk increased.

All at once, paper sailed down from the ceiling.

The words on Edelweiss Pirate flyers tended to be simple, the messages clear. They were printed with phrases like:

PUT AN END TO THE BROWN-SHIRTED HORDE!

SOLDIERS, LAY DOWN YOUR WEAPONS!

WE PERISH IN THIS MISERY. THIS WORLD IS NO LONGER OUR WORLD. WE HAVE TO FIGHT FOR ANOTHER WORLD OR WE WILL PERISH, WE WILL PERISH IN THIS MISERY.

Before the first flyer hit the floor of the train station, the lovers had let go of each other, the Mountain Climber was down on the ground, and the others were safe too. The whole action had probably taken under fifteen minutes. They didn't stick around. They all moved quickly in different directions away from the train station.

The next day, the newspaper had the story: the action at the train station had been committed by a group of criminals.

Jean Jülich — aka Schang

Jean had first noticed them in Manderscheider Square, right next to the school he went to. The square was like a little park lined with trees, central to the neighborhood. Jean had seen the guys and girls hanging out there almost every afternoon. The first thing he noticed was the way they looked. The guys had long hair, not the militantly short cuts he was used to seeing in the Hitler Youth. They also wore short leather pants, checkered shirts, handkerchiefs around their necks, and big wristbands with the Edelweiss flower. Kids weren't supposed to be meeting in groups outside the Hitler Youth. The Gestapo had started calling all of these groups wild and unauthorized, and generally referred to them as *bündische*.

The next thing Jean noticed was that they played guitars and sang songs he'd never heard before. One of the ones Jean liked the best went:

> *If you come to Hamburg to the seaman's bar "At the Blue*
> *   Shark"*
> *You'll see the vagabond drinking, the man called Tall*
> *   Hein.*
> *He'll tell you about Charly and Jimmy, the grasslands*
> *   and prairies,*
> *And sometimes he'll tell you about Shanghai, where they*
> *   met, all three.*
> *It was in Shanghai, in the Ohio Bar,*
> *The three hitchhikers met, who'd traveled around the*
> *   world.*
> *Jim Johnny, he came from Frisco, from Hamburg came*
> *   Tall Hein,*
> *And Charly, the little Frenchman, made the suggestion:*
> *Let's all hitchhike together.*

He liked all the songs: Russian songs; American cowboy songs; and German traditional songs. Jean thought that the blatantly anti-Jewish songs he had to sing in the Hitler Youth were awful. These guys and girls at Manderscheider Square were different from the Hitler Youth, and that was cool. Their outfits looked different from what other people were wearing; the songs they sang were different. They didn't have a leader; they just got to joke around and do what they wanted. They didn't look uptight and weren't into authority.

Jean's friend Ferdinand Steingass had started talking to the kids, who called themselves "Edelweiss Pirates." Like Jean, Ferdinand was also raised by his grandma and grandpa, and also hated that he had to join the Hitler Youth. Ferdinand was outspoken and gregarious, and Jean shouldn't have been surprised that he went up and made friends with a group of kids he didn't know. He wanted freedom like he thought Americans had freedom.

Soon Jean was hanging out with the Edelweiss Pirates in the evenings too. Most of the people in the group went by nicknames, and Jean chose Schang, from Shanghai in his favorite song, and Ferdinand went by Fän. When Jean joined the Pirates, he was still thirteen, and the others he hung out with were pretty young too. For them, going on hikes and trips and just being with one another were the most important things.

The Manderscheider Square Edelweiss Pirates didn't plan political activities like other groups; they mostly sang songs and complained about the Hitler Youth and the Nazis. The actions that they took ended up being more like pranks. The only thing they had in mind was to irritate the Nazis.

One man that annoyed them was a newspaper-stand owner in the neighborhood. Every time they wanted to buy a comic with stories about Native Americans, he'd suggest that they get something about war heroes instead, so they'd be better soldiers for Nazi Germany. Jean and his friends thought the glorification of war in those books was gross. They knew firsthand what bombs falling on your neighbors really looked like. They were convinced that this man was an actual Nazi, who had turned people in for not having proper Nazis beliefs. That was annoying.

One night in the late fall of 1942, when the newspaper stand had closed for the day, they attached a metal chain to the stand, which was just sitting on the side of the road. They attached the other end of the chain to the last wagon of the streetcar, stopped nearby. When the trolley started up again, the chain clanked and became taut, and then pulled the newsstand down the trolley tracks.

Jean burst out laughing. He was proud that he could do some damage to an old Nazi jerk.

Fritz Theilen — aka Fritz de Plaat

The fact that Fritz had once been thrown out of the Hitler Youth when he was thirteen years old still haunted him two years later. Now he had a job at the Ford factory, but someone had told a supervisor that Fritz had been kicked out, and he was called into the office of the foreman, also a leader of the Hitler Youth.

"Listen here, we know that you are in the Edelweiss Pirates. What do you say to that?" Someone said they'd seen Fritz hanging out in the Volksgarten with the Pirates. This was true, but he couldn't admit it. The Gestapo was on high alert for bündische youth group activities. Fritz tried to come up with an excuse, to downplay the whole thing and pretend like it wasn't a big deal. It didn't work at all.

"You know that it is forbidden! That it's against the law. But we couldn't expect better from you, you've always made problems, and we are done with you, you can count on that." The foreman's words and his spit struck Fritz's face.

He knew this sort of tirade was coming.

"As a traitor against the Führer, the country, and the people, the process will be short, and we have our methods."

With the last sentence, a hand smacked across Fritz's face. Fritz's body stiffened instinctively, but he didn't have time to react. He fell backward. Those were the methods.

"To be an apprentice at Ford is a privilege for a German boy, and you will be out of here if you act with so little discipline again. You are not bearable for the German people."

Fritz scurried out of the room. He could hear the foreman and his supervisor laughing behind him. This was just one more reason why he hated the Nazis and loved hanging out with his friends, the Edelweiss Pirates.

Part One
1932–1938

"She will be the one who has to deal with the consequences of this. She needs to understand."

Cologne, 1932

The year is 1932, and you can learn a lot about the city of Cologne by standing on the Hohenzollern Bridge, which connects the west side of city with the east. Look to the west and you'll see the seven-hundred-year-old *Kölner Dom*, or Cologne Cathedral. Almost anywhere you are in the city, you can see the five-hundred-foot-tall spires of the Catholic church piercing the sky. From the bridge, you can also see its flying buttresses, arches, ornate stonework, and stained-glass windows—a perfect example of High Gothic architecture. Cologne is mostly Catholic, and Catholicism permeates daily life and culture. During the days before Lent, these streets fill for *Karneval*, with people dressed up in costumes and parades of floats that wind up from the old town near the Cathedral to the *Neumarkt*. Cradling this center of the city is ring of parks called the Green Belt. The parks are an urban oasis, with little reservoirs and lakes, tiny forests, and a series of forts built just over a century earlier at the end of the Napoleonic Wars.

Look down from the bridge and the Rhine River flows beneath you. South—upstream on the river—leads to castles, forests, and a wine-growing region that has invited romantic notions of the outdoors for generations. For about thirty years, various iterations of unaffiliated youth groups hiked and camped in these green spaces. Before the First World War, the groups were called *Wandervogel*, a peer-led movement that developed into groups called *bündische Jugend* in the 1920s and early 1930s.

Look east and you'll see the Deutz neighborhood, with the new *Kölner Messe* convention hall, where trade shows and meetings are held in an expansive brick building with a clocktower that looks over the Rhine.

While people, cars, and trains move across the bridge daily, one thing that doesn't cross the bridge is military troops. On the Deutz side, you might see a tank, but as part of the Treaty of Versailles, which brought an end to the First World War thirteen years earlier, those tanks are not allowed to cross this bridge. The land that borders France, Belgium, and the Netherlands is a demilitarized zone.

The Rhine flows north, and you may see barges and ships transporting goods to the Netherlands and North Sea. The Rhine Valley is an industrial region, and to the north and south, east and west are factories. In 1931, the Ford Motor Company opened a plant in Cologne to build cars and trucks for the European market. But there are also manufacturing plants and factories of all kinds, and these are the places where people in Cologne work, if they can find work.

Germany's Weimar Constitution promised to bring democracy and a new German republic after the country was destroyed in the First World War, but Germany has been overcome by economic problems and political instability. The Treaty of Versailles also made Germany pay 33 billion* US dollars for damages caused by the war, and in 1921, the first payment alone put the country's economy into a tailspin. In 1929, the Great Depression caused more turmoil, and by early 1932, half of the workforce in Germany is unemployed or underemployed. In Cologne, men stand around during the day, looking and hoping for work. Your dad might have work at a factory this week, but they might not need him the week after that. Apartment buildings are in disrepair. In some sections of the city, your family and two other families would be packed into a single apartment. You could be lucky enough to have running water, but have to use a common toilet in the hall. Some buildings still have only an outhouse in the courtyard.

Throughout German cities, politicians promise to make things better and change Germany's fortunes. Cologne is no different. Cologne's mayor is Konrad Adenauer, a member of the Centre Party,

---

* Over $400 billion in today's money.

a moderate Catholic party popular in Cologne. But the three other parties popular in Cologne are not moderate; they're on either end of the political spectrum. On the liberal side, the Socialist Party (SPD) wants more rights for workers, and more employment. It still has strong membership in Cologne although they have been losing support since 1930. After the Depression worsened and politics became more radical, more people across Germany and in Cologne started voting for the Communist Party (KPD), farther to the left than the SPD. The KPD wants Germany to be like the Soviet Union, where personal property, and therefore inequity, vanish, at least in theory. But even though both left-leaning parties agree on some things, they can't agree enough to work together. The third party, the National Socialist Democratic Workers Party (NSDAP) might sound like they agree with workers and Socialists, and even democracy, but they are actually on the far right side of the political spectrum. This is Adolf Hitler's party, better known as the Nazis.

None of these parties have a majority, and all the parties are having trouble finding enough common ground to build a coalition and work together. Throughout the late 1920s and early 1930s, Parliament dissolves multiple times and new elections are held, some parties gain votes, some lose, and sometimes all parties lose votes because people are tired of politics. From all sides you hear the same comments: That party will take away your freedom. This party will get you a job. This party will bring us into the future. That party will only cause more instability.

In 1932, the NSDAP can't quite win the support of working-class Cologne and doesn't have a majority on the national level, but people are voting for them at an increasing rate. They believe that Hitler can make the country better and stronger, and in 1932, the Nazis have the plurality of the vote nationally, and the most seats in the parliament.

It's important to note exactly what a political party means for an individual and a family in Cologne—and Germany—in this period. The political parties are more than just who your parents vote for on election day; they are a way of life, a part of your day-to-day identity. Your parents go to meetings and rallies. They read the newspapers and magazines put out by their political party. Maybe your dad is a member of the paramilitary group that provides protection for the party. You are a member of the youth organization, like the Young Communist League of Germany or the Hitler Youth.

In the summer of 1932, armed clashes and street fights erupt constantly between the paramilitary arms of the Nazis and the Communists. In Cologne, the Neumarkt is a typical European market square during the day, busy with people selling produce and waiting to catch the streetcars. Kids run around among the stalls. But at night the market is also the marching ground of young men in brown shirts and tall black boots. The men are members of the Nazi Party's paramilitary groups, called the SA and the SS. The SA is the *Sturmabteilung*, the brown-clad paramilitary group that provides protection for the party, and the SS is the *Schutzstaffel*, another protection unit within the SA.

The KPD's paramilitary group has been banned since 1929, and the SA and SS were briefly banned in 1932, but none of those bans seem to matter, and as Nazi support grows, so does the number of street fights between members of the left and right.

If you are five, six, or seven years old and standing on the bridge in Cologne, you don't know about the nuances of politics—even adults don't know what's going on behind closed doors in the capital, Berlin. Sometimes they don't care. They went to war in 1914 and came home to a broken country that still hasn't been fixed. You do know that your whole life has existed in that aftermath: dads who don't have jobs, people upset when your mother has a job, not enough money to buy food, fights in the street. And even if you don't understand, you have the feeling that life is getting worse; life is getting scarier.

1 — Gertrud

Dusk settled into dark over the Cologne skyline. On a broad street in a nice neighborhood of the city, Gertrud Kühlem—no one called her Mucki yet—heard a knock at her apartment door. She peeked into the kitchen, and in the dull yellow light of a petroleum lamp, her father leaned over and gave her mother a kiss.

"We won't be alone anymore," he said.

They had been expecting that knock. Almost every night, Gertrud would watch as a stream of her parent's friends drifted into their spacious kitchen. Chairs filled up around the large wooden table, and dark brown beer bottles and white porcelain coffee cups filled the table. As far back as Gertrud could remember, the adults would talk about politics, but joke and laugh too. By the end of 1932, Gertrud noticed almost all the talk was politics, no laughing. She had turned eight that summer, and her parents let her stay in the kitchen. Words whirled around Gertrud as she sat in the corner, trying to parse what she heard: President of the Reich, monarchist, Weimar Republic, Social Democrat, National Socialist, SA, SS, Nazi, Fascist, Communist.

She knew her parents were Communists. On days when her father was particularly proud of his party, he'd hang a red flag with a yellow star and hammer and sickle in the middle from the window. He was a trained welder, who supported unions and wanted a better world for workers.

The people who came to the apartment were also Communists. That night, a friend named Franz said that the behavior of the SA was scary, but still seemed mild. "How will it escalate?" he asked.

His girlfriend, Ilse, looked worried. "Don't you want to send your daughter out?" she asked Gertrud's mom. "We shouldn't be talking about this in front of kids."

"No, she stays here," said her father. "She will be the one who has to deal with the consequences of this. She needs to understand."

Gertrud didn't understand a lot of what they were talking about, but she did see that the world could be better than it was. Their family was lucky to have a big apartment in a nice neighborhood on the edge of the *Innenstadt*, or Center City. In other sections of Cologne, some apartment buildings looked like they were about to collapse. On the street, men stood around during the day, looking and hoping for work. Those who could sing or play the accordion played whatever tunes they knew and hoped for spare change to be thrown into their cups.

How such people lived and how to make it better was what the Communists talked about.

"All people on earth should have the same rights."

"People are poor and they don't have work. Inflation has destroyed the country."

"When Hitler comes to power, they will say, 'Oh, Hitler is good; he's brought us jobs, and the kids have food to eat again.'"

"People won't realize he's abusing us, at least not at first."

Gertrud knew her father hated Adolf Hitler, the leader of the National Socialists—the Nazis. "He will be a catastrophe for Germany. He is a criminal," he told her once.

Gertrud had also heard the Nazis called Brownshirts, the SA, and the SS. These men hated the Communists, and sometimes the Communists went to the Neumarkt to confront the Nazis. This particular night, her parents had decided to stay in rather than go to the Neumarkt.

There was hard knock at the door of Gertrud's apartment that stopped the conversation. Gertrud's father disappeared into the vestibule and reappeared with another comrade, a man named Walter. Blood obscured Walter's face.

Walter had been at the Neumarkt.

"He was an especially brutal SA man," Walter said as he slumped down on a chair in the kitchen.

Gertrud's mother grabbed a bottle of antiseptic and cotton bandages. Her work at the pharmacy helped in situations like these. As she cleaned Walter's wounds, his whole being—from teeth to fists—stayed clenched, his body ready to fight.

Around him, the conversation came back to Hitler, the Nazis, and what they should do next.

2 — Fritz

Fritz Theilen strained his ears to hear what was going on in the next room. The voices from the cramped kitchen were audible, but hushed. Fritz was sitting in the bedroom of the apartment, where he and his parents had their beds. The apartment was just two rooms. His parents couldn't afford a bigger place since his dad was constantly in and out of a job depending on whether the Ford factory needed him or not, and he didn't earn very much when he did have a job. His father and uncle had inherited the house from Fritz's grandparents, so his whole extended family lived in the four-story building in the Ehrenfeld neighborhood. Though they couldn't often afford to buy meat, Fritz regularly smelled sausages cooking in his uncle's butcher shop on the first floor. Fritz knew that others in the neighborhood couldn't afford the meat either; they paid on credit, waiting until the end of the week when they got a paycheck to give his uncle money.

In the bedroom, Fritz was waiting for the voices in the kitchen to get louder, which they invariably did, so he could overhear what the adults were talking about. His parents were members of the Social Democratic Party, and his dad's friends would come over to the apartment, go into the kitchen, and close the door. Fritz's mother would shuttle him and the other kids who had come over into the bedroom, where they were expected to play. But that was hard to do when they knew secrets were being discussed in the next room. Fritz desperately wanted to know what was going on.

He knew that politics were important, and there seemed to be news every day, and not good news. He knew that around his neighborhood, "Nazi" was almost like a curse word. You weren't supposed to say it, and you definitely weren't supposed to be one. He remembered there had once been a banner that was strung up across Venloer Street, the main street in the neighborhood. He was too young to read the words at the time, but the banner said EHRENFELD STAYS RED, a phrase people said in the neighborhood. It meant that they were Communist and Socialist party members, and had no plans to support the Nazis. He had also seen fights in the streets of Ehrenfeld between the leftists and the Nazis. He didn't hear very much from his parents about what was going on or why these fights were happening, but the hunger, unemployment, and discord didn't seem to be getting any better.

He also knew his parents thought that the Nazis would bring war to Germany again. When the voices in the kitchen got louder, Fritz could tell that the parents were scared.

Fritz was cleaning up in the basement with his dad when he heard the sound. The *boom-boom-boom* was faint at first, and too rhythmic and constant to be someone hammering. The sound got closer and louder. Then he could hear notes, rising and falling: the blasts from brass instruments melded with men's voices in a strong chorus. Fritz and his dad ran up the stairs and outside to see what was going on.

Nazis march in front of Cologne City Hall after the takeover of power, March 13, 1933.

Though he was only five and a half, he had already seen his neighbors rally together to protest the Nazi Party. And protests against hunger and unemployment were among Fritz's first memories. But this sounded more like a victory parade than a protest march.

Fritz and his dad ran out onto the street. The sky was starting to get dark on the short January day. When their eyes adjusted, they saw the men approaching. The brown and black came closer, feet in strict sync. Their right arms were outstretched like they'd never bend again. Their static faces turned toward their right shoulders, sternly looking into the distance. They moved forward in straight lines like an organized swarm of bees. They were Nazis, and they were celebrating that their leader, Adolf Hitler, had come to power.

Suddenly, a metallic clang erupted from somewhere above Fritz. Then, a low whistle, followed by a deafening crash of metal against the pavement. A faint slosh of something spilling. Another crash, somewhere farther off.

A funnel of brightness from a police searchlight shot to the top an apartment building. Someone was up there, rolling full trash cans and throwing potted plants off the roof. The light moved from building to building, trying to spot the culprit.

Over the next days, Fritz saw groups of eight or ten men in Nazi uniforms making their way into apartment buildings and houses, wandering through the streets, looking for Communists and Socialists to arrest.

3 — Gertrud

The streets of the Innenstadt looked different now. Fewer and fewer windows had the little red flags like the one that Gertrud's father put out. In their place were other red flags, with a large white circle and the notorious broken black cross of the Nazi Party, the swastika. On the bridges that crossed the Rhine River—including the Hohenzollern—Nazi flags fluttered in the wind. Over the buildings in the inner city, they draped on old stone. And on the Cathedral, high above the city, a Nazi flag hung from the Gothic arches.

Gertrud cried when Hitler was appointed Chancellor of Germany on January 30, 1933. She cried for the murmurings she heard on the street: "The Communists have to be taken care of. They are standing in our way." She cried for the headlines she saw in Cologne's Nazi newspaper, the *Westdeutscher Beobachter,* that declared the "Eradication of the Marxists"—another word for Communists. A catastrophe was coming; she could feel it.

At the end of February, the Reichstag parliament building in Berlin caught fire. The Nazis quickly attributed the fire to a Communist plot. Gertrud's father told her he thought the Nazis had just blamed Communists so they could round up people who did not agree with Nazis and say that it was to protect the people.

She was eight and a half, and her dad wanted her to know what was happening. He told her how his friends were pulled out of their beds in the middle of the night and thrown into the basement cells of the Gestapo, the secret state police. The Gestapo was above the law, tasked by Hitler to find those who committed treason, sabotage, and other crimes against the government. They decided how strictly to enforce laws, and could arrest someone for listening to foreign radio, or speaking ill of the Nazis, or simply because a neighbor claimed that you did any of those things.

Her dad didn't need to tell her that the Gestapo tortured their prisoners; she had seen the friends who came to her apartment with broken and bloody faces and bodies covered in bruises. People who had come and gone from her apartment as long as she had been alive were being beaten for no other reason than that their views did not align with the Nazis.

"It's only going to get harder for us," said a man named Karl as he sat in Gertrud's family's kitchen, now a makeshift clinic. His words were barely audible from his swollen face and lips. Spread out on the table were bottles of different shapes and sizes, filled with tinctures and medicines. Gertrud helped as her mom cleaned and bandaged wounds.

"The Nazis do nothing but lie," Gertrud's mom replied. "You can't just accept that. Everyone has to be able to say what they believe."

But voicing the wrong opinion was cause for arrest.

4 — Jean

They had been a family: Jean Jülich, his older brother, Franz, his mom, and his dad. The Jülichs had lived in an apartment on Barbara Street on the north side of the city. The apartment was small, just a bedroom, a kitchen, and a hallway. Jean remembered the walls being an ugly blue

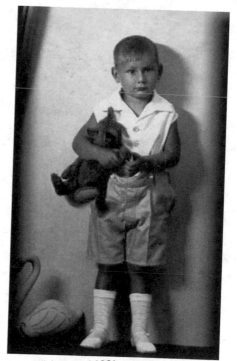

Jean Jülich around 1931.

and the whole place being a little lifeless. But it was home, and they were all together.

In 1933, that changed. Everything changed. Jean's father was an official in the Communist Party and saw what was happening with the arrests and fights after Hitler came to power. He left. Jean's mom couldn't afford to support both children, so Jean went to live with his grandparents. Jean was four, and they doted on him. And he loved his grandparents, and their apartment was nicer and bigger, but his family was broken and would never be put back together again.

5 — Gertrud

One day in the spring of 1933, Gertrud heard a knock at the door. There in the hallway was her friend Margaret, dressed normally in a colorful skirt and white blouse. But there was something wrong with her eyes. They were confused and desperate, searching for something.

"They've beaten her to death! They've beaten my mother to death!" she screamed.

Gertrud pulled her inside. Margaret's mother had often been at the Kühlem apartment, sitting on the very same leather sofa in the living room where they now were. Margaret explained what had happened:

A few days earlier, five men had come to their door, ripped Margaret's mother out of bed, and dragged her from the apartment. Margaret's dad was working in another city, so she just sat there in her bed all night, alone, wondering what to do. She'd heard about the Brown House, where the Gestapo took prisoners, so the next day, she went there to ask about her mother. They told Margaret that her mother had jumped out of a window.

Gertrud and her mom took Margaret to her grandparents' house in the Deutz neighborhood. They were the family that could take care of Margaret now. Losing a parent was something that happened in fairy tales, not in real life. But now Margaret's mother was gone, and she wasn't a character in a book. She was a friend who had sat on their leather couch in the light of the petroleum lamps and talked about Communist leaflets and newspapers. She would never sit there again.

On their way home, marching Nazis appeared on the street—something that happened more and more. Her mom quickly wrapped her arm around Gertrud's shoulder and pulled her closer. At any moment, one of the men could stop and start asking questions, start making demands. *Why didn't you give the Hitler salute? Why did you look me in the eye? What are you doing out?* There might not be a right answer.

The brown-shirted SA troops moved past without noticing them. They exhaled and continued home.

Meanwhile, Gertrud's family was managing. Her parents still had jobs. They had an apartment. They had each other. In the days following Margaret's mother's disappearance, Gertrud wondered if her friend would cry at night now. Gertrud couldn't really imagine living with her own grandparents. She didn't like her mother's parents. They were stiff and formal, and they didn't like her dad because he was working-class and talked about politics. She loved that her dad talked about politics with her and read her political books.

Before dinner one night, she found him reading an autobiography of Communist Party member Max Hoelz. Hoelz was German but had moved to the Soviet Union. She called her dad to dinner.

Gertrud had put out cheese, sausages, and pickles to go with the bread her mother had baked for a light supper. For this place and time, such a spread was a feast. But no one felt like eating; they were too occupied with what was going on around them: the arrests, the beatings, the people going missing, the friends lost.

The silence was broken by a loud crash followed by thumping.

"That sounds like boots," Gertrud's father said.

The noise got louder. Then, a crack.

In an instant, the specter that had been haunting the street was in their home. Four men in uniforms were in the kitchen.

Her father jumped out of his chair. Almost automatically, Gertrud's mother grabbed her daughter and spun around, putting herself between the men and Gertrud.

"We're searching the house," growled one of the men. "Looking for weapons."

"There are no weapons here," said Gertrud's father.

"We'll see about that. Search!"

The soldiers pushed their way into the living room and bedrooms. With unnecessary force, they sliced open the leather couch cushions, the bedding, the pillows. They upended the coffee table, knocked over chairs. Gertrud's mother pressed her closer.

When a man walked into Gertrud's room, she broke away from her mother to see what he was doing. Looking for guns, in her room? There weren't any in there. There weren't any anywhere in the house. But in the middle of the floor was her favorite possession, a dollhouse her great-uncle had given her. Gertrud watched as the big, black boot of a Nazi came down, the wood cracking and splintering everywhere. His foot slammed through the walls. He turned his destruction to the doll family whose home he had just destroyed, and crushed them too.

"You can't destroy my toys! They're not yours!" Gertrud cried as she hid behind an armchair that was now spilling its innards like an exploded goose.

"Kühlem, come with us!" the leader yelled.

"Can I bring my jacket?" Gertrud's father asked.

"You won't need it."

Her mother was silent as the men dragged Gertrud's father out of the apartment.

The fastest way for Gertrud to get to school was to walk toward Rathenau Square at the end of her street, walk along the small park, and then make a right on Lochner Street. Her short hair brushed against the side of her neck, and her skirt swished around her thighs as she hurried to the three-story brick building.

Gertrud often met her friend Waltraud on the playground before school and during recess. On this day, Waltraud had brought Gertrud a doll because she'd heard Gertrud's father had been arrested and all of Gertrud's toys had been destroyed. Gertrud was grateful for a new toy—and for a good friend. She stuck the blue-eyed, blond-haired doll under her arm as she walked across the playground.

Then four or five girls confronted her. They too had heard what happened to her father.

"Your dad is a criminal."

"He's in jail. The daughter of a criminal doesn't deserve a doll," they taunted.

A hand reached toward Gertrud and pulled the doll out from under her arm.

Fury erupted from inside her. She flailed her arms at the girls, and her skirt flew up as she kicked wildly. A high-pitched scream spewed out of her mouth and she cursed at the bullies. Tears welled up in her eyes and rolled down her cheeks.

When the girls finally left, Gertrud couldn't go into the classroom. She just stood outside, alone with her thoughts. Why were these girls so mean? She wasn't a criminal. And her dad wasn't a criminal. She didn't think he deserved to be arrested or in prison. He just wanted to make things better for everyone, especially the workers. These girls were no better than the men who had broken into her apartment.

The girls in Gertrud's class were mean, but they weren't her biggest problem. Nazis had infiltrated the whole school. Students didn't talk about politics in school, unless they were saying how great Hitler and the Third Reich were. The teachers couldn't simply avoid politics. They had to be members of the Nazi Party to keep their jobs. And every morning, they were supposed to lead the students as they raised their hands in the air and shouted, "Heil Hitler!"

Before Hitler, the students at the Catholic elementary school would say "Greetings to Jesus Christ," or "Greetings to God," at the beginning of the day. Hitler demanded a more German greeting and wanted people to be reminded of him—and him alone—daily. So the teachers took down crosses and put up pictures of Hitler at the front of the classrooms.

But Gertrud just couldn't bring herself to salute. Hitler was the reason her dad was gone.

One day,* her teacher noticed she wasn't doing the greeting and sent her to the principal's office, and her mom was called in. The principal's gray suit looked as stiff as a uniform. Gertrud suspected that her teacher was a real Nazi, but she wasn't sure about her principal's views.

"Why does Gertrud refuse to do the Hitler greeting?" he asked.

"You can ask her yourself," Gertrud's mother replied.

The principal turned to Gertrud.

"Gertrud, why did you not say, 'Heil Hitler'?"

---

* I can't precisely date this, because Gertrud just writes it as a thing that happened at some point when her father was gone. Technically, it appears in her memoir right after her description of Kristallnacht, but she jumps around in time even after that to things happening before 1938.

"Hitler locked up my father for no reason, and I'm not going to greet a man like that," she responded.

This was an answer that could have easily gotten her thrown out of school. Or worse.

"All right, go home," he said.

The next day she was put in the other class, but she made sure to sit in the back of the classroom so the teacher didn't see if she said "Heil Hitler" or not.

Gertrud missed her dad, especially after school, at the times when he'd usually come home from work. Before, she would snuggle into the big leather couch with him, where they read books together about Communism and Socialism. His favorites were the *Communist Manifesto* and writings by Ernst Thälmann, the leader of the Communist Party in Germany. Gertrud's hero was Rosa Luxemburg, the first female editor of the *Leipzig People's Newspaper* and founder of the Communist newspaper *Die Rote Fahne*, or *The Red Flag*. She was for the working people's revolution and wanted workers to strike, but she was also a pacifist and didn't believe in violence. She had been murdered in 1919 for her beliefs. Gertrud wanted to study politics, economics, and history like Luxemburg. She wanted to write and bring people together so that they could live peacefully with one another. She could never understand why people who simply had different political beliefs would be killed for their opinions. Now Gertrud had to read Luxemburg on her own.

After nine months in a concentration camp, Gertrud's dad was released and came home in April 1934. He looked different. He had been a big, heavy man, with snow-white hair and a small mustache. Now he was a thinner, smaller version of himself. Before, he had always liked to look good. When he came home from work, he'd change out of his coveralls and wash his hands so he wouldn't have the grime from the day on him. Now, the camp had left him dirty, skinny, and worn-out. She thought he finally looked older than he was.

She noticed his spirit wasn't broken, though; he wanted to keep working for the Communist Party underground. He told her that every time he'd dug his shovel into the dirt at the camp, his conviction to resist grew stronger. Gertrud knew whatever her dad wanted to do was dangerous, but she couldn't ignore his conviction. This was a way she could help him.

"We are going to hand out advertisements," Gertrud told her school friend Waltraud, the one who'd given her the doll. "Do you want to help?"

"Advertisements" was a lie, but she wanted Waltraud's company. When she agreed, they headed to the printer.

Gertrud and Waltraud put the papers in their bags and went to meet Gertrud's dad. As they walked up to him, Gertrud's father gave her a look. She knew she had done something wrong, but she didn't know what. He didn't say anything.

They walked along the streets, going into apartments and slipping the papers under doors, facedown. They didn't go to every house, only to the ones Gertrud's father knew were safe. They also didn't want to just leave the illegal material in a mailbox where someone could accidentally pick it up.

They walked and walked, and after they had given out all of the copies and Waltraud went home, her dad finally said something.

"What were you thinking?" he asked. "You will not do that again, do you hear me? It is too dangerous. Her parents are not Communists. She doesn't belong with us." Her dad had never used such harsh words with her before.

"But it's just a newspaper," she replied.

"Yes, my child, but the Nazis do not like what is written inside."

Gertrud hadn't thought about how dangerous handing out

papers could be, for them or for Waltraud. If Waltraud had been caught, the Nazis might not have believed that she didn't know she was handing out illegal material. Waltraud might also figure out what was going on and tell someone about the newspapers.

Gertrud thought that the truth needed to be told, and *The Red Flag* told the truth about the Nazis. But she also needed to know whom to trust, and to be sure that if she was doing something illegal, the other people with her could be trusted completely. The days of openly flying the red Communist flag outside her home were over.

6 — Jean

Jean had started first grade—his first year of school—in the fall of 1935. In his photo on the first day, his blond hair hangs down his forehead, and his smile pushes his round cheeks up toward his large eyes. He looks like a happy six-year-old. And his grandparents had tried to make him as happy as possible. It wasn't an easy job. Hitler had come to power promising employment and a better life, but his family hadn't experienced that. Jean saw his dad sometimes, but not often, and his mother couldn't visit often either. She worked in an umbrella factory and took work home in the evening to earn extra. Jean's older brother lived in an orphanage because she rented a room in an attic and couldn't afford to take care of him. Jean's grandfather had to work to support Jean and his grandmother. They lived on sauerkraut, potatoes, and green beans. Sometimes they had eggs or fish, but rarely meat.

On the morning of May 27, 1936, Jean's father happened to be in Jean's grandparents' apartment. Jean was getting ready for school when he heard loud footsteps, and then voices. The door to the apartment flew open and two men in black SS uniforms were standing in the hallway.

"Where is Jean? We want Jean Jülich!" They were looking for Jean's father, Johann, who also went by Jean.

When young Jean's father heard the footsteps, he hid himself in the shared bathroom in the hallway of the apartment building. The SS officers looked everywhere on the second floor, and then everywhere on the third floor where Jean's aunt lived.

When the officers eventually found Jean's father in the bathroom, they pulled him out and beat him as they arrested him. Jean's grandmother begged the men, but they only paused to laugh and threaten her. Jean was hidden in a back room so he couldn't see what was happening, but he could hear everything—every blow, every cry of pain, every plea to stop.

Two weeks later, the Gestapo came back to arrest Jean's grandmother and aunt. They were accused of helping his father in a Communist plot. Jean couldn't stay with his grandfather, who had dementia, so he had to move to another aunt's apartment. But his aunt decided she couldn't keep him either.

Jean Jülich and his father in the mid-1930s.

She took now-seven-year-old Jean to the Klapperhof Home for Boys, where nuns watched over boys like Jean and his brother, who didn't have families or whose parents were too poor to take care of them.

Now Jean's family wasn't just broken, it was gone.

7 — Fritz

Our banner flutters before us,
Our banner represents the new era,
And our banner leads us to eternity!
Yes, our banner means more to us than death.

Fritz knew the song, but he wasn't in the mood to sing along. It was the same thing every Saturday, and it made his skin crawl. Since 1936, everyone between ten and seventeen was supposed to be a member of the Hitler Youth or League of German Girls. In 1937, ten-year-old Fritz was supposed to join the youngest division, the *Jungvolk*. His parents had tried to save him from the Jungvolk by saying they didn't have enough money to pay for the uniform. It didn't work, and Fritz still had to show up every Saturday, even though he didn't have the proper outfit.

He had thought the Hitler Youth would be fun at first. He imagined that they would go camping and hiking and play games and have a good time. All of the Hitler Youth on the Nazi posters and in movies were always smiling and having a good time. Fritz thought it might be like the Wandervogel hiking group that Fritz's father had been in as a teenager. These groups were built on freedom and friendship, and rejecting adult life. They were unorganized, without leaders or a political party backing them up; they'd go on adventures and sing songs and play music.

Fritz quickly realized his mistake. In the Hitler Youth, everything was regimented and organized. On Saturday mornings, they had to get up and stand in straight lines for roll call and listen to Nazi propaganda.

One memorable Saturday started like all Hitler Youth Saturdays. A sea of brown outfits stood in front of Fritz: one guy after another in dark brown shorts, a big shiny belt buckle, a khaki shirt with two chest pockets, and a dark brown handkerchief. Since he was the youngest, Fritz had to stand at the back of the lines of other boys. Maybe they wouldn't notice if he wasn't singing.

"Last man, come forward!" the platoon leader yelled when they finished singing.

Fritz ran to the front. The platoon leader was older, maybe sixteen or seventeen. He shoved a briefcase into Fritz's arms and told him to carry it. The platoon leader always brought this stupid briefcase, always made Fritz carry it, and then told Fritz he should be honored to do so. The whole thing got on Fritz's nerves. Why did this guy bring this briefcase? What was so important about it? And why did Fritz have to carry it for him? All the guys that were high up in the Hitler Youth like the platoon leader were in positions of power only because their dads were Nazis and they had money.

Fritz told a friend named Paul how annoyed the briefcase made him.

"Man, you should shit in his bag," Paul suggested.

Fritz loved the idea.

Hitler Youth training took place on a big open field in a park in the city, and after they lined up, sang, and practiced how to march properly, they played field games like capture the flag that were supposed to prepare them for war. That was another thing Fritz didn't like: everything always had to do with the military.

On the edge of the field, everyone piled up the stuff that they didn't need for the war game, which included the platoon leader's briefcase. As the other guys scattered to play the game, Paul and Fritz snuck up on the pile, looked around, and grabbed the brief- case. They ran into the woods that lined the field, their prize in hand. They undid the latches and pulled the briefcase open. What was so important to the platoon leader?

Nothing more than a lunchbox and a crumpled-up piece of paper. He'd just been carrying it around to look more important than he was. This was perfect for Fritz's plan.

Feeling triumphant, accomplished, and possibly a little lighter, Fritz returned the briefcase back to the pile and joined the field game.

The next Saturday, Fritz reported to the field again. The whole troop was told to line up. The troop leader wasted no time.

"Who shit in the platoon leader's briefcase?"

Giggles, then outright laughter, erupted from the line.

"The whole troop will stand in a line! Quiet! The person respon- sible needs to confess, or there will be consequences for everyone."

Fritz and Paul kept quiet, although they might have been laughing a little harder on the inside. The troop leader couldn't get a confession out of anyone, and the responsible party was never found.

For Fritz, it was a complete victory. No punishment, and the platoon leader didn't bring back his briefcase to Saturday trainings for Fritz to carry.

Jean Jülich joined his brother at the Klapperhof Home for Boys in the Innenstadt. The whole place was awful. The nuns in charge were bad: they told the boys scary stories to keep them quiet at night and made them pray three times a day. The food was worse. Red goop, supposedly tomato soup, was on the menu at least every other day, sometimes for days in a row. He imagined that someone must have donated a huge quantity of tomato soup concentrate to the orphanage, so he had to eat it again and again. Sometimes they got waffles, which were only marginally better. They were made with buckwheat flour, but no milk, no butter, no sugar, no eggs. Poor kids didn't get good food.

One day, Jean sat at the table and picked up the cold spoon and took a sip of soup. The sour, acidic taste slid across his tongue and down his throat. Even if he only had to eat the soup once it would have been gross. He took another sip. How many more days would he have to eat soup? Maybe if only the tomato soup could have been dressed up a little bit: piece of bread with butter, or, a pure fantasy, little bits of fried sausage, brown and crispy, sitting right on top.

Jean took another bite. He couldn't stand the taste. The slime hit the back of his throat and it was too much. The liquid was coming back up, his body wasn't letting him swallow another bite. If he made a mess, the nuns might get mad, so back into the bowl the vomit went, with the rest of the soup he hadn't eaten.

A nun had seen.

"Here, we eat what's on the table!" she scolded him.

What was he supposed to do? He didn't have a choice—he ate the soup-vomit mixture.

✦ ✦ ✦

Jean's grandmother and aunt spent half a year in prison, and the Youth Welfare Office took another three months before they agreed to let Jean go back and live with his grandmother in the Sülz neighborhood. Those nine months in the Home for Boys had made Jean frightened, timid, anxious, and unable to concentrate in school. He didn't like this new world he was living in.

9 — Gertrud

Darkness came early on Wednesday, November 9, 1938. The sun had already set when Gertrud stood with her mother behind some bushes just at the end of their street. Apartment buildings lined the park, stately homes with porches held up by Roman columns,

Roon Street Synagogue, Cologne, 2018.

ornate plasterwork, and bay windows. The most magnificent building on the square was the synagogue. The Jewish house of worship was almost like a fortress, made of big cream-colored stones and taking up half a block. In the middle of the synagogue, a large square tower ascended into the sky, high above the five-story apartment buildings. The front of the building had a large, round stained-glass window and was flanked on two sides by smaller towers.

Gertrud and her mother were focused on the destruction of that magnificence. Men in uniform stood in front of the synagogue and had blocked off the street. Clothing, furniture, books, and rolls of the Torah, the Jewish holy book, were scattered about. Nazis had gone inside and ripped out the living quarters of the rabbis, taken the holy texts and thrown them into the street.

Gertrud's mother noticed someone climbing on the roof of the building. He was trying to rip the gold Star of David off the top of the tower. They recognized the man as their neighbor.

"Max! What are you doing?" Gertrud's mother yelled. "This is disgusting!"

"If you don't hold your tongue, I'll report you," he snapped back.

Then, smoke started rising from the building. The whole thing was being set on fire.

"Remember what your father said?" her mother asked her. Hitler would bring destruction, and the beautiful synagogue was being destroyed before their eyes.

They should have gone home. The streets were not safe, but Gertrud's mother wanted to keep walking around to see what was happening. As they walked from Roon Street east toward the center of the city, they saw broken window after broken window. Gertrud knew some Jewish families had already fled Germany, but her mother had told a shopkeeper they knew that everyone had to stay and fight. Now, scrawled on the windows of stores were the words, "I'm a Jewish pig." Her mother wanted to go all the way to Schilder Alley, near the central shopping district, but as they approached, they weren't allowed to go any farther. The whole central part of the city had been blocked off by SS men in uniform.

Her mother was afraid of what they might see if they ventured closer.

10 — Fritz

Darkness cloaked the streets of Ehrenfeld as Fritz emerged from the Neptune Pool building. He walked to Venloer Street to walk the few blocks north to his house, and he noticed something was wrong, very wrong.

Glass lay shattered in the street, glittering and shimmering, catching the light of the streetlamps. What was happening? Along the busy shopping street, extending from the city center out past

Fritz Theilen (middle) with his mother and brother, around 1939.

the Green Belt and the Ehrenfeld train station, someone had broken store windows. There were shoes scattered in front of one shop, clothing in front of another, and people were picking things up and running away.

These were all businesses where Fritz's family shopped, and they turned out to all be Jewish, but eleven-year-old Fritz had never really thought about that before. In Cologne, there wasn't a particular neighborhood that was the Jewish neighborhood. Two years ago, Fritz had a Jewish classmate whose dad was a violinist at the opera. At the time, he had no idea what the classmate's religion was and didn't care. But the Nazis cared.

Fritz heard that people in civilian clothes and in uniforms had smashed the windows and broken into the stores as some kind of retaliation. Even in Cologne, where there weren't so many die-hard Nazis, the anti-Jewish sentiment had been growing. Floats in the Karneval parades had grotesque anti-Semitic caricatures and kids sang anti-Jewish nursery rhymes in the schoolyard. Some Jewish families moved to Palestine, unwilling to be treated so poorly, but many stayed, not wanting to give up their lives and businesses, which were now lying smashed in the street.

11 — Jean

The next morning, Jean Jülich walked to Berrenrather Street in Sülz, past fabric and shoe stores, all destroyed. The glass was broken and the businesses looked like they'd thrown up all over the street. He knew these were Jewish businesses, but these weren't the important stores as far as he was concerned.

Jean ran to the toy store that belonged to a man named Mr. Mangen. Jean loved that store. Whenever he passed by, he'd press his nose against the big window, gawking at all the toys that he wanted but probably wouldn't get. The store was like a paradise, where a nine-year-old could dream even if his family couldn't afford the toys he wanted.

The whole dream was smashed. The big glass window where he'd pressed his nose was shattered, the door was pushed in, and the toys, all the beautiful toys were in the street, broken, destroyed. He knew he could have picked up one that wasn't totally destroyed, but he couldn't bring himself to do it. It was all too upsetting.

An SA officer was standing at the door, watching over who was coming and going. Jean looked at him and felt an instinctive hatred. This was the man who'd done this. What right did that officer have to destroy the toys they dreamed of?

In the days that followed what came to be known as *Kristallnacht*— the Night of Broken Glass—Jean went back to the store to look because he just couldn't believe what had happened. He knew that Mr. Mangen was Jewish, and that was why the store had been destroyed, but he didn't understand. The store was beautiful and he had Jewish friends that were no different from his other friends. But even that started to change. Not long after that night in November, he didn't see his two Jewish friends hanging around the neighborhood as much anymore, then they started wearing yellow stars on their clothing, and then, one day, they just weren't there anymore.

Part Two
1939–1942

"What does it matter to you? Leave us alone."

Cologne, 1939

Hitler has plans. Something has been brewing since troops marched across the Hohenzollern Bridge to the west side of the Rhine in 1936. Hitler wasn't supposed to do that; the Treaty of Versailles after the First World War said that no German troops could be west of the Rhine. Your father, maybe your older brother, had been drafted into the army in 1938, and now more troops are being sent to the border with Poland. Something is coming.

On September 1, 1939, you hear Hitler's harsh voice come over the radio: "Our aims: I am determined to solve the question of Danzig, and the corridor in relation to Poland and effect an arrangement for peacefully living together. . . . One word I have never learned to know. That is capitulation. November 1918 shall never be repeated in the history of Germany. . . . I expect every man and woman to take part in this struggle in exemplary fashion."

One specific thing Hitler believes is that the city of Danzig— which Germany gave up with its November 1918 "capitulation"— is more German than Polish. He's sent over a million soldiers to the Polish border to take the land he wants. Hitler is determined to make his vision for Germany a reality, and in so doing, he wants to erase the humiliation of the end of the First World War. He expects all Germans to share this aim.

In Cologne, an electricity flows through the air. The newspapers have all declared Germany's quick march into Poland as the first step to creating a greater German Reich that includes all people who were ever German, like the citizens of Danzig. All over the city, church bells erupt, clanging through the streets to celebrate and give thanks for the victory, and to acknowledge the losses of German life. You hear the bells go on and on, for a whole hour, much longer than they do on a Sunday morning before mass. And no one has declared war on Germany. Yet.

12 — Fritz

On September 2, 1939, Fritz's mother took him and his brother from Ehrenfeld into the center of Cologne. The streetcar rumbled down Venloer Street, past the Green Belt, and into the heart of the city. They could get off at Neumarkt, where the Nazis liked to march, or continue down into the old part of the city. The Nazis wanted everyone to celebrate, for everyone to support the vision for a greater Germany. But for Fritz, there wasn't anything worth celebrating. His dad had been drafted into the army and was gone. His mother mumbled, "It's all over."

Maybe the fear was why Fritz's mom offered her sons coffee and cake on this walk through the city. The bakeries had rows and rows of fresh cakes, cookies, pastries, and sweets on display in the window. A special treat might take their minds off the dread of what would happen next. They sat at a table outside of a bakery, ready to sink their teeth into the sweet, buttery baked goods.

All of a sudden, Fritz heard a noise coming from the sky. The sound was the grumbling and rumbling of a big motor. Everyone looked up.

"Up there, a plane, it's an English bomber!" a man at the next table yelled.

Someone made a joke about something Herman Göring, Hitler's number-two Nazi, had said about English bombers coming over German airspace. The day before, Göring had declared it would be impossible for British planes to fly over Germany. Clearly he got something wrong.

Fritz's mother didn't think the joke was funny; fear washed over her face. "Fritz, we're going home," she said as she grabbed his brother's arm. They got up and ran home, leaving the coffee and cake untouched on the table.

Report from the Justice Press Office of Düsseldorf

AUGUST 8, 1937

Before the takeover of power, there were wild hiking groups in western Germany that called themselves "Kittelbach Pirates." After Hitler came to power, the good elements joined the NSDAP [Nazi Party], while the organization that remained became more and more of a collecting tank of discontented people against the NSDAP. . . . Despite the dissolution and ban of this group, new Kittelbach Pirate groups have developed in different cities in western Germany. . . . Not only will the activities of the Kittelbach Pirates be strongly punished, but so too will any continuation of the banned bündische youth groups.

Report of the Gestapo, Düsseldorf

DECEMBER 10, 1937

Even if these [bündische groups] can rarely be considered organizationally cohesive, there still exists the potential that they will bond more closely together and this constitutes an instrument that would become, in the hands of the enemies of the state, a danger to the youth and thus to the nation.

Provincial Administration Letter

APRIL 23, 1940

Following a raid by the Cologne Gestapo on the second day of
the Easter holiday [March 25, 1940], 116 boys and 11 girls were
taken to the Youth Prison Friedersdorf in protective custody.
For the most part, they could be released in the following
days after their interrogations. Only 8 young men remain in
custody here.

Gestapo identifying deviant youth in confiscated photo, 1936.

After her father's release from prison, Gertrud saw less and less of him. She thought sometimes that he had been arrested and was in jail, but he could have also been underground, hiding so he could publish and distribute illegal Communist materials. Knowing where he was would have only put Gertrud in danger.

In the summer of 1939, he was definitely arrested again and sentenced to three years in the Esterwegen camp for high treason. Gertrud wasn't allowed to attend the trial because she was only fourteen. Her mother told her that her father had cried during the sentencing. Gertrud had never seen him cry. The idea of him crying surprised her, and scared her a little too.

But as awful as the changes at home were for Gertrud, she found hope somewhere else.

Gertrud wandered through the woods of the *Siebengebirge*, the Seven Mountains, a nature preserve just south of Cologne. The ground cushioned the soles of her loafers as she padded across the leaf litter and pine needles. Overhead, the wind brushed through the trees. If it was a clear day and the sun was shining, the rays peeked through the trees, casting pockets of light down onto the forest floor. When it was cloudy, it was like the woods wrapped a dark, damp cloth around her. No matter the weather, there was a quiet here, a peace that didn't exist in the city.

Gertrud loved the woods, she loved hiking. She remembered going hiking and camping with her parents, who she knew had been part of the bündische hiking clubs when they were young. She had gone on a few hikes with her mother and her mother's old friends in 1936, but for young people to meet up outside the Hitler Youth was totally illegal now. But Gertrud wanted to hike and camp and get out of the city.

By the summer of 1939, Gertrud found other girls and guys that were interested in hiking and camping, and they didn't really care if it was legal. On weekends, they'd wander the mountains and valleys all around Cologne in their anti-uniforms. They wore brown leather shoes or sandals with white socks folded down, flopping around their ankles. Everyone had colorful shirts, sometimes checkered, and the guys liked to roll up their sleeves just so. Gertrud and the other girls wore knee-length black skirts with a zipper and the guys wore leather or corduroy pants. Over their mops of long hair, the guys wore hats, often cocked to the side and decorated with lots of pins. Sometimes, they wore Edelweiss pins, a little metal flower that was a common souvenir.

Most of the friends she was closest to were guys, and they all had nicknames: Jus, Banjo Willi, Ätz, Hadschi, and Ali. Gertrud's nickname, Mucki, came from a bunny in a children's book. A nickname based on a bunny might seem childish, but she liked it. She had a bunny look: the middle of her upper lip pointed toward her nose, making it look like she was scrunching her face, and she had soft, thin, dirty-blond hair.

Gertrud was surrounded by friends as she hiked through the woods of the Seven Mountains. At the top of the rocky hills, she could look down on the Rhine River, and maybe even see the Cathedral in Cologne. The rocky outcroppings were great for climbing and scrambling, and perfect for finding caves and grottoes to spend the night in after a day of hiking. The caves were also a good spot to stay unnoticed.

They set up camp for the night and built a fire to keep warm. Inevitably, someone would pick up a guitar and start singing.

> *Yes, under the Mexican sun,*
> *Was the Wild West, amber-skinned Navajo.*
> *Today my heart is still ablaze,*
> *I think of the Navajo.*

Gertrud (center) and friends on the way to the Liesenberger Mill in the early 1940s.

"Under the Mexican Sun" was a bündische song, an original composition passed around between youth groups over the years. The romanticism of the song was probably inspired Karl May's bestselling books.* Everyone in Germany knew the character Winnetou, an Apache who would rather knock down his enemies than kill them. May's books were truly fiction: he had never been to the American West and had never met an American Indian. But the bündische youth were in love with the stories, regardless of the truth. The Winnetou series was filled with battles and bravery, brotherhoods and beauty, and the books always painted the Native Americans as fighters for freedom, willing to risk their lives. Gertrud's friends from Düsseldorf, Hadschi and Ali, had taken their nicknames from May's characters, and one bündische group called themselves Navajo, either inspired by May or "The Mexican Sun" song lyrics.

---

* See "A Note on 'the Navajos,'" page 271.

The teenagers sang and talked, and the sky turned from a hazy blue dusk to dark, and Gertrud found herself sitting next to Ätz a little ways off from the rest of the group. Ätz was tall and lanky, with wavy, dirty-blond hair, and the only one in the group younger than Gertrud, but he definitely didn't seem like a kid. The war had made everyone realize what was going on, and what was expected of them. Ätz was supposed to join the Hitler Youth, but really didn't want to. None of their friends wanted to be in the Hitler Youth or the League of German Girls.

"My parents are totally frustrated," Ätz told Gertrud. "They've been threatened again that I will be sent to a reeducation home. They've been blamed for doing a bad job since they can't get me to join the Hitler Youth."

"But it's going to destroy you if you join the Hitler Youth. The way you are, you're not going to be able to keep your mouth shut for five minutes," Gertrud said.

The League of German Girls (LGG) would probably have destroyed Gertrud too. She had told a teacher that she didn't want anything to do with the LGG because she wanted to do whatever she wanted, she wanted to wear whatever she wanted. That hadn't gotten her out of her duty as a German. Instead, she had received an official letter stating that she needed to join. She ignored it. Soon another letter came.

Each time she got a letter, her mom wrote that she was sick and in bed. The excuse didn't work for long. She and her mom ended up going to the women's society office and having to hear a speech about how important the loved-by-all Führer should be to German girls and German women. A woman told Gertrud about the role and duty of German females, which was, put simply, to have children—"Aryan" children—preferably with an SS man. That idea was disgusting to Gertrud. SS officers were probably mistreating her father in a camp right now. And she had no interest in having her children believe in Hitler. After listening to a tirade about her bad behavior, she had been allowed to go home.

So Gertrud knew why Ätz didn't want to join the Hitler Youth. He told her that the whole thing had been stressing him and his parents. Even though his parents weren't Nazis, they didn't believe that joining the Hitler Youth would be that bad.

"You have to make that decision for yourself," Gertrud told him. "If it was me, I would only listen to myself."

Gertrud Kühlem in her Edelweiss outfit, early 1940s.

Guidelines for the Hitler Youth Patrol Duty (HYPD)

JUNE 1, 1938

B. Intervention against bündische groups

1.) The bündische youth are, according to the laws of the Reich, fundamentally outlawed. Bündische activity is antigovernment activity. The monitoring of the youth who engage in bündische activity falls to the Hitler Youth and is thus one of the main tasks of the HYPD.

2.) One of the requirements for combating the bündische Youth is that one recognizes them. Following are some distinguishing characteristics:

A.) appearance is casual, unorderly, and unclean;

B.) hair and clothing are unkempt;

C.) The head coverings are frequently cut-up caps and strange hats of all types, decorated with a number of pins, buttons, feathers, etc.;

D.) They wear leather sandals or tall leather boots with
very short shorts, that often have tassels;

E.) other clothing that should be emphasized include
checkered shirts and colorful handkerchiefs

The overall look of the bündische groups is always
uneven. Pocketknives of all kinds are carried. They
stick [tobacco] pipes and combs in the tops of their
boots, and zippers are found on all sorts of places.

3.) These signs may not be found on all bündische groups. On
the other hand, individual signs are also not proof of
bündische activity. However, caution should be used when
intervening.

4.) Bündische activity should mostly be noted during travel
stops. If during such a stop, there is a strong suspicion
of bündische activity based on their type of ID or for any
other reason, the police should be informed based on the
laws and guidelines of the state.

Group of Pirates in
Altenahr, near the
Eifel mountains south
of Cologne, 1941.

14 — Gertrud

May Day used to be a holiday when Gertrud's dad and his fellow Communist Party members would march through the street to celebrate the workers. Now the Nazis used the day to march and show off. On May 1, 1940, the Hitler Youth marched through the Green Belt park to a meeting spot where a big rally was supposed to happen, a spot right next to Gertrud's neighborhood.

Usually, the Green Belt park was another tranquil place where Gertrud and her friends could meet during the week to talk, sing songs, and hang out. Her group had decided recently that they would call themselves the Edelweiss Group, after a flower that grows high in the mountains in the Alps, a flower that was wild and free. She knew the situation on the street had been getting worse. She'd heard about people being followed and attacked by Hitler Youth patrols, totally unprovoked. Gertrud thought it was her friends' love of freedom that pissed off the Hitler Youth so much.

On this spring morning, the grass was green, leaves unfurled from their branches, and flowers dotted the landscape. The Hitler Youth were supposed to assemble near the square reservoir at the bottom of a hill in the park, where they had erected an eagle and a swastika, each two stories tall.

From the loudspeakers, march music boomed. Drums, horns and voices joined together to sing about the beauty of the Reich and the Führer. Gertrud thought the music droned on and she didn't see the appeal. It was boring and all sounded the same, no matter what song they were actually playing.

And people increasingly looked the same too: brown, brown, brown. The Hitler Youth wore dark brown corduroy shorts or black canvas shorts, a dull brown shirt, and a dark handkerchief. Their hair was cropped short on the sides and only a little longer on top. The League of German Girls wore calf-length black skirts with a white short-sleeved collared shirt and a black scarf tied like a neck-tie. They pulled their hair back into braids or buns. They were to look sharp and clean at all times.

Gertrud and her friends Banjo Willi and Jus watched as the ants marched by, one after another. The Hitler Youth always acted like they were better than everyone else.

Then all of a sudden, one of the guys wasn't in line anymore. He bumped into Gertrud's group. Was that a mistake? Why would he fall out of line like that?

A flash of brown was coming toward Gertrud. She felt a tug on her scalp. He had her hair. His fingers dug into her soft, blond locks and tightened around her hair as he made a fist. The front of her neck strained as he pulled his hand back and her head came with it. With the other hand, he tried to grab her arm and pull it behind her back. He was bigger and stronger than she was.

Her body tightened as she gained her strength. She had to get loose from him; she had to free herself. With all of the power she could gather, she threw her leg into the air and kicked him in his shin. He must have loosened his grip, because she threw her head forward, and a blob of spit sailed out from her mouth into his face.

Gertrud felt his hands leave her body. She thought either the spit disgusted him or he remembered his mom telling him he shouldn't hit girls. Being grossed out by the spit was more likely, since the Nazis never seemed to have a problem beating women, like her friend Margaret's mother.

Gertrud scanned her surroundings. The situation was bad. The Hitler Youth were everywhere, and her friends were getting beaten badly. She picked up a stick, and before she could move farther away, another hand came flying toward her. It belonged to another Hitler Youth, one with fewer scruples than the last guy.

His fist hit her squarely in the face. She swung the stick in his direction, made contact, and then she ran.

Her face tingled where the fist had made contact, and she knew the injury would swell. She thought she would have a black eye. Jus and Banjo Willi were worse off. Jus's dark, unruly hair framed his busted face. They'd been beaten with fists and batons. Blood trickled down from both their nostrils and dripped off their chins. She hoped their noses weren't broken.

Gertrud went home, knowing that her mom could help with her eye. She was starting to look like her dad's friends that had showed up at the apartment so many years ago.

15 — Fritz

Fritz had managed to stay in the Hitler Youth for three years. One Saturday in 1940, the new company leader wanted to inspect Fritz's troop. The organization of the Hitler Youth was supposed to mimic the military so that all the German boys would know how platoons, troops, and companies were organized before they were drafted into the army. All of the troops were supposed to march in perfect, straight rows, in strict sync with one another under the watchful eye of the company leader. Fritz thought his troop had done at least a passable job. The company leader didn't share that opinion. Fritz couldn't really figure out what the company commander's problem was, but at the end of the inspection, he held Fritz's troop back and told them they were going to have to do punishment exercises.

Fritz knew these exercises, and no part of them would be enjoyable. To start, the whole troop would run together. Then, all of a sudden, someone would yell, "Tank left!" Fritz would have to shoot his arms out in front of him, drop his body down into a push-up position, his stomach hitting the ground, and then pop back up again. They'd run some more, someone would yell, "Tank right!" and down they went again. Over and over and over.

It was in moments like these that the idea of being obedient and educated as a proper Nazi pressed down hardest on Fritz, tightened around his body and psyche. This was bullshit, and he didn't want to do it anymore.

Everyone else started running, and Fritz just stood there.

"Stop!"

The whole troop stopped running.

"Why aren't you running?"

"I'm not doing any punishment exercises," Fritz said.

They got back in line and started running again. Fritz didn't move.

The company leader told Fritz to hand over his pocketknife, shoulder strap, and handkerchief.

These were his personal belongings, not something that belonged to the Hitler Youth. His parents had bought him those things. Fritz wasn't giving them up.

The company leader told the rest of his troop to take the knife, strap, and handkerchief from Fritz.

His platoon got closer. They were going to use force. Hands reached toward Fritz in a frenzy, pulling and jerking, trying to get his shoulder strap. His body rocked in different directions. He tried to punch back, but the fight was twenty-five against one. They pulled off his shoulder strap. They grabbed his pocketknife.

"Get back in line," the company leader told him once the scrum had cleared.

Fritz refused. He wasn't going to get back in line with those jerks who had just attacked him on an order from some rich kid pretending to be in the military.

"You can all kiss my ass!" he yelled, and then he turned and walked home.

Fritz was asked to apologize for his behavior. Not surprisingly, he refused. Soon thereafter, his parents received notice that because of a lack of discipline, he had been kicked out of the Hitler Youth.

Since Fritz didn't have to report to the Hitler Youth training on Saturdays anymore, he began to hang out with a group of older kids at the sports fields. Most were a lot older than he was. At thirteen, he was still supposed to be in the Hitler Youth, and these kids were either skipping practice or old enough that they didn't have to go any longer. He quickly became close with a guy named Hans and his sister Maria. They seemed to understand one another.

Soon after they met, Fritz visited Hans and Maria's family's apartment. Their parents had been members of the bündische youth and all over the apartment were photos of their hiking and camping trips. They explained the bündische youth movement to him, a movement Fritz had first learned a little about from his father, who'd had been a member of the Wandervogel. The Wandervogel—literally Wandering Birds—was the first bündische youth group, officially created in 1901. They wanted to escape the cities and explore nature. That group soon split into different groups and still others formed their own bündische organizations. The movement grew to include many groups devoted to hiking, camping, singing songs, and developing close friendships with one another. World War I broke up the movement, with over two million young German men forced to fight and die in the trenches across Europe. After the war, groups

Fritz's dad, Anton, as a Wandervogel in 1919.

started appearing again. While some of them became more conservative and even aligned themselves with the Hitler Youth, the bündische tradition continued to be largely anti-authority. By the 1920s, there were over 55,000 members of bündische groups, and they were against the complacency and strict morals of the older generation.

Most of the bündische groups didn't care if members were gay or straight, male or female, Jewish, Catholic or Lutheran. From the beginning, the Nazis particularly didn't like this aspect of the movement. For example, they thought the Wandervogel were internationally focused and homosexual. The group known as *Deutsche Jungenschaft vom 1.11.1929* or dj.1.11 (November 1, 1929, German Youth) were too Russian-influenced for the Nazis to tolerate. They made sure to ban bündische groups in 1933 when they came to power, but illegal groups still formed and gave themselves names like the Lost Gang, Kittelbach Pirates, the Buccaneers, and the Reliables. They did what bündische groups had always done: they hiked, they camped, they sung, they hung out.

The term *bündische Jugend* translates to "free-federated youth," but it became a phrase of its own that the Nazis continued to use for any youth groups that emulated this older tradition and were anti-Nazi. To the Nazis, the bündische movement as a whole was a threat to their authority and power.

Hans, Maria, and their parents taught Fritz some of the now-banned songs of the bündische youth. He soon fell in love with the tradition and wanted to be bündisch too.

In the late summer of 1940, Hans and Maria took Fritz to their meeting of a new bündische group that called themselves the Navajos. Fritz didn't care that the group was illegal. He wasn't alone anymore; he found other people who didn't want to march in straight lines and follow arbitrary orders.

He also thought their outfits were cool. The girls sewed their

Edelweiss Pirates from the Rhine Valley at Felsensee in the Seven Mountains, about 1940.

own pleated skirts from plaid fabric. On top, they wore colorful shirts, windbreakers that hugged their waists, and white knee socks. The guys wore corduroy shorts, colorful shirts, and sometimes white knee socks. There was life and vibrancy to the clothes that the Navajos wore, not just boring brown uniforms over and over again. They wanted to be individuals, with their own style that set them apart.

When they got together, someone always had a guitar, and the guitar straps, and sometimes hats too, were adorned with pins from places they had been. And most of the Navajos either wore a strap around their right wrist or a ring with a skull.

Fritz loved every minute of hanging out with the Navajos. No more military drills and no more harassment from some guy who thought he was better than you and would tell you what to do. Everything here was democratic, they had no real leader, and they made decisions together.

Fritz loved the songs, like "Tall Pines," a song whose original lyrics talked romantically about the woods and a fairy-tale mountain spirit. While the Nazis and Hitler Youth added pro-Nazi lyrics, the Navajos added a sentence that was distinctly anti-Nazi:

Tall pines point to the stars
On the Isar with its wild flowing tide
Lies the camp in the distance
But you, mountain spirit, guard it well
Have you given yourself to us?
You tell us stories and fairy tales
And live in the deepest forest
Taking the shape of a giant
Come to us and the blazing fire
At the Felsensee pond on a stormy night
Shield the tents, the dear homeland
Come and stay with us to hold watch
Hear, mountain spirit, what we are saying to you
In our homeland, we no longer sing freely
So swing your club like in olden days
And break the skulls of the Nazis in two.

16 — Gertrud

Around the city, Gertrud saw more parades, more Nazis marching. Top members of the Nazi Party would come to town: President of the Reichstag, Hermann Göring; Reich Leader of the SS, Heinrich Himmler; Propaganda Minister Joseph Goebbels; and even

Hitler himself. She saw rows and rows of young people screaming "Heil! Heil!" They've been indoctrinated; they don't have reason anymore, she thought.

And in the months since the May Day fight with the Hitler Youth in the Green Belt park, confrontations and attacks from the Hitler Youth increased. They couldn't go tell anyone that these guys were beating them up; the HY would just say they were doing their duty. The Hitler Youth Patrol Duty (HYPD) was allowed to police other young people. Gertrud felt like they could defend themselves, as long as they weren't too outnumbered. Mainly, Gertrud and her friends tried to stay out of their way.

17 — Fritz

Fritz and the Navajos liked to hang out in Blücher Park at a little plaza that sat higher than the rest of the park. The gravel spot was surrounded by a waist-high concrete wall. On each side of the steps leading up to the plaza was a stone lion, crouched on a concrete base, looking like it was ready to pounce.

The park was on the edge of Ehrenfeld, but also close to another neighborhood called Nippes, so sometimes kids would show up from there too. Usually it was about twenty to twenty-five young people, and they were far enough into the park that they could hear and see when others were coming.

Fritz's mom didn't love the idea of him hanging out with the Navajos. The mixed genders bothered her, but she couldn't really control him. Even the Nazis couldn't control him—a Police Order for the Protection of Youth said that children under eighteen years old were not allowed to be in streets or public places after dark, but Fritz and his friends didn't really care. This was the time after school or work that they had to meet. They weren't going to let a curfew stop them.

They'd sit on the walls to the plaza and talk, play their guitars, and sing songs. One of Fritz's favorite songs, which he learned early on with the Navajos, was about a kid dreaming of his dad in prison. It was called "Do You Know, Mother, What I Have Dreamed?"

Next to the very sick child,
The mother sat still and cried,
Because during his life,
The sun had never shined.
She pushed back his golden locks.
The child woke from his sleep.
The slumber had made him cheerful,
And to his mother he softly said:
Do you know, Mother, what I dreamed?
I looked in the prison
And saw our darling father
Walking around inside.
He could not say hello.
He was being watched over carefully.
I only saw a few tears
Dripping down on his striped outfit.
His hair was shorn.
His mustache was shaved.
Tell me, why have I been born?
Tell me, what has happened to us?
Is our father a murderer,
Has he committed these crimes,
Has he broken these laws?
And I have loved him so.

Child, please don't ask, said the mother.
Your father is a brave man.
Only once was he drunk
And he was angered.
He became prey to the law,
And while we are in the German Reich,
Will only the working class be condemned
To the highest penalties.

A voice boomed across the park.

"Stop with the music and get out of here!"

This day there were about fifteen people hanging out, and they hadn't noticed the group of men in uniforms approaching.

"What are you all doing here? You know that this is not allowed," the voice boomed again.

As soon as Fritz knew there was trouble, he dove into a bush nearby. His friends were always worried about how young he was and had told him that at the first sign of trouble, he was supposed to disappear.

Peeking through the leaves, he saw the men in uniforms as they approached. They looked like older guys in SA uniforms and some young guys in HYPD uniforms. The darkness and the plants obscured Fritz, but he could hear what was happening.

"What do you want?" one of his friends retorted.

"You guys have no business here. The songs you are singing are also banned."

"How so?"

Defiance. Denial. Always.

"Get out your IDs," one of the Nazis yelled.

"What do you want? What does it matter to you? Leave us alone."

"How old are you?"

"Older than you think!"

The men got closer and reached out for the guitars. Fritz's friends weren't going to put up with that.

From behind the bushes, Fritz saw bodies colliding. If the SA and Hitler Youth were going to use force, then so were the Navajos. The darkness made it hard to see what was happening, but Fritz knew there was fighting, and he thought his friends were doing a good job defending themselves.

Then, more men showed up. Police. That was the real sign that the fight was over. The Navajos bolted, running in all directions away from the Nazis and into the dark.

To the Secret State Police [Gestapo] Office, Düsseldorf

OCTOBER 7, 1941

According to news received by us, the Bündische Youth groups have had increased activity lately. According to a report from the local district of Niederberg, the so-called Kittelbach Pirates have drawn attention to themselves. In one case, a Hitler Youth's uniform was shredded by one of these trash. The "Kittelbach Pirates" look like a Communist horde and are often in the company of young degenerate women, found in undisciplined hordes dressed in colorful outfits and scarves. Recently, they have frequently been observed in the Neander Valley, for example.

It seems appropriate for the police to have a stronger approach and to use a reinforced deployment of patrols, especially since the Hitler Youth Patrol Duty members are no longer able to combat this increased activity due to increased conscriptions.

Heil Hitler!

NSDAP Provincial Leadership Düsseldorf

Fritz looked out across the water. The Rhine was greenish gray floating under the hull of the small boat that was taking him south on the river. Long, flat barges with coal floated north, to the ports in Düsseldorf or maybe all the way to Rotterdam, in the Netherlands. If Fritz looked south, he could see the Seven Mountains on the left side of the Rhine, which looked like little more than seven soft pillows under a blanket of dark green trees. On one of the pillows, close to the river, he could just make out the brown stones of Drachenfels, a castle that overlooked the river.

The weather was beautiful and his weekend trip in June 1941 would start with blue skies and sunshine. The plan was for bündische groups from all over Cologne and the Rhine Valley to meet at the Felsensee pond on Saturday evening. They couldn't all take the same train or boat without looking suspicious, so they had

Pirates at the campfire during a hike in Loosenau, east of Cologne, 1943. From the photo album of Edelweiss Pirate Max Stahl.

decided that each group would travel separately and not go a direct route. Some people got off in Bonn, which was on the same side of the river as Cologne, and crossed over to Oberkassel and then made their way to the meeting spot.

Fritz got off in Königswinter, which was just south of where they were meeting. The town looked like a scene out of a storybook. Many of the houses were over four centuries old and charmingly irregular, with crooked doors and windows and potbellied walls. Some of the houses were newer, from the early 1900s, when the town was a popular summer destination for city people from Cologne or Düsseldorf. Those buildings were straight and symmetrical, but were painted different colors and had ornamentation on the facades, lining the windows and on the spaces above the doors and the eaves, which all made the buildings look like gingerbread houses. There weren't very many tourists these days, though, and Fritz and his friends liked it that way.

Fritz walked east from the town into the woods to the ponds where everyone had agreed to meet. From the main path in the woods, Fritz walked along a narrow path to get into the area surrounding Felsensee. These ponds—Felsensee, Blauensee, and Märchensee—were not up in the mountains. The ponds were set into the side of a hill, surrounded by cliffs. Once campers reached the ponds, they couldn't see the nearby river or train tracks. In reality, they weren't that far from town, but the place felt worlds away.

Because of the cliffs, there was just that one narrow path to get to the ponds. Fritz and his friends would know if someone approached. The area was also dangerous. The cliffs on three sides of the ponds were made of unstable rocks that could come crashing down at any moment but were also great for diving into the deep water.

When Fritz and the Navajos arrived at Felsensee, there were about sixty others already there, girls and guys from the Wandervogel, and maybe the Fahrtenstenze from Essen or the Kittelbach

Pirates from Düsseldorf. Other guys had names like Whiskey Bill and Texas Jack. Some people had already staked out sleeping spots in caves around the pond, or were pitching tents on the dirt beach near the water.

Making a campfire was illegal because enemy planes might be able to spot it, and Fritz and his friends thought it smarter to avoid any light at night. But they didn't really need the fire; in June, the sun wouldn't set until almost 10:00 p.m. during the longest days of the year.

They sat down to start singing. Fritz didn't have a guitar yet, but someone always had one. They started with a song written for this secret hideaway.

> *Alone and left along a rock wall*
> *There lies a calm water, called Felsensee.*
> *Here the guys from lovely Cologne on the Rhine meet*
> *With their hiking ladies for pleasant company*
> *We are friends from hitchhiking and trips and*
> *A little Edelweiss our sign will be.*

Edelweiss Pirates do a "clothes swap" on a hike in the Berg region, northeast of Cologne, near Wuppertal, 1941.

This was their own oasis, totally undisturbed by the Nazis and the rapidly deteriorating world around them. They had found their people, and this meant the world to them. They would tell stories about things they'd done together, places they'd traveled; those were the happy things. People would also talk about the friends who weren't there, who had already turned eighteen and been drafted into the army. Some of their friends hadn't been heard from in a long time—they'd been arrested by the Gestapo and taken away. Even if they had gotten out, they probably didn't want to come back to hang out with the illegal groups that had gotten them into trouble in the first place.

Every time they talked about arrests, a big discussion followed. How would this affect them? And what were they going to do when it did? They were pretty sure that it wouldn't be long until the Nazis stepped up arrests and more people were taken away. Fritz couldn't imagine going back to a time when he didn't get to meet

Edelweiss Pirate Wolfgang Ritzer wrote "Crazy World" on this generally goofy photo (featuring more clothes swapping) of a hike in 1941 or 1942.

with his friends in the evenings or go on weekend trips. Being together was the most important thing for everyone there. They had all been alone before and now they had finally found other people who didn't want to be Nazis, who wanted to sing, talk, wear different clothes, and just be.

Someone suggested that instead of running away from the Nazis, they should strike back. Not many people liked that idea. The bündische tradition was a nonviolent one. The philosophy was about being who you wanted to be, not fighting. Besides, they weren't really ready to fight back anyway.

Another guy suggested that if they actually went into the SA or became Nazis, then they could just show those IDs when they were on a trip, and then they wouldn't be arrested.

That idea was dismissed pretty quickly, especially by some of the older guys. They had seen that before, and the plan hadn't worked. Their parents, brothers, and sisters thought when the Nazis came to power they would be left alone because they weren't overtly political. That wasn't what happened. Complacency was dangerous, and they shouldn't let that type of naïveté harm them again, they said.

The conclusion this time was to wait and see what happened with the war, and then make decisions.

The next morning, they went about their usual camp-life activities. Some people stripped down and plunged into the Felsensee. The pond was really deep, and cold at the beginning of the summer, but that couldn't keep the brave from swimming and splashing around. Others just sat out in the sun that reached the ground through the clearing in the trees. Sometimes the girls and guys swapped clothes as they posed for photos. There was unending comfort in just being able to be free and do whatever they wanted.

Suddenly there was a rustling from the path entering the

campsite. A moment's fear was settled when the sound proved to be just the arrival of another group from the Kalk neighborhood in Cologne. When the campers from Kalk started talking, though, the fear grew again.

Their news was shocking, and bad. Hitler had decided, without a declaration of war, to send the German army into the Soviet Union. Good moods and comfort blew away with the breeze. There would be no quick end to this war. Two years ago, Fritz believed the propaganda that Germany would win whatever war they started. Now, his mom's words that the invasion of Poland was just the beginning of the end seemed to be more true. More planes, more bombs, more drafts, more death.

Some of the older guys who were on vacation from the army almost immediately packed up and left, knowing that their leave was over. But before the first people left, everyone agreed that they would try to meet on the first Sunday in September, at Felsensee, if possible.

19 — Jean

The first five or six years his father had been in prison, Jean had been too young to visit him. Then his father was assigned to a work detail in a nearby quarry. Jean could go to the worksite and bring his dad food and warmer clothes, even though every part of that was illegal. Jean had hardly seen his dad since he was four and hadn't seen him at all since he was seven. Jean was now twelve, and sometimes he felt like the man in front of him was a stranger, but he still loved his dad and wanted to visit him, to talk to him.

"Kid, we are going to lose this war," Jean's father said one visit.

Jean couldn't believe that the Germans wouldn't win the war. The war had just started and a German victory followed each battle. Every day, he heard special reports on the radio about sunken ships, at school they followed the forward movement of troops, and in every newspaper there was a euphoria that Germany would win the war.

"Our troops are on the front and winning—France, Poland, Norway, and in Africa. How could we lose this war?" Jean asked.

His dad didn't buy the propaganda the Nazis blasted on the radio, in newspapers, and on posters. He didn't think the Germans would win.

20 — Fritz

Getting kicked out of the Hitler Youth was probably the best thing that had happened to Fritz. If that hadn't happened, he would have never become a Navajo. But not being in the Hitler Youth also made things harder for him.

"Well, you know that if you want to be an apprentice you have to be in the factory division of the Hitler Youth," his principal had told him at the end of the school year in the spring of 1941. He was supposed to start vocational training when he graduated Volksschule, the equivalent of eighth grade, and he had planned to get a position as a tool-making apprentice at the Ford factory, where his father had worked. The Ford factory was built by the American company in 1931, and the Ford Motor Company had continued to make investments and lobby for contracts to make

German military trucks until the war started in 1939. After that, the company became a German subsidiary of the American company, known as Ford-Werke A.G., but everyone still just called it Ford. Fritz had applied for the job even though he wasn't in the Hitler Youth. He had been denied. He got a job as an errand boy instead, and he thought running errands in his white uniform was kind of fun. Sometimes he got chocolate and candy from the secretaries. But being a page at Ford wasn't the road to a career, and he needed a plan.

Fritz was supposed to be officially on the roster as a member of the Hitler Youth by October 1, 1941, in order to be considered for an apprenticeship. But the Nazis kept very good records, and Hitler Youth leaders knew that Fritz had disobeyed orders and told his superiors to kiss his ass. His records showed that he had been given many opportunities to apologize for his bad behavior and that he'd taken none of them. When Fritz's dad went to the Hitler Youth leaders to see if Fritz could get back in, they reminded him of that history, and in response, Fritz's dad lost his temper. Fritz's dad thought they were being disrespectful of someone who was in the army. Yelling at them probably didn't help Fritz's case.

A few days later, his dad tried a different approach. He went to an old colleague at Ford, who was an apprentice supervisor, and asked him to put in a good word for Fritz. It worked. On the positive side, Fritz now had a job. On the bad side, he also had to report to Hitler Youth training from 7:00 a.m. to noon every Saturday, again.

The sirens had started and Jean and his grandparents ran down into the bunker in the basement of their apartment on Sülzburger Street. During the winter of 1941, the bombings had become more frequent and on this night the bombs were falling again. The whole room shook, like a train roaring past at full speed.

Jean was in the first bunker of the house, in the basement between the front part of the building that faced the street and a back garden house. The basements were always damp. In the winter that meant the air was cold and you could never get warm, and in the summer it meant that it was muggy and wet and you could never get dry. Jean had heard soldiers on leave from the front say being here was worse than the battlefield. There, at least they could move away. In the bunker, everyone was just waiting for death. Everyone was sitting, on the bunk beds or chairs or benches, too afraid to sleep.

First, Jean heard the droning of airplane engines followed by the whirling whizzing of a bomb falling from the sky, coming closer and closer. Then, everything happened almost at once. The room lurched out of place and the air pressure changed inside the bunker. A loud pop exploded, followed by a rushing noise.

A rumbling and cracking came from above as the ceiling buckled down. Stones fell to the cement floor and dust clouded the room. Then, the lights went out. Screams erupted from every direction. People were afraid and confused. They thought that the house was going to collapse, that they were going to be buried alive.

The noise stopped, no more crashing. After a minute, calm settled on the bunker. Jean thought people believed the ceiling would hold.

"No open flame! The gas lines have been hit!" someone yelled in the dark. They had to get out of there before something exploded or they were all poisoned by the fumes.

Jean made his way through the dark hallway to the stairs, but he realized his grandmother wasn't with him. He went back into the bunker and heard someone coughing. In the dark and clouds of dust, Jean could see that his grandmother was standing behind the rubble where the ceiling was collapsing. She'd lost her way in the dark. He pulled her and led her out of the bunker, trying not to breathe too deeply.

They broke out into the night and Jean started taking deep breaths. His lungs had been filling up with the thick air in the bunker. The planes were still dropping bombs, but they stayed in the courtyard of the building anyway. The building and the bunker seemed ready for collapse at any moment. When the sirens stopped, his family went to his aunt's house a few blocks away.

The next day, Jean went back to his apartment and saw the full extent of the destruction in the morning light. People were there, clearing the rubble and pulling out bodies. Parts of the building were still standing, and he was allowed to go in and quickly gather some belongings. He couldn't be inside for very long; the building was still at risk of collapsing. Then he spotted his neighbor who lived on the third floor. She'd been trapped under a steel truss that had protected her from more rubble falling on her. She found out her daughter wasn't that lucky, and she just screamed over and over again, "Why do I have to live when my child is dead?"

Memorandum of the Reich Youth Leadership

SEPTEMBER 1942

Since the beginning of 1942, all of the HY-groups of Düsseldorf have observed that youth of both sexes are increasingly joining into cliques that take trips together, many times putting themselves into open opposition against the HY and the work of the unit leader of the HY. HY-leaders have been attacked, accosted, and even shot at. The outfits of the cliques resemble that for the former Bündische Youth. Particularly loved is the Edelweiss symbol.

A large-scale monitoring operation on May 3, 1942, had the following results: in 8 excursion locations around the area, 55 groups with between 7 and 15 members were observed.

22 — Fritz

Fritz Theilen was on the lower bunk of a hospital bed resting after a hernia operation when he heard a humming. It wasn't the humming of an approaching bomber or of a machine at the factory, no, this was a melodic humming, like a song. He knew this song. He started humming along.

A head popped down from the top bunk.

"How do you know that?" the head asked. The guy looked a little older than Fritz, maybe fifteen or sixteen years old.

"Well, how do *you* know the song?" Fritz asked without directly answering the question. Something from the other guy's way of acting made Fritz trust him. The boy introduced himself as Mac, and Fritz confided in him that he had been in a bündische group, where he'd learned the song, but that the group really wasn't meeting anymore.

"Man, then you have to come with us to the Volksgarten, that's where the Edelweiss Pirates are," Mac replied, and told Fritz about his friends.

23 — Gertrud

Every month, a letter arrived for Gertrud: a little piece of paper, wrapped in an envelope, with a little picture of Hitler in the corner for the stamp. The letter came from the Esterwegen camp, from her dad. Inside, the words were almost always the same: He was doing fine; he was getting enough to eat; and he had learned a lot of good things from the Nazis.

Lies, all lies. Gertrud and her mother knew it. Gertrud's mother said that she didn't think the Nazis could change who he was; he was too obstinate, too determined, believed too strongly in the cause of giving power to the people. What was written in the letter didn't even really matter that much, but the piece of paper did. Every letter they received meant that he was still alive on the day that he sent it.

Once a month, they wrote him a letter back. The stuff was always boring too: a gray-and-white-striped cat had run up to them, her mother had made a nice dress. If he read the letters, he knew they were okay too. He wasn't here, with them, but he wasn't gone either.

She couldn't tell him about her new friends or how she refused to join the LGG, no matter how much she wanted to. She thought he would have been proud she wasn't giving in to the Nazis. Gertrud knew she would have to wait for him to come home before she could tell him about the Edelweiss Group and what she had been doing with her friends.

In May 1942, there was no letter.

Mail came twice a day then, but day after day, nothing. Gertrud didn't know why there was no envelope from her father. Was it because he had done something, and he wasn't allowed to write anymore? Her mom was less optimistic. She told Gertrud she feared the worst.

No, he's alive. They must have moved him to a different camp, Gertrud thought.

Part Three
1942–1943

*"If you don't want to be a soldier, and
you don't want to burn up, then you have
to actively do something, become a part
of the underground, commit sabotage."*

Cologne, 1942

In the spring of 1942, the war is here in Cologne and the war machine is all-encompassing.

On the right side of the Hohenzollern Bridge, the Messe building vibrates with the coming and going of bodies. Polish, French, and Russian soldiers are brought here and held as prisoners of war, forced to work in factories that surround the city, factories like Ford-Werke. Since fall 1941, the Messe has also been a departure point for tens of thousands of people who are being deported from Cologne. This spring alone, 44,000 people are sent from the Messe to Theresienstadt, a camp-ghetto where they face almost certain death from disease or further transport to extermination camps like Auschwitz, Majdanek, and Treblinka.

As the German army marches forward and occupies land, they send back not just prisoners of war but laborers too. The Reich needs people to work in factories, to keep producing cars and trucks and rubber and guns and bullets. Tens of thousands of people arrive in Cologne from France, Belgium, Ukraine, Poland, and Russia. You see these people arrive in the city. They are young, sometimes as young as thirteen, and many of them are women. They live in unsanitary camps and are given tattered clothing and wooden shoes. They are enslaved to the Reich.

These camps and sites of terror are not just in the city. Outside Cologne in the town of Brauweiler, there is a prison that morphs to fit the needs of the Nazis. Years ago, it was an old-school penitentiary where prisoners had to work off their sentence. Your parents might threaten to send you there if you misbehaved. The joke isn't funny by 1933, when the prison becomes a concentration camp. In 1938, hundreds of Jews from Cologne were held at Brauweiler before being transported to the concentration camp Dachau. By 1940, when the cells at Gestapo headquarters swell with bodies,

Brauweiler is used as a prison to hold young people arrested during raids of bündische youth groups. Most of the time young people are let go with a warning and a fine, but sometimes they're transported to youth reeducation camps.

Just after midnight on the evening of Saturday, May 30, 1942, a full moon shines down on Cologne. An all-too-familiar noise rises across the city. First you hear a whirring, then the sound rises to a note that isn't quite in the scale, then dips back down, oscillating between two screaming tones. These airwaves against your eardrums instinctively make you uncomfortable.

All the residents of Cologne know what the sound means: an attack is coming; planes are coming; bombs are coming. In every building, residents clamor down staircases into the basement or out into the streets, heading for the nearest bunker. For a whole apartment building, there might be a single room where you press yourself together with all your neighbors and pray that the building won't collapse. The bunkers are either cold and dark or hot and dark, depending on the season. They smell bad year-round. There are no comforts, but there might be a bunk bed for the kids to lie down on, some chairs for others to sit on. Still, you might not even think about how uncomfortable the physical space is. Instead, you look up and listen for the rumble of planes and whistles of bombs, wonder if your home will still be standing. Ninety minutes in the shelter feels like an eternity.

On this night in 1942, the Allied bombers fly over Cologne in formation, covering the night sky like a flock of birds. You've never seen this many planes flying together. The moonlight means both that the British planes can see their targets and that the German air defense can see the planes, but only the Brits seem to gain an advantage. The British planes fly overhead, a bomb dropping every six seconds. Now the war finally feels like it has come to Cologne.

24 — Jean

Jean moved back in with his mom after his grandparents were evacuated from Cologne, and the two of them had spent the night in the apartment's bunker on May 30. The next morning, they had to climb from the basement through other bombed-out houses, to a stairway that finally took them up to street level.

Out on the street, the burned homes left a sweet, toxic odor. The air was thick and hot as flames flipped in the wind and smoke clouded the streets. He found a piece of paper, dunked it in a bucket of water, and put it over his head.

They needed to get out of the street and into a square or park quickly. The wood inside the houses was burned and the heat had expanded the metal. The buildings could buckle and collapse at any moment. They ran through the falling and burning joists, stones, and rubble to Eifel Square, where the buildings were less dense. Only when they could stop and look around did they see how bad the neighborhood looked and realize they'd narrowly escaped death.

25 — Fritz

When Fritz emerged from the safety of a bunker after the night of 1,000 bombers, the acrid, earthy smell of burning filled his nostrils. Smoke billowed up from piles of stone and wood where a building used to stand. The smoke filled up mouths and lungs, causing people to cough and choke. Flames climbed up walls, illuminating the predawn gloom more than the moon ever could. People cried out in despair, desperately searching for missing loved ones.

Fritz was in an emergency firefighting brigade with other men and boys who weren't on the front. His job was to go around with a fire engine and save whatever there was to save. With every moment that passed, that seemed to be less and less of the city, as the fires raged and buildings buckled in on themselves. Fritz's most important task was to make sure that the entrances to shelters and bunkers were clear so no one was trapped underground.

Fritz found himself in front of a bunker where a bomb had broken through the shelter and destroyed everything—and everyone— inside. He couldn't imagine the gruesome scene when people realized they were about to die. This war was bringing everything to an end, it seemed.

Fritz couldn't stop and think for long in front of a place where there was no one to save while there were others who were still alive and trapped. His brigade needed to move on.

As he moved through the city, the destruction didn't stop, and neither did the death. Fritz helped load bodies into a truck. He looked at the crumpled corpses, mangled from the fire, some barely recognizable as human forms. Their skin was black and red and blistered and even white where the flesh burned to the bone. People out on the streets tried to cover their noses and mouths with handkerchiefs to not inhale so much smoke, but the sweet, meaty smell of so many burning bodies was probably too thick to filter out. The smell wasn't like the meat and sausages Fritz's uncle had cooked and sold in the butcher shop; this was sour, metallic, wet, thick, and made his stomach churn.

This was hell, and he wanted to get out. It didn't matter where, he just wanted to get away. He wanted to scream. But his stomach was somewhere in his throat, and the disgust and the nausea made it so he couldn't even open his mouth. Parting his lips might mean emptying his stomach.

"Hey, sissy!" one older policeman yelled from behind Fritz. Fritz hadn't realized he had just been standing there, staring, trying not to puke.

"Get those bodies moving and don't stand here like a dummy! You'll see a lot worse than this out on the real front!" the man yelled as he pushed Fritz against the wall where they were stacking bodies.

One night of bombing had made the city look abandoned for hundreds of years, like the ruins of Rome. Almost five hundred people had died, tens of thousands were left homeless. This was what the war was giving them: death, destruction, chaos.

Fritz thought back to the previous trips with the Navajos. They hadn't managed to meet again at Felsensee in September. So many of those friends were now dead, wounded, missing, or in prison. He hadn't understood their fear at the time; being old enough to be a soldier felt like an eternity away. But now, just a few years later, the war had pulled him in. How would he survive?

"If you don't want to be a soldier, and you don't want to burn up, then you have to actively do something, become a part of the underground, commit sabotage," one of his friends told him. Fritz wasn't so sure about that. He wasn't sure what he was willing to risk, and he still feared the repression and terror of the Nazis.

26 — Jean

The day after the 1,000-bomber raid, Jean walked the streets of the city. Little fires burned under collapsed buildings. Bodies lay in the street, sometimes totally unrecognizable as anything except a soft, organic mass. He was scared, but he was also young enough that these attacks quickly became a normal part of life. He'd already seen a girl in his apartment building crushed and a friend in school had died after an earlier air raid.

Hitler was also shocked by the death and destruction, even though the propaganda machine kept saying that Germany would win the war. What the government was really afraid of was losing a future generation of soldiers in bombings. So in the summer of 1942, Jean was sent to the countryside with his school class of eleven other boys in a Nazi program that relocated children for their safety.

Jean was away from his family again, but this time, he wasn't meek and scared like he'd been at the boys' home. There, other kids had picked up on his weakness and had no problem bullying him or beating him up. In the country, all the boys became equal. Jean realized that the other boys weren't any smarter or stronger than he was. He came home more self-confident and more respected by his peers.

27 — Gertrud

We have to do something.

Gertrud had been thinking that for months. The feeling probably grew a little each time something happened: her father's arrest; the destruction of neighborhood Jewish businesses and the synagogue on Kristallnacht; the bombings; her friends becoming soldiers. Not only was the Nazi power touching every part of life, the harm they caused was more and more apparent and things weren't getting better.

"Can't we do something?" Jus seemed to read her mind. She was hanging out with her hiking friends, and they felt the same way she did.

"What can we do against the brown horde?" Banjo Willi asked skeptically. They were just teenagers, and they had seen what had happened to people who resisted the Nazis.

"I think we should distribute flyers," said Jus.

Gertrud's eyes lit up. Yes, this was an idea. She wanted to make people stop and think, so that they weren't just going about their business as usual. She'd seen her parents do it, so this type of action wasn't unfamiliar.

"I think that's a great idea," she said.

Jus had a connection with a printer, who agreed to get the flyers for him. To remain anonymous, they called him Tom. Most of the time, they just printed slogans in big lettering, like:

PUT AN END TO THE BROWN HORDE

SOLDIERS, LAY DOWN YOUR WEAPONS

They had no idea how dangerous what they were doing was.

Gertrud could barely see the top of the Cologne Cathedral if she stood outside and looked straight up. The dark stones ascended into the sky, with hooks and points and edges sticking out like sugar crystals growing in a glass. This building was something from the past, when people would come from hundreds of miles to pray inside the Cathedral at the bones of the Three Kings from the Bible story. This church was visible for miles around, from the Ford factory to the Seven Mountains. And it was easy to spot from high in the air, where American and British planes dropped bombs.

The heavy doors opened, and Gertrud stepped inside. The large sanctuary unfolded in front of her as the doors shut out the light from outside. Almost no matter the weather, the large open space, thick stone walls, and stained-glass windows kept the sanctuary cool and dark. This was a perfect place to hide flyers where people would find them.

People shuffled around, everyone looking up and around at the magnificence, the light shimmering through the red and blue and yellow glass, putting visitors in a trance. They were not paying attention to Gertrud and her friends.

Gertrud had a shoulder bag full of flyers, already folded up, ready to go. She picked up a hymnal and carefully placed it into her bag. Then she opened the book without looking down and slipped in a flyer among the pages of holy songs. She took the book out of her bag and placed it back on the rack on the pew. No paper could be sticking out, and no one could see them picking up the books or putting them back. The Catholic Church had also suffered at the hands of the Nazis, but anyone here might think

In the fall of 1942, Gestapo in the cities of Cologne, Wuppertal, and Düsseldorf found anti-Nazi graffiti attributed to the Edelweiss Pirates. Phrases included "The Bündisch Youth Live," "Down with Hitler," and "The High Command of the Wermacht [armed forces] lies."

what they were doing was suspicious and report them to the Gestapo anyway.

She moved along the pews, doing the same trick over and over again, all around the massive sanctuary. She didn't have many flyers, but she needed to get rid of all of them right then and there. Nothing could be found on her person.

When Gertrud and her friends didn't have flyers, they had other plans. They would meet up at night, and move through the black, empty streets. No lights could shine, and there were no streetlights and no stoplights. Every house window had to have a blackout curtain, and cars weren't supposed to drive with headlights. The city was supposed to be hidden from the bombers flying overhead. The cloak of darkness also meant the Edelweiss Group could sneak through the streets with their buckets of white paint and scrawl messages on the sides of buildings.

One of the newer members of the group, Sepp, had compared the Nazis to shit because of their brown shirts. So he wrote:

IS YOUR NOSE STILL FULL OF BROWN SHIT?

and

AS BROWN AS SHIT.
THAT'S HOW BROWN COLOGNE IS.
WAKE UP!

Once, the day after a night of graffiti, they heard someone say something like, "Those pigs, destroying the houses. It was definitely the Communists, those scumbags," as if the messages they were writing on the houses were worse than the destruction the Nazi war was causing. On the other hand, when they heard people supporting the graffiti, it made Gertrud happy. The more they did, the bigger impact they could have, even if it also meant more

"Heil Navajo" graffiti, a reference to the bündische youth group, found in Cologne's inner city on the night of September 13, 1942.

danger. That was when they decided to drop flyers at the main train station in Cologne.

Months had passed, and Gertrud and her mother still hadn't received a letter from her father, or from the camp in Esterwegen explaining why the letters had stopped. They thought about whether they should travel north, up to the camp, but they thought there was a strong chance they would be turned away at the gate.

On a Sunday afternoon in September 1942, Gertrud and her mother were sitting down for a cup of substitute coffee—a mix of roasted roots, grains, and water that was brown like coffee, but tasted like wood chips. Their lives were so different now than they had been nine years ago. They used to sit and talk at their big, wooden dining table. Now they hardly ever had a chance to talk to each other. They used to have that big dining room where friends could come and enjoy themselves; now they had a tiny two-room apartment. They used to sip real coffee and eat cheese and sausage for dinner; now they had substitute coffee and butter was a delicacy. Once Gertrud's father had been arrested as a political prisoner, they weren't allowed to get ration cards, and no ration cards meant no food, not that there was much food around during the war anyway, regardless of whether you had a ration card.

There was a knock at the door. They didn't get many visitors, but Gertrud's mom answered the door anyway.

A man stood in the hallway. He held a black hat in his hands, and his thinning gray hair stuck to his scalp. His face was narrow and thin, and his skin was a sickly yellow. He didn't look healthy, but somehow he still looked strong. He was out of place, and he didn't try to hide it. They didn't know who he was.

"Are you Mrs. Kühlem?" he asked nervously.

Gertrud's mother nodded. From the kitchen table, Gertrud couldn't see her mother's face, but she noticed her shoulders were tight and flexed, a woman ready for the worst.

"I promised your husband I would come to find you," he said.

Gertrud's father knew this man; that made Gertrud's mother relax.

"Come in," her mother offered as she stepped aside. She closed the door.

He sat down in the kitchen, in the third chair, the chair Gertrud's father used to sit in.

He said his named was Pater and that he knew Gertrud's father from Esterwegen. They had worked together in the peat moss fields around the camp. At night, Gertrud's father had shared stories about his family. They had promised each other that whoever got out first would go to the other's family.

"I was let out all of a sudden," Pater told them.

"Where is my husband? How is it going for him?" Gertrud's mother asked in a soft voice. Gertrud thought she sounded like she already knew the answer.

"I came from Berlin," he said. He looked down at the black hat in his hands, twisting it around. He seemed like he didn't want to meet their eyes.

"He's dead." Gertrud's mother said it for him. "They've killed him."

"Yes," he said.

Gertrud didn't believe it, couldn't believe it. Was it a joke? He wouldn't joke about someone dying, right? This couldn't be real. Was he an actor? Was this a play? This wasn't a play. How could it be a play? This had to be real.

When her father had stopped writing in May. That was when he died.

"What did they do to my dad?" Gertrud asked. She couldn't imagine that anyone other than the Nazis was fully responsible.

"I don't know. One day I didn't see him anymore, and I asked a block guard what had happened. They said he was in the infirmary." When he had asked more questions, he didn't get answers, just threats. Pater told them how awful it was in the camp. People sick, dying, buried in mass graves.

He kept talking, but Gertrud wasn't listening. She thought of sliding next to her dad on the leather couch and reading Rosa Luxemburg. He'd petted her soft hair and called her his little laughing dove. He'd never call her that again. They'd never walk together along the Rhine again, he'd never tell her about his days fighting the Nazis in the Communist Party, she'd never get to tell him about how she was fighting the Nazis now. In that moment, she promised herself she wouldn't give up, and she wouldn't give in.

Later, Gertrud and her mom received a letter from Esterwegen with a note that her father was shot trying to escape. That was all, no more details. Gertrud's mom told her it couldn't have been true. Her father knew he would have been shot if he tried to escape, which would have left them without him.

But it might have been true. The camp might have been too much to handle, or he might have thought he could get away.

28 — Jean

By the fall of 1942, Jean was thirteen years old and had returned from the countryside and started at the school on Manderscheider Square in his old neighborhood of Sülz. It was at the little park in the square where Jean and his best friend, Ferdinand Steingass, who went by Fän, first saw the kids in the funny clothes. They looked so different from the Hitler Youth. Their outfits were playful and carefree, not strict uniforms. They seemed like they didn't fit in, but in a way that Jean thought was cool. The kids allowed Jean and Fän to join their group. They called themselves the Edelweiss Pirates.

Jean loved the songs they sang, and gave himself the nickname Schang, from his favorite song, "It Was in Shanghai."

Jean and this group of Pirates were around the same age—young enough not to be in the draft or to face many wartime duties. So, like the Edelweiss group that Gertrud was in, Jean and his friends went on longer weekend trips south on the Rhine, to the Seven Mountains or Drachenfels.

One weekend, Jean and his new friends took a trip out to the Seven Mountains. Jean's way of getting there was almost always to take the train that went along

Jean (bottom right) and friends in Beethoven Park, 1943.

Top: Pirates at Felsensee, early 1940s.
Bottom: The Drachenburg Castle, in Königswinter, 2017. From 1943 to 1945, the castle served as an Adolf Hitler School.

the Rhine River south to Bonn, then the streetcar to Königswinter, and then to hike up the hill to the ponds tucked away in the side of the old rock quarries. He loved finding a cave to sleep in and building a campfire. Like Fritz and Gertrud and dozens of other kids, he enjoyed being away from the city and the destruction of the war, in an oasis of people with whom he got along. He didn't have to worry about how he felt or what he said. He and his friends would sit for hours in the calm of the forest and sing songs and talk. He could talk to girls too, and here, their conversations were never interrupted by air-raid sirens.

The sun was shining on Sunday morning as they walked to Königswinter with a plan to hike up the Drachenfels, a storybook castle ruin at the top of the mountain. Someone had brought a picnic—potato salad and sandwiches—and the plan was to eat and enjoy the view of mountains sloping down into the Rhine.

They didn't make it that far. Between the top of the mountain and the town of Königswinter on the Rhine was the Drachenburg Castle, which was being turned into an Adolf Hitler School, an elite training academy for Hitler Youth. Before they could start up the mountain, Jean and his friends ran into a group of guys marching in straight lines.* Their short hair was parted to one side, and they wore black shorts and shirts and red-and-white-striped bands on their arms.

The Nazis had long ago given Hitler Youth patrols the authority to police other young people, and this patrol asked Jean and his friends for their IDs. The Pirates refused. They hadn't done anything, so why should they have to submit to that request?

They weren't afraid to get in a fight with the Hitler Youth, most of whom were from families that had money and could pay for high school, while the Pirates had to work as apprentices doing manual labor. Even before the Nazis came to power, there was a

---

* Although the school didn't open in the castle until 1943, the boys were in a school in Königswinter and working on the reconstruction of the castle after a bomb attack.

tension between young people from different backgrounds, and the authority the Nazis gave wealthier teenagers only made things worse. Jean thought his friends were the strong ones.

Someone threw a punch and a fight started. The Pirates had knives, but this time they settled for using their fists to fight. Knuckles sank into flesh and hit bone, arms wrapped around bodies, heads ducked out of the way, bodies fell to the ground. Jean thought they could win like they'd done in the park in the city sometimes, but this felt different. This didn't feel like their turf. The castle ruins could become a trap, and the Hitler Youth could call in backup from the SS and police before the Pirates would be able to get out of there. They pulled back and made a run for the trolley back to Cologne.

When they finally made it back to the city, they decided to skip their normal stop and then backtrack to their neighborhood. They had a bad feeling about what had just happened and didn't want to risk being ambushed at the train station.

Curiosity overtook them. When they got back to the neighborhood, they couldn't help peeking at their normal stop, where they saw Hitler Youth, men in trench coats, and SS officers waiting on the platform.

Jean knew they'd been lucky this time.

29 — Gertrud

The air was crisp and cool, and clouds danced across a milky yellow sun. A gust of autumn wind made Gertrud pull her windbreaker closer. She and her friends met at 8:00 a.m. on a fall day in 1942 to take the train from Cologne east across the Rhine to the town

Pirates on a hike at Königswinter, 1941 or 1942.

of Bergisch Gladbach. From there, they hiked through the hills of the Berg region around the town. Their goal was the Liesenberger Mill, which wasn't really a mill, but an inn where they could stay.

Gertrud liked the gentle hills and the slow hike to the Mill, where everyone felt safe. The smell of burning buildings left their nostrils, the sound of air-raid sirens stopped blaring in their ears, and there was no rubble to climb around. Here, they felt the cool air against their faces, heard wind rustling and birds chirping, and saw old houses with slate siding, rock mined from the hills around the area. The only other people they encountered were farmers.

Even so, they couldn't help but talk about what was going on at home.

"The Nazis treat forced laborers worse than farmers treat pigs," Jus said as they walked.

Gertrud agreed. She had seen a camp where Russian and French prisoners of war and forced laborers were being kept, and another with mainly Ukrainians. She couldn't believe how young they looked—younger than she was, just kids. The thin, pale faces with big eyes had stared at her through the metal fences. A while back, Gertrud and her mom had come up with a plan to get sugar cubes to the starving prisoners. Gertrud's mom got the sugar from the pharmacy where she worked, wrapped it in brown paper, and Gertrud would casually drop the tiny packages from her coat pocket as she walked by the fence in the early evenings. One day, Gertrud had seen a guard standing around, looking suspiciously at her. Her mom stopped the whole plan, saying it was too dangerous. Gertrud hated that the women and girls were still malnourished and suffering, but she hadn't come up with another plan.

"I've heard that the browns are afraid the forced laborers will desert or join together with a resistance group," said Lolli, another girl from Cologne who hung out with Gertrud at the Volksgarten. Lolli's real name was Käthe Thelen, but like Gertrud—Mucki— she went by a nickname in the group.

"Is there really no way to help?" Gertrud asked.

"We could try to get more rations from food supply trains," Ellie suggested.

"Do you think the trains are open and you can just waltz right in?" Lolli replied. She said what they all might have been thinking. Their actions had been nonviolent. Leaving flyers, painting graffiti, those were actions to make people stop and think. Yes, Gertrud had hit that Hitler Youth, but he had hit her first. She was against provoking violence, and that's what stealing would probably do.

Jus said the forced laborers weren't likely to get more food; their treatment was murder on installments. The laborers would be worked harder and harder, with less and less food and little medical care. They would get skinnier and weaker, and then they would die, for no other reason than that they were from the Ukraine or Poland, or a prisoner from France, Belgium, the Netherlands, or Russia.

As they hiked, they started coming up with a plan to get the food out of the trains and to the forced laborers.

One of Gertrud's friends had been strumming his guitar as they walked. They wanted it to look like they were just walking and singing, not doing anything suspicious. All of a sudden, he broke into song:

> Forests and pines swim in the morning fog;
> We wander silently through the homeland.
> We see hills, meadows, villages, and fields
> As it has been for many years.
>
> And this earth, born to us,
> She holds us tight with invisible bands.
> You often thought, we had lost her;
> You often thought, a foreign land beckoned.
>
> In our hearts, a holy will stands;
> In our blood, a command throbs.
> You saw too little, you saw only the shell,
> Because in us lives a song with deep desire.

They were getting close to a farm where an old farmer was sitting on a tractor, and around him were two women, some children, and a couple of chickens picking at the ground. Some Pirates had been arrested on hikes, just for the way they looked. The song they were singing seemed innocent enough, a decent cover for kids out on a hike. They kept walking away from the farmer and the music faded.

"Some other groups have gone so far as to steal explosives to get food out of the trains," Gertrud said, even though she was totally against that idea. She thought it sounded like arrogance more than a thoughtful action. She suggested that next time they were writing graffiti on trains, they should check to see if there were any wagons that were open.

One source says this is Gertrud (left) hiking east of Bergisch Gladbach with friends from Cologne and Wuppertal around 1940, while another says Gertrud is hiking with members of the Volksgarten Edelweiss Group in the Seven Mountains in 1941 or 1942. The photo could have been mislabeled or misidentified, or this could be the result of how two different people remembered the trip.

Ellie didn't think it was a good idea to attempt anything in Cologne. She'd heard that kids from Ehrenfeld—Fritz Theilen's neighborhood—had been doing something similar, and that it had gotten notice from the Gestapo. They decided it might be better to try it in a nearby smaller city, like Wermelskirchen. They knew a group there that might help them.

"Not without batting your eyelashes at the boys," Lolli teased.

Everyone let out a laugh. Ellie was a master of getting the information she wanted and wrapping guys around her finger when she gave them the right look. Gertrud admired that about her.

They arrived at the Mill in the early evening, the haze of a long, slow sunset unfolding before them. They settled into their rooms, and after dinner Gertrud, Lolli, and Ellie plopped down in front of the tile stove in the common room. The burning logs popped and crackled and the warmth radiated out into the room.

"I want to be, like, really in love," Lolli said, her dark eyes gazing into the flames. "I don't know what it is . . . love."

"Be happy. Before you know it, you'll be married and have two, three kids," said Ellie. "And besides, you haven't seen anything of the world."

"I envy you, Mucki," Lolli said to Gertrud. Her voice had a longing in it. "You have Gustav." Even though Gertrud and Banjo Willi had played lovers when they dropped flyers, she and Jus were actually a couple. They had left flyers and painted graffiti together, and when they were camping, Jus would sit next to her at the campfire. He'd slip his fingers between hers, and they would sit, holding hands, watching the fire.

"You guys flirt with each other, without him wanting to rush into things. You just look at each other and seem to understand each other's thinking," Lolli continued.

"Flirt?! They've kissed," Ellie exclaimed.

Gertrud felt a warmth in her cheeks, and not from the fire. Ellie was right; Gertrud and Jus had kissed. Her whole face was flushed. Lolli noticed.

"Ring the bells, why don't you," Lolli said.

"No one heard me," Ellie replied. The guys were all doing their own thing.

"Do you know how your true love is supposed to look, Lolli?" Gertrud asked.

"He has to be blond."

"And with eyes so blue and deep like an unending ocean, with broad, wide, shoulders?" Ellie couldn't keep her sarcasm to herself.

Ellie and Lolli went back and forth, playfully, almost forgetting that there was gossip to be heard.

Lolli pulled her attention back to Gertrud. "So, have you and Gustav . . . "

Gertrud turned even more red. They didn't normally talk about guys, and they definitely didn't talk about sex. Sexuality in general was a taboo, and none of them really knew anything about anything. "Normal" sexuality fit into a small box in Nazi Germany: anything other than being heterosexual and cisgender was considered deviant. The role of women was to marry and have babies, and anything outside of that was not acceptable in the eyes of the state. Women who had sex before they were married were said to have loose morals and could be sent to prison. Women and men who didn't want to get married and have children, for whatever reason, were seen as detriments to the growth of the country.

Everything that the girls knew about their bodies was from gossip at school or on the street. When Gertrud got her first period, her mom told her that she shouldn't get into bed with a man now, because if she did, she'd soon have a baby. Gertrud didn't really understand what "into bed" meant, and her mother didn't clarify.

"What are you talking about?" Gertrud asked Lolli. She was playing dumb, but also hoped that Lolli might explain something she didn't know. "I'm not engaged," she added.

"What does one thing have to do with the other?" Ellie asked.

Gertrud and Ellie didn't get their questions answered. The innkeeper suddenly pressed himself down in between them.

"So girls, are you talking politics? Someone looking at you would think you're trying to conquer the world," he said. "Or am I wrong?"

What an ass. Had he come over to sit with them because they were cute and young, or was it worse than that? Gertrud thought he might actually be trying to find out about their politics, a risk she wasn't willing to take.

"Politics? Who's interested in that? We hike—or gossip about cute guys," she said in her high-pitched voice, maybe adding an octave to attempt a vapid, girly tone.

He wasn't convinced. He told them he'd heard Jus talking about the Navajos.

They didn't believe him. Jus wouldn't have been talking about another group like that out in the open; that was way too risky. There were other groups here that went hiking and sang songs they weren't supposed to, but they weren't political. Talking about a group that had been specifically banned by the Nazis was dangerous. Was this guy laying down a trap?

Lolli noticed Gertrud's apprehension with the innkeeper's probing and did her best to seem unaware of what "Navajo" meant in a political context. The innkeeper definitely wasn't talking about Karl May, but there was no way to be sure whether he was on their side or the wrong side.

The innkeeper eventually gave up, and later Gertrud asked Jus if he had said anything about the Navajos. He shook his head.

Wrong side.

After spending the night at the Mill, Gertrud's group decided to hike on toward their next destination. The encounter with the innkeeper had given her a bad feeling, but she pushed it to the back of her mind as they hiked north to Altenburg.

Just as they reached the top of a hill, Gertrud's stomach sank. Standing across from them was a group of Gestapo officers.

Gertrud and her friends were loaded into a truck and brought in for questioning at the Gestapo office. Soon, they were released. After all the flyers, all the graffiti, all the things she and her parents had done, she'd likely been arrested because of the inn-keeper's suspicions, although she didn't know for sure.

This run-in with authorities was supposed to scare the Edelweiss Group into behaving. The next time Gertrud met with her friends, the question was the same for everyone. Do they keep going? Or quit before things get worse?

An die geknechtete deutsche Jugend!

Deutsche Jugend, denke an deine alte gold'ne Zeit der Pfadfinder denke zurück an die sonnigen Tage der Fahrten und der Lager. Dieses alles ist euch heute versagt. Warum? Das heutige Nazi-Deutschland will euch in die "Hitler-Jugend" stecken. Wo ihr militärisch und fachlich ausgebildet werdet im marschieren, Schießen, Karten- und Geländekunde u.s.w. Das Ziel worauf dieses alles zurück geht ist: Kanonenfutter für Hitlers unersättliche Machtgier!

Deutsche Jugend erhebe dich zum Kampf für die Freiheit und Rechte eurer Kinder und Kindeskinder, denn wenn Hitler den Krieg gewinnt ist Europa ein Chaos, die Welt wird geknechtet sein bis zum jüngsten Tage. Bereitet der Knechtschaft ein Ende ehe es zu spät ist.

Herr mach uns frei!

Flyer discovered by the Wuppertal Gestapo, 1942. The text translates as follows:

To the subjugated German youth!

German youth, think of the golden days of the scouts, think back to the sunny days of trips and camping. This has all been denied to you.

Why? Today's Nazi-Germany wants to stick you in the Hitler Youth. Where you will be trained in military and technical skills like marching, shooting, map-reading, and orienteering, etc. The goal of all of this goes back to: Cannon fodder for Hitler's insatiable greed for power!

German youth, bring yourself to the fight for freedom and rights for your children and your children's children, because if Hitler is to win the war, Europe will be in chaos and the world will be as enslaved as it was in its youngest days. Bring the bondage to an end before it is too late.

Lord free us!

30 — Gertrud

Just a few months after the run-in with the Gestapo, the damp chill of November air swirled around Gertrud and her friends as they finished distributing flyers in Düsseldorf, the next city north from Cologne on the Rhine.

"Does anyone have any more flyers?" the Mountain Climber asked.

Everyone shook their heads.

They looked down at almost-still water in the canal in Düsseldorf's main shopping district. The canal would freeze soon, and the Mountain Climber wanted to throw more flyers into the canal. Their messages might be frozen there all winter, even more indelible than the graffiti they had written a few days earlier.

"A nice image," said the Mountain Climber. "But only a dream."

With nothing left to do, they decided to go to the home of a fellow Pirate named Pepita. They would spend the night with her before they made their way back to Cologne in the morning. They walked a few blocks south to the narrow street where Pepita and her parents lived. The cold air had penetrated the living room where Pepita had spread out wool blankets for Gertrud and her Cologne friends. The chill put Gertrud to sleep almost immediately.

Gertrud felt someone pulling on her shoulders. She blinked her eyes open and saw that the curtains were still drawn and the light was faint in the apartment. She scanned the room. Only about an hour had passed.

She opened her eyes a little wider and saw there were about fifteen people in Pepita's apartment, including Hadschi, the Mountain Climber, the Guardian, Lolli, some of Pepita's friends, and a few more people from Cologne. Two or three people had brought guitars.

Pepita brought out two big plates of sandwiches and a pitcher of water from the kitchen. Someone had brought a little keg of beer too. The Gestapo always used drinking and mixed-gender groups as examples of the degenerate behavior of the Edelweiss Pirates. If anyone was worried, though, they didn't show it. Sometimes, in moments like this, it was easy to forget the war, the bombings, the Hitler Youth, the missing friends and parents. Just like in the woods, they could just eat, drink, talk, and sing.

A guy named Pico strummed his guitar. Gertrud noticed his coarse, floppy hair as he started "We March Along the Rhine and Ruhr." The original was a Hitler Youth song, but they had changed the words for the better:

> We march along the Rhine and Ruhr,
> We are fighting for our freedom.
> The Hitler Youth, break them in two!
> Edelweiss march, watch out—the streets are free!

The song brought back reality. There was a war, and they were a part of it. Pico mentioned posters with anti-Nazi messages they had posted, and they talked about what they had been up to. Gertrud had dropped flyers from bridges so the paper would float down the rivers and canals, and the Nazis would have a hard time knowing where they came from.

They had written, "Soldiers, lay down your weapons, there is no point, your home is no longer here!" and "Stand up, end the war and stand up against Hitler!" Guys in the group had hidden flyers in their pants and taken them to the nearby city of Wuppertal to distribute.

The war kept going; buildings kept burning and crumbling after bombings. There was less and less food and freedom. And everyone in that small apartment felt it was more important than ever to fight the Nazis. Gertrud felt she had to continue what her father had started.

"We were sitting in Jonny's bar, playing cards and drinking schnapps . . . " Someone had started another song, and everyone joined in.

Then, a crash. SS and Hitler Youth Patrol Duty officers barged in and snarled at them.

"We heard you from outside," one of the SS officers boomed. "Looks like there's a nice little party here. Singing bündische songs? You all know that isn't allowed?"

Silence.

"Lying is pointless, we heard you."

Silence.

"Who lives here?" a second SS officer asked.

"I do, together with my mother," said Pepita.

"And does your mother know what's going on here?"

"Yeah, she lets us come here. She thinks it's better that we are here than wandering around on the street." Pepita was calm; her words were clear. Maybe confidence would make the men leave. Maybe confidence meant they weren't doing anything illegal.

"What are you trying to tell me?" the first man yelled. He wasn't buying it. He gave an order for the men to search the apartment and everyone in it.

No one resisted, and no one panicked—though they knew they had reason to be sacred. The Gestapo did not need a reason to act. Anyone who expressed doubt about the war or that Germany would be victorious could be arrested, and anyone talking about or handing out illegal propaganda would definitely be arrested.

The men stomped around the apartment in their leather boots and brown uniforms, shoving their hands in pockets, turning the pockets of jackets inside out, rooting through the girls' bags. One officer pulled a paper with song lyrics and a skull ring from Pico. Some of the groups that called themselves Pirates wore the skull rings or wristbands with skulls on them. From Pepita's room, another officer took an Edelweiss pin, a letter, a diary, and a notebook.

The SS officer looked at the kids. His cold, gray eyes pierced the gazes of Gertrud and her friends. He demanded they sing a song.

"What song would you like to hear?" Pepita asked.

"Hm, what about 'Show Me the Way to Go Home'?" he asked. This was a German folk song, another one that they had changed to have anti-Nazi lyrics, a version they would not be singing right now.

"We don't know that one," said Hadschi.

"Are you refusing to comply?"

"No," said Jose quickly. He hummed the first couple of notes. Everyone joined in and sang along. Gertrud was careful to sing the lyrics the SS officer wanted to hear.

"There's no problem here," said the officer. "Bring them in. And early tomorrow those from Cologne and Wuppertal will be brought back to their cities."

With that, Gertrud was taken to the Düsseldorf Gestapo office. The officer accused her of having a party with beer, which she denied. Early the next morning, she and her friends from Cologne were loaded onto trucks.

❈ ❈ ❈

Before long, they were unloaded at the Gestapo office in Cologne. The EL-DE House sat on a corner in the middle of the city, across the street from the courthouse, right around the corner from the police station, and a few blocks from the main shopping district. The building was like a fortress: solid beige blocks and thick stone frames around the windows. The windows that seemed to sink into the concrete sidewalk at the very bottom of the building were the scariest. They had metal bars and could barely open. People walking by might get a whiff of a foul stench coming from below or hear the cries and screams of the people in the basement.

The EL-DE House was the Gestapo office, but also where some members of the Gestapo lived and where they kept their prisoners. No one who was arrested by the Gestapo knew how long they were going to be kept there. That was part of the power of the Gestapo, and the terror.

Cell at EL-DE House, 2017.

As the officers took the Pirates down the stairs, Gertrud knew she would be separated from the guys.

Banjo Willi winked. They were in this together, even if they weren't together.

The basement was dark. The building had electricity, but the lightbulbs provided hardly any light. The air was cold but thick with damp and the smells of mildew, bodies, and disinfectant. The floor was cold cement, the walls were green and yellow.

An officer pulled on the heavy metal door of the cell and opened up a black hole. He shoved Gertrud inside. The warmth of other bodies—too many bodies—radiated throughout the room, which was no bigger than a small bathroom. The cell was big enough for one or two people at most. Gertrud thought there were at least eight women here, but she couldn't see any of their faces.

She asked how long they had been there. One voice said she had been there two days. Others couldn't or wouldn't answer.

Her eyes adjusted to the light. One face looked familiar, but Gertrud couldn't quite tell if she knew her. The girl's eyes were swollen. Gertrud looked again. *Agnes.* She was seventeen—a year younger than Gertrud—and in another Edelweiss group from Cologne.

Gertrud didn't say anything to her, but when Agnes finally looked up from the floor and their eyes met, Gertrud could tell she was surprised. Gertrud wrapped her hand around Agnes's and they slumped to the floor. They still couldn't speak. Words, acknowledging each other, that was dangerous: those words could be used against them. Anyone could be listening.

Time passed. Maybe an hour, maybe less, maybe more. Gertrud didn't have a way to tell.

The door opened again, and a faint, yellow light snuck into the cell.

"Gertrud Kühlem."

She stepped out into the light of the hallway and looked around at the other cells. She didn't know where her friends were.

"Faster!" the guard yelled. He gripped her arm and pulled her up the staircase. She could see a window, the outside. He kept pulling her up. Once they were out of the basement, he led her down a narrow corridor with a door and another door and then another door. From behind the doors, she heard bodies slamming against hard surfaces, heard those bodies' screams. They arrived at another door—her door—and a man in a uniform opened it.

The room looked like an office, only not quite. It had a wooden table and chairs, but no papers on the table, no typewriter. Gertrud felt uneasy. This was some strange place, not an office at all, but what was it?

"You're a piece of shit, you know that?" the voice erupted at her.*

She didn't say anything. She wasn't going to say anything. She looked down at her winter boots, the leather scuffed and worn.

She felt the blow before she realized what was happening. Someone else's boot slammed into her. Her whole body lurched forward from the force, and she crumpled downward. He hit her again in the ribs, knocking the air from her lungs.

"Who prints your flyers? What's his name? If you tell us, we'll let you go."

Did they actually know she had handed out flyers? Had someone else talked? Or were they just trying to get her to confess and then give other names?

Her throat was dry, her tongue was sticky and heavy. She hadn't had anything to drink or eat in what felt like forever.

"Can't you open your mouth, you slut?"

The Nazis always assumed the bündische youth were sexually deviant because guys and girls hung out together.

"You are an Edelweiss Pirate. Give it up! You are part of this criminal gang."

---

* In her memoir, Gertrud writes that this man is Josef Hoegen. However, Hoegen was at the time serving with the Einsatzgruppen B in Smolensk, and did not return to his duty at the Cologne Gestapo until October 1943.

She kept her head down, looking at her boots. Her mind floated, her thoughts tried to leave this room even if her body couldn't. She wanted to ignore them, pretend like she wasn't here, like this wasn't happening.

"Get out! Back to the cell!"

She looked up. The man's face was red and puffy.

Back in the basement, Agnes's face turned blue and purple with bruises.

More women were taken out of the cell for questioning and returned half an hour later. The look in their eyes terrified Gertrud.

"Be strong," she told one of them.

Those were the words she may have told herself when she was brought back to the interrogation room.

"Ah yes, here we have our little criminal," the officer said the next time Gertrud was brought upstairs. "Tell us the names."

Who were they?

No answer.

A blow to the side of the head.

Where did they meet?

No answer.

Another smack.

At the second interrogation that day, she did speak. She asked if her mother knew she was there. She didn't get an answer.

"It is clear that you are an Edelweiss Pirate; everyone knows that."

He was trying to sound friendly this time. Good cop, bad cop— only the same person—and you don't know which one you are getting moment to moment.

"All you have to do is sign, and then you are free."

"What do I have to sign? That I am an Edelweiss Pirate?"

"Oh! She can speak!"

Gertrud clenched her body together, tightened her muscles in anticipation of a blow. It didn't come.

"Sign it!"

"Never," she said. "Why should I sign something that I don't know anything about?"

"I'm warning you. Sign it!"

"No."

"Get out of here, you bastard! You whore!"

She went back into the cell.

The next words she heard were, "You can go." The guard just let her walk out of the cell. Gertrud couldn't understand. She hadn't signed the paper. Why was he letting her out? She ran up the stairs as fast as she could.

"Stop!"

They'd make a mistake, she wasn't going to be let out.

"There's one condition to your release. You have to work in a wartime job."

"What's that?"

"You have to work in the Humbolt factory. A munitions factory. In the grenade division. Tomorrow."

"That's too far from me," Gertrud lied. She hated the idea of working for the Nazi war machine. But that was what the Nazis needed: they needed obedience to win the war, to create their thousand-year Reich. "There's a cardboard box factory near my house. Can't I work there instead?"

"Fine. Cardboard box factory."

After three days, freedom.

Even after the run-in with the officers at Pepita's apartment and their brief detention at EL-DE House, Gertrud and her friends distributed more flyers than ever. But each day was increasingly difficult. Some people left the group because they thought it was too dangerous. A bunch of the guys received draft papers. They had orders to report to the army and were being transported to the front. This is what they had been fighting against. They had wanted the war to stop, and now they were going to have to participate. Gertrud knew that none of them considered not reporting or leaving once they showed up. That was desertion and the penalty was death.

"Who knows what's going to happen to us or if we'll see each other again?" Gertrud said to her friends one night. She wanted there to be one last big meet-up. They decided to go to the Schmidt Bar at the edge of the Volksgarten, part of the Green Belt. They wanted one last time to be together, one last time to sing songs, one last time to laugh and enjoy the night.

The bars in Cologne were dark and homey, with the classic look of an old German tavern. Spread out across the checkered tablecloths were light and dark beers in big steins. Sometimes the girls mixed the beers with apple juice for a drink called *schorle*. Before the war, there might have been cheese, butter, and sausages as part of the spread, but on this December night, all they had was bread and pickles.

About twenty people showed up. Some were Gertrud's age or a little older, but a few were as young as fifteen. They were crowded together in a little room at the back of the bar. Gertrud had her guitar on her lap and her flower-decorated strap around her shoulder.

Even though they were all there together to sing and drink, the mood in the room was heavy. The last weeks had been hard. They had been doing more actions, but fear was growing too. Gertrud wanted a future; she wanted to be an adult and have a family. They had all hoped for an end to the war, but now the guys were headed to the front. The bombings were getting worse, and the city really looked like a war zone now. There was no escaping the war. Every day, it was something different, but all of it was bad: an apartment building burned down; a home destroyed; a friend lost.

They held hands and sang a melancholy song that also gave them hope: "It Was in Shanghai." This was Jean Jülich's favorite song, about friends, travel, and better times.

The door to the back room flew open and smacked against the wall. Men stomped into the room. They weren't wearing uniforms. The Gestapo.

"Weapons on the table! Stand up, hands high! Understood?"

No one moved—they didn't put anything on the table.

"We don't have any weapons," said Jus. That was true; they'd even left their pocketknives at home.

The men continued yelling at them. They wanted them to shut up and hand over their guitars.

Gertrud pulled the strap off her shoulder and handed over her guitar. The Gestapo officer's hands wrapped around the instrument and his arms went up into the air. She must have flinched; they all knew what was coming next. The guitar hit the table, splinters flew in every direction. The Nazis were good at destroying her things.

"You can't do that with the guitars! That's crazy!" Jose erupted. God, he was brave.

Smack! Another Gestapo officer hit him from behind.

"What are you saying, you scumbag, you pig?!" There was a terrifying fire in the eyes of the Gestapo officer.

A line had been crossed. Gertrud was convinced this was the end. They would be sent to a concentration camp now. Jus was standing next to her and tried to comfort her.

Someone must have ratted them out. There was a traitor in the group; there must have been. How else could the Gestapo have known where they were? The Gestapo had spies everywhere. They were the most cruel and cunning detectives, willing to go to any lengths to get the answers they wanted.

They were all marched out of the bar and into the street, then loaded into a truck.

Excerpt from the Arrest Reports

DECEMBER 1942

Restaurant Jakob Schmidt:

At this location, 23 people of both sexes were encountered. They were playing music and singing. A search of all persons was also conducted here and the material recovered is being kept by the police. The following were present:

1.) Vorhagen	Marianne	4.4.25 Cologne
2.) Blankenheim	Paul	16.6.25 Cologne-Sülz
3.) Gerling	Wilhelm	28.1.24 Cologne-Bickendorf
4.) Wiese	Johann	2.5.25 Cologne-Ehrenfeld
5.) Coenen	Kurt	29.8.26 Cologne-Riehl
6.) Schwanenberg	Karl-Heinz	28.4.25 Cologne
7.) Rockenfeller	Fritz	29.5.25 Cologne
8.) Kramer	Hans	23.9.27 Cologne
9.) Krick	Hans	29.7.27 Cologne
10.) Bauer	August	2.6.23 Cologne-Ehrenfeld
11.) Voosen	Friedrich	9.6.23 Cologne—currently a Soldier
12.) Gilles	Karl	25.10.25 Cologne-Sülz
13.) Kirchenturm	Franz	29.12.26 Cologne
14.) Hanss	Alexander	29.8.24 Cologne
15.) Hitdorf	Jakob	9.10.21 Cologne
16.) Schwalm	Käthe	18.3.24 Cologne-Bickendorf
17.) Menden	Rudi	2.6.26 Cologne-Ossendorf
18.) Ritzer	Wolfgang	25.6.25 Cologne-Deutz
19.) Steffens	Heinz	23.8.25 Cologne-Sülz
20.) Reinhardt	Alfred	22.11.25 Cologne
21.) Kühlem	Gertrud	1.6.24 Cologne
22.) Thelen	Käthe	31.5.25 Cologne-Nippes
23.) Kröly	Werner	18.12.26 Cologne-Ehrenfeld

Everyone listed above was taken to the Gestapo offices.

Excerpts from the Interrogation Report of Käthe Thelen [nickname Lolli]

On the next Saturday, November 21, 1942, we traveled to Rosrath in the evening.

Those who participated on this trip:

From Düsseldorf:

H a d s c h i e

J o s e

H a t t e

From Cologne:

M u c k i

B i l l a

M a r t h a and I,

S t e f f

R i o and W o l f.

We stayed for a little while at the restaurant zum Sülzthal, and then we looked for a place to spend the night, which we found in a barn.

In this barn there were about 4 or 5 guys, including Klaus B r e u e r, K u r t, and Paul. One of them asked me if I had spent any time at Leipzigerplatz, which I denied.

We girls spent the night separated from the boys in the barn.

During no occasion did I hear that we called ourselves or that others called us "E d e l w e i s s P i r a t e s." I did not see a small flyer with the words "Edelweiss Pirates" on this trip.

At the goodbye party for L u k o, P i k o—(Goldberg)—
said that flyers with antigovernment messages had been put
up in Wuppertal. I do not know of and have never heard of any
flyers or posters that have antigovernment messages or have
to do with the Bündische Youth.

My answers are the truth.

—Signed—

Käthe Thelen

Brauweiler, December 8, 1942.

31 — Jean

Before Christmas break in 1942, when Jean would have been in eighth grade, everyone was supposed to go up to the principal and say, "Heil Hitler!" before they were dismissed.

"Jean Jülich!"

Jean walked to the front.

"Goodbye, Mr. Principal," he said in a soft voice.

"What did you say?" the principal yelled back.

"Goodbye, Mr. Principal."

Jean couldn't bring himself to do it. Hitler was the reason his father was in jail, Hitler was the reason his friend was dead, Hitler was the reason he had to eat his own puke. Nope, no Heil Hitler.

The principal turned away and talked to a few other teachers and then yelled, "Look here, German boys and girls, there stands a cancer on our National Socialist society that must be removed and eradicated!"

But the principal didn't have Jean removed or eradicated, and he didn't report him to the police. Jean's luck held out again.

32 — Fritz

Fritz had gotten in trouble for being kicked out of the Hitler Youth and was in trouble again at his Ford apprenticeship for being a member of the Edelweiss Pirates. His friends were getting arrested, other groups were constantly harassed by the Hitler Youth patrols, and he could lose his Ford job if he didn't stop hanging out with these illegal groups. He should have kept his head down to stay out of all that trouble and gone calmly back to his job.

But he didn't stop. He wasn't hanging out with the Edelweiss Pirates in the Volksgarten anymore, but had found a new crew that gathered in the bunker at Taku Square, not far from where he lived in Ehrenfeld.

Gerhard, one of the guys in the group that met at the Taku Square bunker, wasn't just fighting the Nazis with songs and guitars. Fritz had always heard people talking about taking action, even back to his days with the Navajos, but most of the time people were too afraid to do anything against the Nazis. Everyone knew bigger actions could mean arrests, interrogations, beatings, prison or concentration camp, and that was too scary. Gerhard hadn't exactly explained what he and his friends were doing, but he'd invited Fritz along. Fritz was curious, so he went.

"We're giving out flyers against the Nazis and if you want, you can help us," said the guy everyone called Hermann.

Fritz had gone with Gerhard to an apartment at Barbarossa Square near the central part of Cologne. The apartment belonged to this guy Hermann, who looked like he was about forty years old. Fritz knew his name wasn't really Hermann, but he also knew enough not to want more information than was necessary.

Fritz didn't need much time to think about what Hermann had asked. He was there, at the apartment, so he'd already made his decision to help. He said yes, he'd help out. He wouldn't realize until much later how dangerous this decision was.

After the arrest at the bar, Gertrud and her friends were taken to the EL-DE House again. Gertrud was shoved down the stairs and a Gestapo officer stepped on her arm. She was sure it was broken. She was interrogated again, and then in the early morning following the night of her arrest, Gertrud and the others were loaded into a convoy of transport trucks along with other prisoners. Foreigners were put in the first two trucks, Germans in the third.* They were warned that anyone who tried to run would be shot. They weren't told where they were going.

When the trucks stopped, it was obvious they were not in Cologne. Wide expanses of lawns unfolded before them, dotted with barren trees. There was a beige church with a slate roof and spires that towered over everything else. Next to it was a complex of white buildings that almost looked like a country manor home. This place was meant to be beautiful, a place of God, a church and former Benedictine monastery. But Gertrud knew that this place was going to be difficult, not pleasant. This was Brauweiler, a prison, a concentration camp, a place for breaking people.

A female guard threw Gertrud into a cell and said, "Talking is forbidden."

There was no one else in the cell. Who was she supposed to talk to?

This was still a prison, but maybe a better prison than the EL-DE House. She got water and brown bread. She could see the sky through a window in the cell. Bodies weren't pressed together, the stench of human suffering wasn't thick in the air.

✿ ✿ ✿

---

* Gertrud's memoir says this happened three days after being at the EL-DE House, but another Gestapo record says they were brought almost immediately to Brauweiler.

One wing of the prison at Brauweiler, 1945.

Soon after she arrived, she began to lose track of time. Days melted together. She was taken from her cell to the interrogation room, questioned, beaten, taken back. Day and night didn't matter anymore.

"You were at the train station! You and a few other rats. Who was there?"

"You'll save yourself a lot if you just open your mouth."

"Give it up, you are the leader. You concocted everything."

"Where are the meeting places?"

"Don't pretend to be more stupid than you are, you disastrous, devious bitch."

Slut, bitch, whore.

Edelweiss Pirate, Communist, traitor.

Filthy, worthless, scum, trash.

We'll come after your mother, your family.

These were the types of things that the Gestapo spewed at Gertrud and other prisoners to see if they would talk. The Gestapo spoke as if they knew everything, and could do anything they wanted. They made general accusations, wanting prisoners to feel uncertain about what it was they had done wrong so they would admit to something, anything. They promised freedom if you were willing to say what they wanted to hear.

Gertrud talked now, but she denied everything.

"Who printed the flyers?"

"How should I know? I don't know anything about flyers."

"Tell us where you hid the flyers."

"I said I don't know anything about flyers."

A crack of pain radiated on the side of her head. The Gestapo beat prisoners, but weren't allowed to write down on reports what their enhanced interrogation techniques were. According to Gertrud, they hit her so many times in so many places that her skin was shades of blue, violet, red, or green, depending on where they'd hit her and how hard. She thought the Gestapo must have been scared. They had arrested so many people, and the beatings meant that they needed answers. Maybe the flyers had finally made a difference.

"Where did you commit the actions? In which cities? It wasn't just Cologne. Where else?"

"We didn't do anything."

A blow to the back of the head.

"You went hiking. In your group, you were all Edelweiss Pirates, right? Admit it."

"I didn't notice that. We just sang songs and enjoyed nature."

A wooden chair leg slammed into her body.

They were, she said, Wandervogel, Nature Friends, just kids who wanted to enjoy themselves. They were not distributing anti-Nazi material; they were not subversive.

Not saying anything almost became easy. The weaker she felt, the easier it was to not say anything, to not react.

"If you don't know any names, which we don't believe, just give us nicknames."

Gertrud said nothing.

The chair leg collided with her right shoulder, then with her left.

"Solitary!"

She was in a walk-in refrigerator. Gertrud could stretch out her hands and touch all the cold cement walls without moving her feet. There was a bucket in the corner for a toilet. The guards only came and emptied it once a day. After one day, the bucket smelled awful. She smelled terrible too. The interrogations left her covered in sweat and blood, and she hadn't changed clothes or washed her body in days. When she asked for clean clothes, she got a blank stare. She got her period and asked for a sanitary pad or rag. The guard didn't give her anything and didn't really care if blood was running down her leg. *Worse than pigs*, those were Jus's words.

She wanted to laugh, talk, and sing with Jus and her other friends. She wanted to be back in the mountains beside a warm campfire by the deep waters of the little Blauensee, where she had slipped her fingers in between Jus's. In her imagination, she felt the bright sun shining down on her face as they hiked up to the Drachenfels ruin. She looked across the Rhine River, reflecting the blue sky. They went on a longer trip and hiked for days in the mountains. She played her guitar and sang a favorite song, maybe Pico would start, and then they'd all join in. Together.

She wasn't there. She was alone. She was in the dark. She was in a cold cell, waiting for something.

Fritz believed more than ever that Germany was going to lose the war, sooner or later. Since the 1,000-bomber raid in May 1942, bombing raids by the Allied planes had grown more frequent, even though there was less standing to bomb. In February 1943, the Soviets beat the Germans at the battle of Stalingrad. Now the losing was really starting, and that might have been one reason Fritz was willing to risk his life for flyers; the other was that he was fed up with the Nazis controlling his life and telling him that he was undisciplined and needed to be punished.

He was ready to help distribute flyers with Gerhard, Hermann, and the other members of the underground he'd gotten into contact with. They had an elaborate plan.

Herman knew of a place in Cologne that offered shelter and cheap meals. In the charity house's big dining room, they could get a hot meal and be surrounded by lots of people for good cover. Fritz and a couple of other Pirates met Hermann at the entrance and each bought a meal ticket to go into the dining hall. They stood in line, got their food, and sat down together. Fritz might have been paying attention to what was going on around them, who was coming and going.

After a little while, Hermann got up and disappeared into a side room. Now Fritz was nervous. He imagined that everyone who looked at them was a Gestapo spy. And who was to say that Hermann wasn't a spy? A double agent? He was getting up to betray them, to get out of the way before the police barged in and arrested them all. Or maybe he wasn't a double agent at all, but someone else had tipped the police off. Or maybe someone else had just done something stupid, something that would get them all caught.

The worst thing was to look nervous, to invite suspicion that they had done or were about to do something wrong. So Fritz and his friends kept eating, trying their best to pretend like worry wasn't pushing down on their chests, making eating and breathing hard.

Hermann reappeared. No police. Hermann didn't seem nervous or upset; he came back to the table and sat down. They kept talking, as if nothing had happened. Hermann put some packages right in the middle of the table, as if they didn't contain illegal material that could get them all arrested. They ate the rest of their meal, as if they weren't coconspirators in treason. Finally, they stood up and Fritz grabbed one of the packages from the table, as if it weren't something dangerous. Everyone went their separate ways, just friends leaving lunch, totally normal.

Part one of the plan was complete.

In May 1943, Fritz was supposed to take one of the packages and deposit the flyers at an antiaircraft installment in the Ossendorf neighborhood, north of Ehrenfeld. The place wasn't just an antiaircraft gun sitting on top of a building somewhere; it was a base with barracks and soldiers.

Most of soldiers on the base were young, and Fritz figured he might find a former Edelweiss Pirate among them who wanted to help. He knew this plan was risky, but the whole operation was risky, and he knew it would be even harder without help. Before too long, he found a guy he knew from school who had also been an Edelweiss Pirate. His name was Joseph.

Some Edelweiss Pirates in the area would take Allied flyers and shove them into mailboxes. Others stuck them under doormats. But Fritz thought his flyers were different from those he had seen the Americans or British planes drop on Cologne. Those messages were geared toward women, urging them to convince their husbands that this war was started by Hitler and that there was no way to win it. In July 1943, the British would drop flyers all across Germany telling the story of the Scholl siblings and how together with their group the White Rose they spread anti-Nazi leaflets in Munich. Fritz's flyers looked like a small newspaper, but had the title *The Soldier's Newspaper XYZ*. Fritz and others listened to British Broadcasting Company (BBC) news briefs on the radio—which was also illegal—and learned that what the Nazis offered as news was pure propaganda designed to hide the truth of the war. The newspapers Fritz and his friends were handing out had political and military news on the front page taken from the illegal radio broadcasts or other illegal foreign news sources, and on the inside, they put images pasted together with words that made the Nazis look bad. The British had once dropped flyers with a photo of Hitler on a field of dead bodies with the caption, "I feel so fresh, the spring is coming."* Fritz and his friends wanted to make flyers that looked like that.

The Germans couldn't be sure if a plane was dropping flyers or bombs, so either way an air-raid siren would go off when enemy planes flew overhead. Fritz and Joseph decided that was the perfect time to hand out *The Soldier's Newspaper XYZ*—either the young guys at the installment would be distracted by manning the antiaircraft guns and trying to shoot down enemy planes or they would be in the bunker, trying to avoid having bombs dropped on them. The barracks would be the perfect place to deposit the flyers.

The first time, his plan worked.

35 — Gertrud

Gertrud stood in front of her house on Boisseree Street. The building was still there. The Cathedral was still standing too. Given the

---

* This was really a British propaganda leaflet that was dropped in 1942 over Germany, but as an adult, Fritz believed it looked similar to what he and his friends created.

number of bombings that Cologne had suffered and how much had been destroyed, these were miracles. Had magic brought her home? Or was this a dream?

The Gestapo just let her go from Brauweiler. She never admitted to distributing flyers, writing graffiti, or anything else. She didn't really even know how long she had been there. The official Gestapo record said she was only there for nineteen days, but she swears she was there for nine months. It's not hard to understand why Gertrud's memory and the record don't match. The days and nights ran together in the prison. Sometimes she was in a dark cell all day and under bright interrogation lights all night. The Gestapo interrogated people in the middle of the night, or made them stand in the hallway, just waiting for hours. The disorientation helped the Gestapo get confessions, even if the prisoners' words weren't true.

The Gestapo didn't tell her why she was being released. She couldn't even remember if she had walked home or taken a streetcar.[*] All she thought about was the sky, the fresh air, the space around her, and whether her mother and her house would still be there.

She went into the building and walked up the stairs to her door. She didn't have a key.

She knocked. She hoped her mother was there.

"Who's there?"

"Me, Gertrud."

The door opened slowly; her mother's eyes stared back at her. Could this be real?

Gertrud's mother grabbed her and pulled her close. Gertrud felt the warmth and softness of her mother's body. They stood, embracing for a while. This wasn't a dream; Gertrud was home.

"I wasn't allowed to write," Gertrud said.

The Gestapo had asked her mother questions, but she denied knowing anything.

---

[*] Later in life, she would sometimes say one, sometimes the other.

"I'm sorry that you've had to suffer because of me," Gertrud said.

"It's not so bad. We are both alive—that's the most important thing. And we are both free. Let's wash you off, and then you can go lie down and you can sleep properly," her mother said.

Her mother ran cold water in a wash bin and got soap and a sponge. Gertrud took off her clothes and revealed her devastated body. She hadn't been fed nearly enough. Her skin was blue and green from bruises fresh and healing, and she probably couldn't tell how bad she smelled after sporadic showers and dirty clothes.

Gertrud's mom rubbed soap over her back. The soft sponge pressing lightly against her skin and her mother's gentle strokes—they were everything. Loving human touch had entered her life again. Every time someone in prison touched her, it had been to grab, to force, to beat, to abuse, to hurt. Here, a loving touch penetrated her skin, muscles, bones, entering into the deepest parts of the mind and relaxing the body.

It had almost been ten years since her father's first arrest and she was eighteen now, an adult. Her whole life had been consumed by terror and fear. Gertrud wanted to be loved and taken care of, to slip back into being a child again.

After the bath and some bread, Gertrud lay down in her bed. A bed with a mattress. A real mattress, with a comforter. Not a concrete slab. Not a thin, lumpy mattress on metal frame. Not a cheap blanket, or no blanket at all. She shut her eyes and the world was gone.

A knock woke Gertrud. Not again, not another knock—knocks were followed by men, by arrests, by torture. This must have been a dream. The knocks kept coming. Gertrud's mother was pacing the kitchen, unsure of what to do.

"My God. Do they want to arrest us again?"

"How late is it?" Gertrud asked softly.

"Three. Three in the morning."

Another knock.

"What are we going to do?" her mother whispered.

"Mom, open it. They'll just come in. If they're standing out there, we can't do anything about it."

Her mother turned the key in the lock, pulled back the chain, and opened the door.

Marianne was in the hallway, alone. The relief must have flowed over Gertrud and her mother. Marianne was an old friend of the family who had been a member of the Socialist Party. Years earlier, she had gotten into a relationship with an SS officer. No one could figure out why, but she said she was in love. Now she was standing in the hallway outside Gertrud's apartment at three in the morning.

"Come," she said. She wasn't supposed to be here. "Grab your jackets and coats and let's get out of here. You have to disappear from the city. They could be here any minute. You are on a list—"

"How do you know?" Gertrud's mother asked.

"I'll explain later. We need every minute. Hurry up!"

Gertrud and her mother dressed, put more clothing into a back-pack, and grabbed the bag that Gertrud's mother usually took with her to the bunker.

As they walked through the dark, deserted streets, Marianne looked left and right at every corner. The neighborhood was quiet. Gertrud's mother pressed her again about how she knew about a list of names.

Wasn't it obvious? Marianne's SS boyfriend had been feeding her information. He was basically a spy. When he heard that some-one they knew was going to be arrested, Marianne warned them. Marianne's actions were risky, and she clearly didn't get everyone out all the time. This time, though, her risk had paid off.

Marianne told them to walk to Kalscheuren, which was outside the city on the southwest side. There, they could get on one of the freight trains.

They did just that, and when the freight train started rolling, they had no idea where they were going. Gertrud thought if they were headed south she might see mountains.

36 — Fritz

Fritz had been doing actions with the guys from the Barbarossa Square apartment for months, and everything had gone smoothly. No arrests, no mistakes. Now it was August 1943, and he had once again picked up flyers in the city and was on his way to the antiaircraft installment to distribute them. He was sitting, watching, and waiting for an air-raid siren to go off. It had been an hour, maybe more, and nothing. That sound came every night—or it felt like every night—and now, nothing.

People practically lived in the bunkers these days because the alarms went off so often. They figured a whole night in dark, crowded holes was better than being woken up by the screaming siren and rushing to a shelter so crowded they'd have to stand. Or worse, not getting to a shelter at all. Not that a bunker was a guarantee of survival. Earlier in the summer, Fritz's first Navajo friends, Hans and Maria, died in a bomb attack.

Maybe that feeling of inevitable death made Fritz less scared when he waited to give out the flyers. He knew that he had to wait for an alarm so that the barracks where the soldiers slept would be empty. As he waited, he watched the area the whole time. He saw the guard posts change, men coming and going.

Three hours passed. Still no alarm. Maybe no alarm would come tonight. He would still have to get rid of the flyers—bringing the illegal material back into the city was way too dangerous.

He peeked over the earthen wall that separated him from the base. Yes, he could do this. He could jump over, sneak around through the dark, dropping flyers, and then escape unnoticed. A certain cavalierness, or maybe just disregard for authority, led Fritz to believe he could do it. His plan was dangerous and more than a little stupid. Somehow, though, it still seemed safer than bringing the flyers back, and better than wasting them.

He jumped over the wall and almost landed in the arms of a watchman. Where did this guy come from? Fritz hadn't seen him before. His heart was racing and he froze. The watchman seemed just as surprised as Fritz.

Leistungswoche

Der

Bündischen

Jugend

Bezirk 1

Kommt Zurück

Jugend Erwache

"Leadership Week of the Bündische Youth - District 1 - Come Back - Youth Awake!" In November 1942, the Cologne Gestapo found around 2,000 flyers with these words, sometimes with District 2 or District 3. The "37" visible in the top right corner was likely written by the Gestapo for their records.

Slowly, Fritz opened his clenched fist and let the package of flyers drop on the ground. He must have been praying that the flyers didn't make a sound. He lifted his hands up into the air. He wanted his body language to say don't shoot. But sometimes body language doesn't matter to a guard.

"What was that?" he asked. He'd seen the flyers.

Fritz couldn't open his mouth, as if someone had glued his lips together, taken out his tongue, and thrown it away.

The watchman asked again. He moved closer to Fritz.

Fritz had to say something. "Flyers," he whispered finally.

His mind was so muddy that he wouldn't remember what the guard said except, "That is not for kids. Get out of here as fast as you can before someone else sees you."

Fritz didn't have time to think about what the guard told him. He turned and sprinted away from the base.

He'd have to tell his friends what had happened. Handing out flyers at the antiaircraft installment would be too dangerous, and Fritz's face could now be known. The consequences could be severe for everyone. But telling everyone also meant that he'd probably be asked not to participate, and he really didn't want that.

He decided to keep the incident to himself.

Fritz would meet up with his friends as often as he could, and sometimes they'd meet up with other Pirates in other neighborhoods. One day in the fall of 1943, they sang and walked east through Ehrenfeld on their way to Blücherpark to meet another group. When they came across a group of Hitler Youth, they couldn't help but laugh when they heard the leader yell, "Sieg Heil!"—the salute to Hitler. Here were a bunch of guys marching in straight lines, with bland uniforms and blind obedience. They looked stupid. The Pirates kept walking, loudly singing one of their favorite songs, knowing exactly how provocative it was:

The black shirt we all wear
With our Edelweiss pinned on
We want to take risks
We won't give the Patrol a break
Ti-ra-ta-ta-ta, Ti-ra-ta-ta-ta, Ti-ra-ta-ta-ta,
Ti-ra-ta-ta-ta, We are the
Masters of the World, The E.P. From Ehrenfeld!

They felt invincible.

37 — Jean

Since 1941, Jean's father had been held at a labor camp as part of his prison sentence. The Nazis tried to save money by building camps for prisoners near where they worked, so they wouldn't need to use trucks and fuel to transport them back and forth from prison. For the two years Jean Sr. had been working at a stone quarry, Jean had been able to visit his dad. They mostly talked about the war and politics, and his dad, despite being a political prisoner, never stopped being critical of the Nazis.

Jean was eager to tell his dad about the new friends he'd met at Manderschieder Square, about singing and hiking, and fighting the Hitler Youth. His group wasn't specifically political, but he knew that resisting the Nazis would make his dad proud. While other Pirates might be afraid to tell their parents about illegal activities, Jean knew his dad would want to hear about his anti-Nazi activity. Any action Jean told him about, his dad approved. And one day in 1943, Jean Sr. introduced his son to another prisoner he thought Jean needed to meet.

The man was Michel "Meik" Jovy, a former bündische youth who was in prison with Jean's dad. Jovy was only about ten years older than Jean, but to Jean, he was the sort of older mentor figure whose stories of his own exploits made everything fall into place. Jovy had been thrown out of the Hitler Youth in 1937 for organizing an unsanctioned trip. That same year, he traveled to Paris, where he connected with political dissidents who had left Germany, including the political writer and former bündische youth Karl Otto Paetel. Jovy's group was being watched, and in 1939, he was arrested for treason and sentenced to prison the following year.

After his father introduced them, Jean and Meik became fast friends.

At night, Meik could sneak out of the camp and meet Jean and a few friends in tunnels near the quarry. Meik would tell them stories about his time in the bündische youth, the books he and his friends read, and how he smuggled anti-Nazi literature into Germany. He recited lyrical, mystical poems by Rainer Maria Rilke, like "The Love and Death of Cornet Christopher Rilke":

> Riding, riding, riding, through the day, through the
> night, through the day.
>
> Riding, riding, riding.
>
> And courage is so tired and longing so great. There
> are no mountains anymore, hardly a tree. Nothing
> dares rise up. Strange huts crouch thirstily at wells
> where the water has gone bad. Not a castle in sight.
> And always the same picture. You have two eyes

too many. Only in the night do you think you know the way. At night, do we go over the stretch that we worked so hard to cover in the foreign sun? Maybe. The sun is heavy, like it is at home in the depths of summer. But we said our goodbyes in the summer. The women's clothing shone in the green distance. And now we have been riding for a long time. It must be autumn. At least where the sad women know of us.

He taught them the songs he knew and told them about the songbook he'd made. Jean felt like Meik was showing them a whole new world and connecting them to a tradition of youth resistance. Jean couldn't get enough.

Meik wanted Jean to get his balalaika, a guitar-like instrument commonly used in Russian folk music, from Meik's mom outside of the city. Jean, Ferdinand Steingrass, and another friend dressed in their colorful checkered shirts, white socks, fedoras, and prominent Edelweiss pins and picked up the instrument from Meik's mom's house.

On their way home, they were stopped by a Hitler Youth patrol, who brought them to the police. Luckily, the police officer on duty was old and not very sympathetic to the Nazis.

"What have these three done? Broken a window, jumped people?" the officer asked.

"No, no," said the Hitler Youth.

Jean's friend Ferdi "Fän" Steingass at Blauensee, 1943.

"But you can see yourself how they're walking around."

"I mean, everyone can walk around however they want," the officer replied.

The Hitler Youth was not about to give up.

"And what kind of instrument is that?" he asked.

"A balalaika. A Russian folk instrument," Jean said. The words slipped out of his mouth before he realized what he had said. Everything that was from Russia was dangerously foreign, and even a Russian instrument could be a Communist threat. But the police officer still didn't seem to think that a couple of kids in strange outfits with an instrument were a real threat to the Reich. He let them go. Three times lucky.

38 — Fritz

Fritz's mother handed him a letter. She was agitated and nervous, so he could tell it wasn't good news.

The letter said he needed to appear at the Gestapo offices regarding an unfinished matter. Fritz started going through all of the transgressions the Gestapo might be upset about to make sure he wasn't caught off guard. First, he tried to ask Hermann, Gerhard, or any of the other guys involved with the flyers if they had received a notice. He couldn't find any of them.

On his way home, he ran into another Pirate who hung out at the Taku bunker. He went by Helmut and he had also received a notice. Helmut hadn't been involved with distributing the flyers, so Fritz knew that couldn't be it. But Helmut wasn't sure what to make of the letter either.

When Fritz returned home, two of his mom's acquaintances were putting up wallpaper in the kitchen. When the older guy saw the letter in Fritz's hand, he warned Fritz that the Gestapo wasn't messing around and there wasn't a guarantee he'd come back from that.

"Of course he's coming back," Fritz's mother said.

"So what's it about?" the friend asked.

"I don't know," Fritz said, which was true. He really didn't know what the Gestapo wanted from him.

"Always stick with your first story! Don't ever say anything else. Don't change your story. The best is when you don't know anything and keep your mouth shut, even if they beat you. If you don't know anything, how are they supposed to keep questioning you?" the friend offered in advice.

The friend got back up on the ladder and busied himself with putting up the wallpaper again.

On a day in late October 1943, Fritz went with Helmut to the Gestapo offices at the EL-DE House. They still didn't really know what the notice to appear was about, but they knew they should show up and be questioned instead of evading the appearance, seeming guilty, and suffering the consequences.

They walked up to the main entrance on Appellhof Place. The painted letters "EL DE" shone in gold on the glass above the doorway. This building was well-known as one of the worst Nazi lairs in the whole city. It must have taken Fritz a lot of courage to not run away at that moment. He might not have known why they were calling him in, but he did know that he'd done many illegal things, and that the Gestapo was cruel and arbitrary in attempts to make the people fear the Nazi state.

Fritz and Helmut entered the front foyer and walked up a few stairs. The building was less than ten years old, and by some miracle hadn't been destroyed by bombs yet. The whole entryway was marble and tile and stone, strict and clean.

They registered with the doorman, who sat behind a glass window like a movie theater ticket seller. The man sent them to an office, where they found familiar faces. Some of their friends from Ehrenfeld had received the same summons, and were just as clueless as to why they were being brought in for questioning.

Everyone gave their personal details to Gestapo officers named Fink and Manthey.* These two were well-known in Cologne. When the Pirates met up, they talked about the officers they met in the EL-DE House, the Hitler Youth to watch out for, and how to avoid arrest. Manthey and Fink were both officials in a special division of the Gestapo that was responsible for opposition from youth. They led Fritz and his friends down the narrow staircase into the basement, just like they had with Gertrud and her friends in December 1942.

Fritz still didn't know what was happening. The basement was barely lit and smelled distinctly of bodies and disinfectant. Along a hallway were doors, heavy and wooden with big bolts and metal hinges that stretched the whole width of the door. Fritz had just been outside, completely free, and now he was staring at cell doors in a basement prison.

Then everything started happening quickly.

The man who had brought them down into the basement yelled, "Line up, in size order!"

Then another man—a short, ugly man with bulging eyes and greasy, black hair—started laughing. His informal clothes caught Fritz off guard. He was wearing a shirt, pants, suspenders, and boots, but no uniform or suit jacket. He was standing right in front of them, and he was holding a whip.

In a loud voice, he explained where they were, as if they hadn't realized. He went down the line, looking at each person and asking,

---

* While Hugo Manthey's full name and date of birth are known, I could only find reference to Fink's last name.

Graffiti in a basement cell of the EL-DE House, 2017. The date the graffiti was created is unknown, but likely between 1942 and 1945. Many writings on the walls of the cells include phrases, songs, and mottoes of the Edelweiss Pirates.

"Why were you brought here? Why are you in the basement?" Except he wasn't really expecting an answer right away. He was just there to terrify them into coming up with an answer. Fritz and the ten or twelve other guys were whipped, punched, and verbally abused before they were shoved into a cell originally intended for only two people. Three or four men were already inside. They couldn't sit; they could barely move. He had no idea how long the other people had been in there, but the air was thick with humanity. Not just the physical bodies, but the remnants of bodies, the exhalation of breath in a poorly ventilated room, the sour smell of unwashed sweat, or the acrid odor of urine that lingered on fabric when prisoners weren't allowed to leave the cell to use the bathroom.

Fritz recognized a few guys as Edelweiss Pirates. They said they'd been arrested the previous night in a raid and had been interrogated, tortured, and then stuck in this cell. They'd been there less than a day, but the experience already sounded way worse than what Fritz had been through. The stories scared him.

One by one, names were called, and people were pulled from the cell.*

Finally, they called Fritz's name. He was taken back to the first office, where Fink and Manthey were waiting for him. Everything happened so quickly.** The officers asked questions like they already knew the answers and were just waiting for Fritz to tell them what they wanted to hear.

"Since when have you been a member of the Edelweiss Pirates?"

"Who are your leaders, are they Social Democrats or Communists?"

Sometimes, they were off base with their understanding of the Pirates. Questions about membership and leadership, about political party didn't make sense in the context of the Pirates.

"Come on, tell us. Who are your leaders?"

But he couldn't simply tell the truth and say, "We don't have any leaders. We are not part of a political party." That would be admitting he knew about the Pirates in the first place.

Back in the cell, the whispers floated between ears and mouths, hoping that guards outside weren't listening. Everyone wanted to share what had happened in the interrogation. They all said that throughout the questioning and beating, no one had said anything about the Edelweiss Pirates.

"Be careful! I think they're listening to us," a voice said in the dark. The voice said he'd been there for a couple of days, and they had beat him during the night. Even in the dark, Fritz could see that above his right eye, there was a fist-sized swelling, and his arms were covered in blue splotches.

"What did they want from you?" Fritz asked.

---

* In the oral history interview, Fritz says that they weren't interviewed any further at the EL-DE House, and it wasn't until they arrived in Brauweiler that he was questioned again.

** He wrote that he was questioned, but also said later that they weren't questioned at all at the EL-DE House.

"I have no idea! One of the Gestapo men explained to me that I could simply tell them that I was in the Edelweiss Pirates. And I don't even know what that is!"

Fritz looked at the others in the cell, and he knew what this guy was trying to tell them: he was trying to protect everyone. If the Gestapo really was listening in on the cell, they needed to deny knowing about the Pirates in here too.

After two days, officers took Fritz, Helmut, and a few others out of the basement of the EL-DE House to a truck waiting to take them to the Gestapo prison outside the city, the place Fritz knew as Brau-weiler. Officers Fink and Manthey had told Fritz and the others that this new camp was a place where they could think about what they wanted to say.

On their way to the trucks, though, the officers made sure their prisoners had something very specific to think about: they left the basement cell through the courtyard where the Gestapo had built a gallows.

At Brauweiler, the cell was better than the one at the EL-DE House. Fritz didn't get a cell to himself like Gertrud had— possibly because they had more male prisoners. He only shared the space with two others, though: Helmut and a guy named Emil. One small window let in light; they were aboveground now. In the room, there was also a little table and a chair, a stool, a bed that folded down from the wall, and best of all, three straw mattresses on the floor with blankets. A bed was a luxury after the days where there had been nowhere to sit and barely enough room to stand. The building was quiet too, except for a repeated smack-smack-smack sound that was always in the background. The noise was rhythmic, like hammering, sometimes close by and sometimes farther away.

Still, it was the most comfortable they'd been in days, and as soon as Fritz, Helmut, and Emil got into the cell, they collapsed on the straw beds.

Though they could now rest more comfortably, they still hadn't been fed. Three days? Was that how long it had been? Their stomachs gurgled and pleaded for food. Quietly, they discussed their situation among themselves. Since the Gestapo had no proof they were Edelweiss Pirates, they agreed they needed to deny it and say that they had been unfairly imprisoned. They didn't know how long they might be held there.

Fritz pursed his lips and started whistling a tune. He couldn't explain why he was doing it, he just was. His cellmates joined in.

A guttural sound erupted from somewhere in the prison. They didn't think about the sound; the cell block had a large, open space in the middle, and they heard yelling, grunting, and screaming from throughout the prison all the time. They kept whistling.

Smack, smack, smack. The inexplicable sound was getting closer.

Then the door to the cell opened with a crash.

"Who is whistling here?" a deep voice growled at them. His country dialect made Fritz think he was a farmer.

Fritz, Helmut, and Emil just stared back. Then they laughed. Fritz thought the serious way this farmer reacted to their whistling was just ridiculous.

In an instant, a rubber baton slammed into Fritz's head, arms, legs. Fritz heard Emil crying and screaming. They all knew they couldn't fight back; they just had to accept what was happening. The next moments evaporated from Fritz's memory. He didn't remember the beating; he just remembered being aware that he was on the floor of the cell and his whole body hurt when the beating stopped.

They finally realized what the smack-smack-smack sound they'd heard was: as the guard walked on his rounds, he hit the rubber baton on the walls and the staircase railings, just to make sure inmates remembered.

That night, Fritz finally got food: two pieces of bread, coffee, and watery soup, and a glob of butter that was supposed to last all week.

On the third night in Brauweiler—or maybe sooner, maybe later; like Gertrud, Fritz found time moved differently in the prison—someone brought him from the cell to an interrogation room. Fritz was half asleep as he stumbled in the darkness after the guard.

The room was small, or at least it looked small. Fritz couldn't see much of it, only a chair, a table, and a lamp on the table. He sat in the chair and the bright light shone directly in his eyes. He could hear the voice of the man sitting on the other side of the table, but he couldn't see him. Then it started.

"So, you lousy kid, your time for thinking is finally over, and now I want to know the truth. Lying is pointless. I know exactly about you and your friends, and now I want to know what went on during your meetings and weekend trips."

Fritz said nothing.

"Okay, friend, the platoon leader of [Hitler Youth] Platoon 46 from Ehrenfeld made a statement that this summer a couple of bullies made it so that he couldn't do his official duties. He described the kids, and you fit the description. Now, let's talk; who were the others and what else have you punks done?"

That rat. The platoon leader knew that Fritz had been thrown out of the Hitler Youth and wanted him to pay. Maybe he had also seen Fritz with the guitar in the park and had the whole group arrested by the Gestapo.

Fritz didn't know what to say next, and he didn't want to implicate himself.

"Well, I know that a fight happened, but I don't really know how it happened. I'm sorry," Fritz said.

"And what's with the Edelweiss Pirates?"

"I don't know anything about that," Fritz replied. "I have heard something about them. I've also seen them, but I've never been a part of the group. Truthfully, you have to believe me." With the last part, Fritz tried to sound as convincing as possible.

Fritz signed his interrogation report and went back to the cell.

When Fritz got back, they took Emil to interrogation, and Fritz whispered to Helmut what had happened. Fritz told him that he needed to make sure he denied that he was an Edelweiss Pirate.

The next night, they were woken up and brought in for interrogation again. The Gestapo thought the sleep deprivation might help get confessions. Now Officer Fink asked Fritz who the leaders were, whether they were Socialists or Communists. Fritz said he didn't know, since he wasn't a member.

Fink gave him a photo album and told him to point out the people he knew. Fritz did recognize some faces, even some Pirates that had helped out with the flyers.

"So, do you recognize anyone?" Fink asked.

Fritz shook his head no.

Then he felt an enormous pressure sink into his right shoulder that immediately turned to pain. Someone had hit him from behind.

"Open your mouth, or I'll kill you!" a voice erupted. It was the growl of the man with the rubber baton who had beaten him in the cell. During the whole interrogation, he had been sitting there, watching, observing, ready to strike.

Fink asked the same questions, and Fritz gave him the same responses.

"Who gave out the leaflets?"

Fritz felt his whole body freeze. Did they actually know about the flyers? Had someone in the group at Barbarossa Square given him up? Emil and Helmut and the other Pirates from Ehrenfeld knew nothing about those actions. Why would the Gestapo be asking if they didn't know anything? Were they trying to trick him?

Fritz acted surprised, like he didn't know what they were talking about.

"I've never heard anything about any flyers, so I couldn't answer that question."

Back to the cell.

Back to the interrogation room.

Back to the cell.

Over and

over and

over.

They wanted Fritz to sign a confession that he was responsible for the flyers. He refused. They beat him. They showed him a paper where his friends had said that he was responsible for the flyers. He denied it again; they beat him again. Smack, smack, smack, smack. It was endless. Their capacity for beatings and brutality seemed to have no limit.

Frtiz's body was bruised: yellow-brown older bruises, blue-purple fresh bruises. He was sore from clenching his muscles to brace himself against the blows. But the pain didn't quell Fritz's rage, even though he could barely move.

"How could you say such things and have done this to me? You're fucking crazy!" Fritz yelled when he was back in his cell. His friends had ratted him out. "You assholes, do you know what they did to me?"

Helmut was ready to yell back at Fritz, but Emil tried to calm the situation.

"Listen, we didn't say anything; they wrote that confession themselves to try to outsmart us," Emil said. "How many papers did you have to sign before they stopped the interrogation?"

"Four, I think," Fritz said.

"You see, one of those was blank. When you were outside, they wrote something on the blank sheet and said we were the informants."

The Gestapo could do whatever they wanted and would do whatever they wanted to get confessions.

Fritz picked up the bucket and hurried toward the bathroom. A day's worth of excrement from three people was nauseating to say the least. For the guards, the running of prisoners with buckets of shit was a game. Fritz stepped into the bathroom and the guard standing at the door stuck out his leg. Fritz's forward momentum spun out of control as his leg collided with the guard's. The bucket flew out of his arms and hit the floor, which the guards had made slippery with water. The mixture of shit and piss splashed out of the bucket and into Fritz's face. Another guy came from behind with his bucket, tripped on Fritz, and more feces spilled into the room. Soon, everyone was covered in brown liquid.

That was worse than the beatings, worse than the mental stress. His rage against the guards in that prison and the Nazis wouldn't end, even if he got out of the prison.

"You'll be released today," Fink told Fritz about three weeks after he'd been brought to Brauweiler. "But first we have some formalities to take care of," he added.

They wanted Fritz to sign a piece of paper that said he had been treated well by the Gestapo.

Fritz refused.

"Well, you can think about it, we have time."

Emil signed the paper and was let out the same day.

A few days later, Fritz agreed to sign the paper. He also had to agree to not be in the Edelweiss Pirates anymore, even though he had denied being a Pirate the whole time, and every Sunday, he would have to go to the Justice Office on Reichensperger Square to report for parole, which meant he couldn't go on weekend trips to the countryside anymore.

Part Four
1943–1944

"ONE PEOPLE, ONE REICH, ONE WRECK."

Cologne, 1943

Half a year has passed since the loss at Stalingrad against the Soviets in February 1943, and the war is at a turning point. The Axis powers surrender in North Africa. Then Allied troops invade Italy and the Soviet troops start retaking land they lost to the Germans. Guys you know who used to be in the Hitler Youth are now joining the military. This is total war.

The Nazis increase fortifications along the Westwall—or the Siegfried Line as it is known in English. The Westwall is Hitler's dream to stop incursion from the west, a 390-mile fortification with 17,000 bunkers, miles of trenches and small cement pyramids to stop tanks, and antiaircraft installments to shoot down planes. It doesn't always work.

Cologne is relatively close to the border and every day you hear an air-raid siren; every day bombed buildings collapse into rubble on the street. The whole city looks like a dump, like piles of garbage. Iron beams that held up buildings are crushed and twisted. The clockface from a church tower is mangled and stopped at the hour of the bombing. Stones and bricks and dirt pile up as high as buildings. Forced laborers and concentration camp prisoners clean up the debris and clear a path so you can still move through the city. Lines for water, electricity, and gas are damaged or completely inoperable. Every day people die; every day there is less food.

Is this Hitler's vision for Germany? No, he imagined broad avenues and modern buildings, not paths through piles of rubble. But the Nazis' arrogance and belief in German supremacy have created this desperate landscape. This war is going to end, and by this point few people believe there will be victory for the Germans. This is a slow-motion car crash; you can see where the action is heading, and looking away isn't going to stop it.

But maybe there is a way to make the crash happen faster, speed up the motion, and get the destruction over with.

Report of the Public Prosecutor on Activities of the Edelweiss Pirates in November, 1943

JANUARY 16, 1944

Two of these proceedings were submitted by me, the public prosecutor, to the people's court in Berlin because of suspicion of highly treasonous activities. . . . [sic] In the second case, one young man was creating an opposition 'Edelweiss Pirate' group in the area of Geilenkirchen, with clear tendencies as an enemy of the HY. After he increased the anti-HY feelings of his friends, he acquired by stealing a machine gun from a shot-down American bomber and 500 rounds of ammunition, and more ammunition, and the necessary explosives. Then he prepared with his accomplices to blow up a HY barrack, in which the HY members were assembled on the occasion of the celebration of the 9th of November 1943.

39 — Fritz

After Fritz was released from Brauweiler, everything was worse than it was before. His mom had been convinced he was dead. She'd gone to the Gestapo building, and they said he wasn't there, that he must be at home. After three days, she still hadn't seen him, and a police officer finally told her, "Your son is in custody." Then the Gestapo came to look for incriminating evidence. They toppled cabinets over, smashed pots, looked inside the sugar bowl, rifled through the refrigerator, cut a hole in the mattress. A neighbor said the apartment looked worse than after a bomb attack.

Fritz's hatred for the Nazis was stronger than ever. They'd ruined everything. He had gone back to the group at Barbarossa Square, but none of those guys had been arrested and they didn't want to see him anymore. They thought even knowing him was too risky, and now Fritz didn't have a place to escape.

He also had to go back to work at Ford, but that was awful too. They put him in a punishment brigade with Russian prisoners of war and Ukrainian forced laborers where he worked more than ten hours a day. Seeing how the forced laborers were treated just made Fritz hate the Nazis even more.

It seemed like everywhere, at every opportunity, the enslaved workers were treated like garbage. The forced laborers were given wooden shoes and worn-out clothes to wear. Fritz also couldn't help noticing their hunger. On Fridays, when they served soup in the canteen for the German Ford employees, some of the young Ukrainians would try to sneak in. They'd sit on top of the roof, looking down through the windows, waiting to get the leftovers from the Germans. Fritz would throw bread rolls out the window or he'd open the windows wide and someone else would pull the guys down into the room so they could eat and get out before being caught. But they were often caught.

One guard was particularly sadistic with the starving forced laborers. When he caught someone, he'd shove their faces into the bowls and hit them on the back of the head. Fritz saw another guard kick a pregnant laborer in the belly for talking back. Others were simply worked to death.

When Germany invaded Poland and Russia, the Nazis forcibly transported millions of people back into Germany to work at factories all over the country. German propaganda told Fritz that the Eastern European workers—like the Ukrainians, Poles, and Russians—were subhuman, and it was okay to treat them like this. Working at the factory alongside Ukrainians, Poles, and Russians, Fritz realized these laborers weren't inferior to the Germans. One woman Fritz worked with actually taught German. The laborers could speak German, but Fritz didn't know any Russian. The propaganda was all lies, built on the belief that the Nazis assumed people were ready to be superior and hate others.

Fritz's coworkers also saw how poorly the forced laborers were treated, how they were all working for a machine that they didn't like. Anti-Fascist and anti-Nazi sentiment was growing, but no one was really willing to do anything about it. They were all too scared of the consequences. They lived in a society where a safer choice was to put your head down and let it go.

Fritz couldn't let it go. He was being forced to be a part of this war, of this system that he didn't agree with. He couldn't just put his head down.

The Ford factory sprawled alongside the Rhine between Cologne and Düsseldorf, and when the whistle blew at the end of one workday in November 1943, everyone else filed to the time clock or the changing rooms. These were the days when it was dark when Fritz arrived at work and dark when he left. On this particular day, he didn't mind the dark so much; it was perfect for what he and his friend Hans had planned.

Fritz and Hans made their way through the dark to the wooden crates stacked up next to the river. Fritz knew that inside the boxes he'd find replacement parts for the trucks the factory had built, and that the boxes had already been inspected and were ready to be shipped to the eastern front.

Fritz snuck up to one of the boxes, pried it open, and looked inside. After working at the factory for years, he knew which parts were the most important. He grabbed an ignition coil and slowly walked over to the concrete wall that bordered the river. He opened his hand and the part fell into the black water with a splash.

After they'd dropped the parts in, Fritz and Hans nailed the box shut again. He could imagine the men opening the box on the front, saying, "What good is this? We got everything, just not the most important part!"

Action inspired action. Fritz was listening to the BBC's German-language radio, which, like the flyers the Allied planes dropped, was supposed to encourage German rebellion. With Fritz, it worked. One friend told him that the Pirates were mentioned on a broadcast, which spurred them on to more actions. They'd turn messages they heard on the radio into flyers. Fritz felt he could do more than he'd already done.

40 — Gertrud

In the fall of 1943, after Marianne's warning, Gertrud and her mom had taken the train from Cologne to Ulm, in the south of Germany, but staying there wasn't a good option. Just traveling around wasn't all that dangerous, since lots of people were trying to get out of the cities to escape the bombings, but at some point, they would have to show their papers, and if their names really were on a list, they could be arrested anywhere in Germany. Gertrud's mom suggested they go to Rulfingen, where Gertrud's brother had spent some time, and the farmers had been friendly even though they knew he was a Communist.

When they arrived at the farm, the two women looked like hikers, with backpacks and hiking boots. A man appeared in front of the barn. Gertrud thought he had probably seen her and her mother approaching.

"Can we stay with you tonight?" Gertrud's mom asked the man.

"Sure, if you can work," the farmer said.

They could.

"You can sleep in the barn. There's a room in there that used to be for the farmhand," he said.

They hoped they would be safe there.

41 — Fritz

At the beginning of 1944, all boys born in the year 1927—the year Fritz was born—were called "A Birthday Present to Hitler," because they would turn seventeen. They could start serious military training, and on Hitler's actual birthday, they would be added to the Nazi Party's official register.

The whole idea disgusted Fritz, but there wasn't much he could do about it. Fritz and his friends got draft notices, and when the Pirates got together, they'd talk about how they could get out of being forced to join the army. The only real option would be to go underground, to start living illegally. But that didn't seem like a feasible option for Fritz: the police state was too powerful and he feared what the Nazis would do to the rest of his family if he did something wrong.

In February 1944, he went to a military training camp for four weeks at a former airfield a little over an hour south of Cologne. Ironically, it was in the Eifel mountains, one of the places that Pirates sometimes went for longer hiking trips. The whole thing was like the Hitler Youth: exercises, marching, drills. Fritz hated it and the weeks passed slowly. He left more disillusioned than ever.

Back at work, Fritz and Hans decided that just throwing truck parts into the Rhine wasn't enough, so they started burying broken milk bottles in the dirt road that newly finished trucks had to pass over on their way out of the factory. A truck's rubber tires would run over the shards of glass and with a pop and a rush of air, the truck was worthless. Tires were expensive, and Fritz and Hans could cost the Nazis trucks and money with only a little broken glass. The sabotage worked well, until the factory started noticing the milk bottles and increased watch over the area.

They had just been trying to bury more broken bottles when the two guards spotted them.

"We have to be really careful, run to the hall, and pretend like we didn't see them," Hans whispered. "I'll run after you so that it looks like I'm following you. When they stop us, just let me do the talking."

Fritz took off in a sprint and Hans followed him.

The men were standing on the edge of the square.

"Stop right there!" they yelled.

Fritz and Hans stopped, and the men started asking them questions. Fritz wasn't sure how much they had seen, but he hoped it wasn't much.

"What are you doing here when you know that's not allowed?" one of the men asked Fritz and Hans. "Are you the ones who have been committing the sabotage? Out with it, what are you doing here?"

"We were fighting, and I ran, but he followed me," Fritz replied.

"And why did you come here?"

"I hoped he wouldn't follow me, since we're not allowed to be here."

The guards didn't buy the story. They grabbed Fritz and Hans by the arms and led them to the factory security office. The plant foreman called the Gestapo.

Fritz was panicked. He knew that destroying trucks was serious sabotage and that he was known to the Gestapo already. They could prove that Fritz and Hans had been somewhere they weren't supposed to be, but they couldn't prove the sabotage. For his part, the plant foreman also didn't believe that just two kids were solely responsible for the buried milk bottles—he imagined a big conspiracy. The supervisor believed that Fritz and Hans had just been fighting and happened to end up somewhere they weren't supposed to be. They were let go.

Hans had to go join the military since he was a few years older than Fritz, but Fritz got a stamp on his ID that said he was *wehrunwürdig*, or unworthy of military service, which he knew would cause him problems in the future. One of the guards said to him, "Here now, you can get rid of that stamp. You only need to go volunteer for the Waffen-SS." That was one way the Nazis got young men to volunteer for the Waffen-SS, a military division of the SS. Fritz didn't answer. He wasn't crazy or desperate enough to join one of the worst regiments of the SS.*

---

* The Waffen-SS would later be found responsible for some of the most brutal atrocities of the Third Reich, including the murder of civilians in Eastern European towns.

This was the end of Fritz's sabotage efforts at the factory. There were too many guards now. But he didn't want to hold back.

Now or never, he had to do something. Sitting in the Green Belt park with his friend Lang and some Edelweiss Pirates he'd just met, Fritz helped hatch a new plan. The others weren't afraid to take real action. "We build a Molotov cocktail, a burning bottle. And during the next air raid, we smash it into the office of the local party while all the Nazis are in the bunkers, shitting their pants," Lang had suggested the day before.

Fritz had met two of the guys in the park during his military training: Bartholomäus Schink and Franz Rheinberger, whom Fritz knew as Barthel and Bubbes. They'd introduced him to Lang, whose real name was Hans Balzer, and Günther Schwarz, whom everyone called Büb. There were some other guys and girls who hung out with them at the Körner Street bunker, but Fritz didn't know them as well. They were all from Ehrenfeld and came from anti-Nazi working-class families, like Fritz and most of the Edelweiss Pirates. But they were willing to go further than most of the Pirates Fritz had hung out with.

Mainly, they wrote anti-Nazi graffiti on the destroyed city. They were funny about it, and wrote messages like:

FOR THIS WE THANK OUR FÜHRER

or

ONE PEOPLE, ONE REICH, ONE WRECK

Like Gertrud's group, they created flyers. For the text, they drew on information they heard on the BBC radio broadcasts, first with handwritten pages and then by cutting out lettering from newspapers.

They stirred together flour and water to make a paste to stick them to the buildings, and when the flour ran out, they used plaster from collapsed walls mixed with water. They wrote:

THE ALLIED TROOPS ARE ADVANCING ON ALL FRONTS

or

THOUSANDS OF GERMAN SOLDIERS KILLED BECAUSE OF HITLER'S MADNESS

Fritz and his friends hoped this would make the end of the Nazi regime come faster, but the actions didn't always feel like enough. These were just words, after all. And the beatings and arrests they suffered at the hands of the Gestapo and party members seemed to be getting worse and worse. Now the Pirates wanted payback, and maybe they needed more than words.

No one had been able to siphon any gasoline to fuel the bottle bomb, but they'd found a canister of diesel in an unlocked taxi. They put some in a beer bottle, stuck a rag in the top, and left the park.

Right before they got to the Nazi Party's office, an air-raid siren went off. They didn't go running toward a bunker, though; this had been part of the plan. Fritz and the others hid in the garden across from the office. From there, they could see the house, the street, and the surroundings. Lang got the short straw and was going to be the one to throw the bottle. Everything seemed calm, no patrols moving through the streets. Then the tack-tack-tack of the antiaircraft guns started. This was the moment.

Fritz stood in the garden, waiting. Lang lit the rag in the bottle; the bottle left his hand and careened through the glass window with a crash. Then almost immediately there was a smaller crash as the bottle hit the floor inside, broke, and the diesel fuel spilled out onto the floor of the office and caught fire.

All of a sudden, a couple of men came out of the house. Why the hell had they been in there? Why weren't they in the bunker? Lang, Fritz, and the others had been spotted. They ran in all directions, faster than the Nazis who'd come out of the office, luckily.

They didn't get caught, but Fritz was still disappointed. They hadn't achieved their goal either: the fire was put out before it did much damage.

"Um, I'd like to go with some friends to Felsensee over the weekend. The weather will be nice, and it's going to be great," Fritz said to his mom.

She looked at him suspiciously. He wasn't supposed to be hanging out with the Pirates anymore. But now that it was spring, he really want to go hiking with his friends. He hadn't really asked her a question, or even asked her permission, but he did need her help.

Fritz had still been regularly checking in every Sunday since his arrest in November, and the most important thing for him was that he at least had a good excuse as to why he didn't show up. He needed his mom to go to the office and tell them he was sick and couldn't check in.

His mom couldn't believe what he was asking.

"You put me in the most impossible situations," she told him.

After some convincing, she agreed to call them, but she wouldn't go to the office.

He failed to mention that with an excuse like that, he probably also needed a note from the doctor. Still, no one would have probably said anything if the shit hadn't hit the fan coming home from Felsensee.

The weekend was wonderful, with good weather and good friends. Fritz set up a tent, and they sat inside with a fire going, singing songs and talking. But there was a cloud over what should have been a good time. They didn't know if they were ever going to have a weekend like this again.

On Sunday morning, they went back down from the hidden-away oasis of Felsensee to Königswinter, where they'd take the boat back across the Rhine to Cologne, or what remained of the city, anyway.

Fritz noticed the dock was full of men in uniforms. They looked like SS, Gestapo, police, everyone. Some of the other groups they'd been with had seen Hitler Youth on the way in. They must have sent for reinforcements.

"Come on, guys! Let's go!" Fritz yelled.

Everyone bolted in different directions. Fritz saw a wall, hopped over it, and hoped no one had seen him. He peeked his head back over. Men in uniforms were loading his friends into trucks. Fritz was sure they were heading straight to the EL-DE House basement or to Brauweiler.

Those who hadn't been arrested took the train back to Cologne, and it wasn't long before the Gestapo was looking for Fritz, which meant either someone had given his name or they were just arresting anyone that had previously been associated with the Pirates.

When Fritz received a notice to appear, his mom didn't understand why. She had said he was sick, and she thought that excuse would work. They walked together to the EL-DE House. Fritz knew what could happen if he walked through those doors, but he felt compelled.

Officer Fink was there again. Fritz tried to explain that he was sick that Sunday, that he had the doctor's note to prove it, and that he wasn't with the Pirates at all over the weekend.

"I know that despite the warning you received at Brauweiler, you've been in contact with the Edelweiss Pirates. I also have witnesses who say you were at Königswinter on Easter during the fights the Edelweiss Pirates started with the party members, and the government is also aware of this," Fink said.

"No, no, that's not right, I was in bed, I've told you," Fritz pleaded.

"Man, quit with the lying, or I will end you."

The interrogation was making Fritz's mother hysterical. She yelled that they needed to believe him, that he had been sick.

"You keep out of this! You should be happy that you're even allowed to be in here," Fink yelled at Fritz's mother. "Sit down now!"

This gave Fritz a moment to think. He had been here before and he had dealt with these people before. And making up lies to get him to confess was a familiar Gestapo technique. They thought if they said, "We have someone who says you were there," then Fritz would probably believe them and confess. But knowing this classic interrogation technique, Fritz said those other guys must have been liars, and that the information had to be wrong. The look in Officer Fink's eyes said his patience was wearing thin.

Fink yelled that Fritz's answers were cheeky and that Fritz was a liar, while another officer started beating on him. He'd been through this before, but now his mom had to stand there and watch. The smacks and yells were joined by the screaming protests from Fritz's mom. She tried to run to Fritz, but Fink held her back.

"By assisting him and lying you are committing punishable offenses. If you don't shut up, I will let them lock you up too. Those who are in Adolf Hitler's National Socialist Germany and protect trash and rogues like your son are punishable, remember that!"

The color drained from her face and her lips turned from red to blue. She gasped for air.

"Mom!"

She had a bad heart, and now they'd killed her just by yelling at her. The guy must have stopped beating Fritz, because Fritz ran over to his mother. The two Nazis just looked confused and left the room. *The things you put me through*, is that what his mother had said?

He got her a glass of water, and after a few minutes, her color came back. Fritz told her not to say anything. He meant to sound compassionate, but he also didn't know if someone was listening.

Officer Fink and the other officer came back into the room, along with the foreman from the Ford factory where Fritz worked, who became the good cop.

"So, Theilen, what's going on now?" A fatherly tone, the same question. "You're having problems, I hear. We'll find a solution."

His solution and Fritz's solution were not the same thing, and Fritz didn't give him the answers he wanted.

"So, my friend, nothing will happen to you if you tell us who the leader is. Just a couple of names and then you get to move on."

Another classic interrogation technique: promise the person who has been arrested something in return for talking. Of course, if he gives any names, he has admitted his own guilt. So Fritz stuck by the story that he had not left the house on Easter and that he wasn't a member of the Pirates.

After more questioning, Fritz finally got to go home with his mom, but not without Fink warning him that the next time he was arrested, he'd be sent straight to a camp.

Fritz and Bubbes walked from Ehrenfeld toward the Innenstadt. Fritz had received the warning from the Gestapo just a few days earlier, but something about the world around him made it impossible to stop resisting. He felt like his friends were being hunted like animals by the Nazis, and he wanted revenge. He also might have thought that he didn't have much to lose.

Death is inevitable, but in 1944 Germany, death came at full speed. An air-raid bombing, deployment to the front: sudden death was everywhere. For Pirates like Fritz, at least if they were fighting back against the Nazis, they might die doing something meaningful. And there was another thing: Fritz might have realized that the one thing the Nazis didn't actually want to do was kill him. They might have wanted him and his friends dead, but they would be happier to see them killed by Allied bullets on the Westwall when they were old enough to join the army.

Fritz and Bubbes walked past a group of men, a chain gang of Russian prisoners of war. A person could also die by being worked to death, and that was the path those men appeared to be on. Their skinny bodies were lost in prison clothing, their cheekbones and chins were angular, their eyes sunk deep into their skulls.

"These Nazi shits. Look at them, the prisoners clearly haven't eaten in a week. What makes me really want to puke is that the Nazis always think they are gentleman," Bubbes said as they passed the men.

When Fritz and Bubbes met the rest of the guys at their new hidden hangout at the edge of the Green Belt by the train tracks, the foreign laborers were all they could talk about. What could they do to help?

The evening turned to night, and the air-raid sirens would start soon. On that night, even before the sirens started, they could hear the tack-tack-tack of antiaircraft guns going off in the distance and the slow, oscillating rumble of American bomber planes.

Bubbes slid from the top of the train embankment where he'd been looking down into the train yard. He said he saw a detached locomotive coming closer. The train stations were among the most dangerous places to be during an air raid. From the sky, the Americans used the Cathedral as a central location in the city, and right next to it was the Central Train Station. From those landmarks, the pilots could navigate along the hashmarks of the train tracks to the next train station and drop their bombs. The locomotives were uncoupled from the trains and moved away from the station to safer locations.

The Pirates scrambled back up into the community garden in

the Green Belt so they could watch the train tracks. The locomotive slowed to a halt, and with a screech and a clack, it stopped right in front of them. They saw the Nazi slogan written on the side of the train:

WHEELS MUST ROLL FOR VICTORY!

In the distance, they could hear the whirring of bombs dropping from planes, and then crash-boom and the ground-shaking that followed.

Bubbes thought the slogan was particularly stupid and that they should change it.

Everyone loved the idea. Now they needed something to write with.

Someone found a paint bucket, and Bubbes hid it in his basement until the next night, when they met up again at the train tracks.

Right after midnight, the siren started wailing. With antiaircraft guns going off in the background, Fritz and Bubbes ran down to the locomotive, gravel crunching under their shoes. Fritz had a funny feeling in his stomach, nervous excitement overwhelming his body.

They got up next to the train, Bubbes held out the bucket, Fritz grabbed the brush. They knew the faster they could get this done, the less risk there was of getting caught. Fritz smeared the paint on the train, adding their own touch to the party slogan.

NAZI HEADS WILL ROLL AFTER THE WAR.

When they were finished, it took about an hour for the train to be hooked up again, and when the locomotive rolled past with their slogan, they couldn't have been more proud. Plus, they relished the thought of how the Nazi bozos, as Fritz called them, would be upset that someone had messed up their beautiful message.

As satisfying as this action was, though, the Ehrenfeld Pirates were ready to plan something bigger and better.

The weather was beautiful but the atmosphere was awful. The day was April 20, 1944, Adolf Hitler's birthday. Fritz knew that on holidays like this, the Nazis would celebrate with parades and marches, and the Pirates should stay away from public areas. Fritz and others had decided to spend the afternoon hanging out in a part of the Green Belt that was between Ehrenfeld and a neighborhood called Nippes. The normal discussion topics of trips on the weekend were superseded by talk of how much they hated the Nazis and how they could fight back.

Barthel had an idea. He wanted to give Hitler a "birthday present." Barthel was the middle child of five siblings and worked as a roofing and plumbing apprentice, earning a low salary. Like Fritz, he had been in the Hitler Youth and his dad was in the army, deployed in Italy to fight the invading Allied troops. But those facts didn't mean he was a Nazi or had any Nazi sympathies.

One of the memories that stuck with Barthel's sister Caroline the most was when Barthel broke down while witnessing a Jewish barber named Moritz Spiro being beaten and dying from a cracked skull on Kristallnacht. Barthel had screamed, "Dad! Dad, help Spiro!" but their dad was crying and said, "I can't help him. If I helped him, they'd smash me and kill me too." Barthel couldn't understand why someone who had been so kind to their family had been beaten like that. The Schinks were poor, and Spiro had always cut their hair for a discounted price. He had died, and there was nothing ten-year-old Bartholomäus could have done about it. That was probably when his hatred for the Nazis really started. Barthel had met Bubbes (Franz Rheinberger) and started hanging out with the Edelweiss Pirates in Ehrenfeld in 1943, and now he felt he could do something with the hate he had for the Nazis.

Barthel's idea for a "birthday present" for Hitler was to derail a train. They could damage a train; take its cargo for themselves, forced laborers, and others in hiding; and it would cost the Nazis valuable supplies—all in one action. Fritz thought he was crazy and Bubbes had no idea how they would accomplish such a big heist.

Then, one of the guys in the park spoke up. Keunz was an apprentice with the Reichs Train Improvement Section and explained an easy way to derail a train using worn-out brake shoes from off another train.

"Huh, there it is. We're doing this," Barthel declared. They went to find the brake shoes.

Just like the day had been beautiful, so was the night. The stars shone like pieces of glass across the dark sky. Even though the city was blacked out and the moon was just a sliver on its way to nothing, Fritz could see the length of a soccer field in front of where he

Barthel Schink (right with hat and guitar) and Franz "Bubbes" Rheinberger (left with hat and guitar) with friends near Königswinter, 1943 or 1944.

was standing on the train tracks, all the way to where the train police were and where the goods trains were loaded in the train yard.

Fritz and Barthel crouched down to see if anyone was nearby. Then they scurried toward the tracks, the sounds and shakes of explosions surrounding them. The air raids were perfect and terrible, offering an opportunity to take action, but signaling death and destruction at the same time. The boys placed a brake shoe down right before the track switch, just like Keunz had told them. Barthel yelled, "Let's get out of here!" A train loaded with wood and trucks was slowly creeping along the tracks.

Fires erupted around them. The bombers were dropping metal cylinders, bombs that looked like dried beans falling one by one and growing larger as they got closer to the ground. When the canisters hit, they exploded into a cloud of thick gray smoke that lifted to reveal fires. Then Fritz heard a sound coming from the train tracks. The sound wasn't like a bomb going off, more like metal colliding and crumpling and twisting. He couldn't go back, he couldn't look, but he was convinced that he had just derailed the train.

Fritz kept running, through the smoke, through the fires, but he wasn't going to make it to the Körner Street bunker where he usually went, so he made a dash for the Taku Square bunker, hoping it wouldn't be full.

Later, when he heard that police were called to the train tracks, Fritz was even more convinced that they had been successful. Even better, none of his friends were brought in for questioning. After a few days, though, Fritz's mom told him that the Gestapo had been at the house, looking for him.

Fritz, Lang, and Bubbes all decided that if they were to be arrested by the Gestapo again, that would be the end. No more warnings, no more short stays in prison. They decided they couldn't go home, and they couldn't go back to work. Those places were too dangerous. They would have to go underground and live completely illegally.

Not going to work also meant no ration cards. No ration cards meant no food. Fritz sarcastically said, "What are we supposed to do, go and say that we are Edelweiss Pirates, and that we live illegally and are fighting against the Hitler Youth and Gestapo?" Asking their parents or friends for food wasn't really an option either, since you only got enough rations for yourself, and even that wasn't very much.

Every time they talked about food and rations, Fritz thought about the prisoners of war and forced laborers who begged Germans for food, even if they knew both asking and giving were dangerous and illegal. Getting extra food was dangerous and illegal for anyone in 1944, but Fritz didn't feel like he had another choice, and unlike the POWs and forced laborers, he could access food more easily. During all their time watching the train tracks, Fritz and the Pirates had seen food being loaded in and out of trains. But this action wouldn't be as simple as painting a car or derailing one. To begin, they didn't know how to get the food out of the locked train cars.

"Maria got me in contact with two men, and I'm meeting them later tonight," Bubbes told Fritz and the others not long after they'd starting making plans to get food. Maria was a friend, and Bubbes trusted her.

"Do you know them?"

"No, Maria just told me that they have a connection to the goods trains. I don't know any more, not even their names."

Meeting these guys was stupidly risky. They either knew the risk and were willing to take it, or they had no idea how risky it really was. Fritz, Bubbes, Barthel, and another Pirate went to the soccer field in the Bickendorf neighborhood, where Maria's contacts were already waiting for them.

"Just so we are clear, we make the decisions what will happen and how it will happen, okay?" the guys said right off the bat.

Barthel explained their situation.

"We don't want anything to do with the foreign workers, and definitely not with the Gestapo, who will probably skin you if they find out," said one of the guys.

The Pirates weren't willing to take no for an answer. They went back and forth, and finally the guys agreed they would help Fritz and the others get food if they promised to follow orders. The Pirates agreed.

The first theft went well. Maria's friends got food, including sausages, out of the train. Bubbes snuck food to the Russians, and the Pirates kept some for themselves.

The next time was different. Something hadn't seemed right from the beginning, and when they saw cigarette smoke seeping out of one of the train cars, they called off the break-in. Bubbes was the only one who wanted to know what was going on, so he went back and waited.

Nothing happened. Then he threw a stone against the side of the car. The clanging of rock hitting metal was followed by a louder clang of the door opening, and the crunching of gravel as a bunch of men in uniforms jumped out of the car. They searched the whole area, but Bubbes managed to get away.

After that, Maria's connections didn't want to help. They thought what the Pirates wanted was too dangerous. But Fritz and his friends still wanted to keep going, to get food and share it with the prisoners. They also realized that their recklessness was becoming dangerous.

"What are we going to do if they start shooting at us?" Barthel asked. "As fast as they shoot, we wouldn't be able to get away." He paused. "I guess the best thing would naturally be if we could shoot back."

"Man, if they find you with a gun, then it's over. It'll be a short trial," Bubbes said.

"And besides, where are we supposed to get weapons and ammo?" Fritz said.

"Yeah, yeah, you guys are right, but I'm tired of being a sitting duck," Barthel said.

Fritz and Bubbes couldn't argue with that.

"Just in case," Bubbes added. They would only use the guns defensively.

They all agreed and started figuring out how to get weapons.

"We have to do something. We can't just sit here and wait for things to get better," said Lang.

That was easier said than done. Now more than ever, Fritz and the Ehrenfeld Edelweiss Pirates felt like they were being watched by the Gestapo and SS. The invasion of Allied troops into Normandy, France, in June 1944 had given Fritz an increased hope that the war would be over soon. But in the late summer of 1944, Ehrenfeld was bleak. The people who remained mostly lived illegally in bunkers, shelters, or basements of burned and bombed-out houses. There were deserters who didn't want to return to the war, escaped French and Soviet prisoners of war, escaped forced laborers from other countries, and common criminals.

All of those people—people who didn't have ration cards and would be arrested if they were caught on the street—took food, clothing, cigarettes, and alcohol when they found it. Stores and private citizens noticed food disappear, and they'd blame the crime on Edelweiss Pirates, since the Nazi propaganda said they were criminals. Sometimes people even lied and said food had been stolen so they could get more rations. Everyone left in the city seemed to be doing something illegal, and some people were just waiting for the American troops to move closer and closer across France, into

Germany, and then into Cologne. Lang thought they needed to make that happen faster.

"The only meaningful thing left would be a bomb attack against the Nazis," said Bubbes. Then, almost as if he was talking to himself, he said, "I have no idea how you get dynamite or hand grenades, and we can't do much with just our guns."

He threw his gun in the air, caught it, and stuck it back in his pocket. Their plan to get firearms had been successful. Fritz had an easy time taking a gun his dad had hidden in the basement. But mostly, the weapons were thanks to the girls they hung out with, who flirted with soldiers in bars and pocketed the sidearms they carried.

"We gotta get these party fat cats out of the way," said Barthel.

"What, you mean . . . " Lang stuck his index finger and thumb out from his fist and made a shooting motion.

"Yeah, that's exactly what I mean. We can try it, right?"

"You're crazy. You can't just stand on the street and shoot a Nazi!"

42 — Gertrud

Gertrud and her mother had been at the farm for some months and were getting used to their new life. The farmer's wife had died some years ago and his son and farmhand were in the army, so Gertrud and her mother's labor helped keep the farm going.

Gertrud's mom had been right: they were safe here. The Americans had no reason to bomb the countryside, so they were safe from air raids. The farm was isolated, but provided them with food. And they had each other.

One day in July 1944, the farmer came back from town with a newspaper under his arm.

"Has something happened?" Gertrud's mother asked. "I mean, the newspaper . . . "

"An attack. They tried to kill Hitler," he said.

Was that possible? Had Gertrud heard him correctly?

"Who dared? And did it work?" The words escaped Gertrud's mouth before she even realized what she had said.

The farmer looked at her. She thought that maybe his silence meant he was thinking the same thing.

"Graf von Stauffenberg was said to have brought a suitcase with explosives to a meeting at the Führer's headquarters at Wolfschanze," the farmer said. "In the newspaper, it said that the Führer sees his survival as a destiny from God."

That seemed like more words than the farmer had said the whole time they had been with him. And God, what if it had worked? The Allies had landed at the beach at Normandy in France and were getting closer and closer to the German border. The end of the war felt like it was coming, but how soon?

"They had a real plan," he continued. "Stauffenberg escaped to Berlin, thinking that Hitler was dead, but he was caught. In the same night, Stauffenberg and four others were executed."

That night, Gertrud couldn't sleep. What if the attack had been successful? Wouldn't fear infiltrate the Nazis now? Would they be afraid of who they could trust? How were the others, the Pirates who remained in Cologne, doing? Were they still fighting?

43 — Jean

The Germans were losing the war, and Jean could tell the regime was becoming desperate. Even though his friend Meik was a political prisoner, he was sent to the front in a battalion made up of criminals. The Nazis would take almost anyone they could get as expendable bodies in this war. Jean managed to visit Meik twice at the new military camp, but traveling inside Germany was becoming harder.

Jean with his guitar in Beethoven Park, about 1944.

And after the assassination attempt on Hitler, the Nazis were more desperate than ever, more brutal. Just going outside meant he or anyone else faced a threat. Jean saw Hitler Youth patrols everywhere, ready to stop him and his friends if they looked suspicious. The Hitler Youth would beat them up, and the older Nazis were worse.

In the late summer days of 1944, Jean would walk along the street, minding his own business and not doing anything wrong, and a swarm of SS or SA men in uniforms would surround him, force him to stand against a wall. Thoughts of what would happen next invariably ran through his head: They'd search him. What would they find? Did he have something to hide? Could they plant something on him because they felt like it? Was something he was wearing cause for arrest? It was an exhausting cycle.

The days of fighting almost felt like they were over. The

thrilling sense of connection to a larger resistance movement he'd gotten from Meik had nearly gone. The SS and SA had weapons and would use them. He was fifteen; how was he supposed to get weapons to defend himself?

He knew of the Ehrenfeld group that Fritz was a part of—he'd met Bubbes and Barthel on a trip to Blauensee and sometimes they came to visit in Blücherpark—but he didn't know what they were up to.

44 — Fritz

Fritz, Barthel, Bubbes, and Büb walked along the ruined streets at the end of the summer of 1944. Their world was decidedly different than it had been even six months earlier. Barthel, Bubbes, and Lang had all been forced to report for military service on the Westwall, but had come back to Cologne. They didn't want to sit in fortifications at the French border, waiting for the Americans to arrive. With nothing else to do, the Pirates had just been hanging around a lot.

On this late summer day, they were on their way to Sülz to meet some friends at a bunker in Herta when a truck full of Nazis approached. Fritz and the others thought the truck would stop them and ask for IDs. No one wanted that hassle or to have to explain why they were on the streets, so the Pirates made a run for the reservoir in the southern part of Beethoven Park.

"Goddammit. I do not want to spend the night here," said Büb.

Bubbes told him they had no choice. Going back out onto the streets was too dangerous now.

Büb's nickname meant, essentially, "little dude." He was the youngest in the group, but had already evaded arrest many times and was living more dangerously than any of the other Pirates in his circle.

Büb's father was Jewish, which made him and his older brother, Wolfgang, undesirables in the eyes of the Nazis. His dad had tried hard to protect Büb and Wolfgang from anti-Semitic Nazi laws. First he took them out of a Jewish school and put them into a Christian one. Then he divorced his wife, Büb and Wolfgang's mother, and sent them to live with their non-Jewish maternal family. In the end, none of it worked.

Büb and his maternal aunt had been at the train station when family friends and the rabbi were loaded on trains bound for the Litzmannstadt Ghetto, friends they never saw again. Büb didn't understand why they were being taken away. And when he and his brother were supposed to show up for deportation, they just didn't go. They had to live in a city where they were no longer supposed to exist.

Both Büb and Wolfgang had joined the Edelweiss Pirates, and even though they were half Jewish, their friends in the Pirates didn't care. On all their adventures, they were treated exactly the same as everyone else. Büb was outgoing and loved to be around other people; he was a daredevil and provocateur who was friends with everyone in the neighborhood. Wolfgang was more withdrawn. Büb and Wolfgang were both living illegally by 1944. They didn't have ration cards and had to get food from others or steal, which was easier if they had connections to criminals and others living underground. By the fall of 1944, who was decidedly political, who was just anti-Nazi, and who was just trying to survive were blurry categories. Wolfgang grew closer to a group of political activists, while Büb kept hanging out with the Ehrenfeld Pirates.

After almost getting caught, Büb, Bubbes, Barthel, and Fritz had to wait in Beethoven Park until it got dark and then walk back north toward Ehrenfeld. As usual, the air-raid sirens started, and so did the bombs. They must have taken a slightly roundabout way to get back, because they found themselves near the Müngersdorf train station, west of Ehrenfeld.

There, on the tracks, were train cars toppled by a bomb strike.

"Come on, let's get closer and see," said Barthel. "Maybe we'll find something to eat."

They found packages of rice and canned vegetables. This was too good to pass up. Getting food was usually a lot riskier than just picking it up off the train tracks. They each grabbed a box and started walking back to Ehrenfeld, which was still half an hour away on foot.

Not far from the forced-labor camp in Ehrenfeld, a civilian patrol yelled at them to stop. The Pirates were close enough to home that they knew the streets and thought they could escape. But as they sprinted away from the first patrol, another patrol appeared and yelled: "Stop right there!"

Günther "Büb" Schwarz (front) as an apprentice in Cologne, November 1942.

They'd never escape carrying the boxes, so they had to throw them away. The food would have probably fed them and their friends for a month.

They ran toward Helio Street.

Fritz thought something must have been going on that night, since it seemed like on every corner there was some sort of patrolman out on duty, keeping watch for something.

Darkness surrounded them, and so did the authorities. Someone fired a gun in their direction. This was getting to be too crazy. The four split up; Fritz and Barthel stayed near the glass factory. But that wasn't a good hideout. Soon, a couple of officers appeared.

All of a sudden, Barthel pulled his gun from his pocket and fired two or three shots in the direction in the patrol. Fritz couldn't figure out why he'd done that. He had no idea that Barthel had a gun on him—Fritz hadn't brought his—and besides, shooting at the people you are hiding from is a terrible idea. But Fritz didn't have time to think about what Barthel had done for long. The officers started looking around for the shooter.

They ran as fast as they could to the community garden plots in the Green Belt near Nippes. The two boys spent the rest of the night there, trying to figure out if he'd hit one of the officers.

The Gestapo was seriously worried about illegal activity in the Ehrenfeld neighborhood and had been on high alert, just as Fritz suspected. Probably because he had been arrested before, Fritz was rounded up a few days after the shooting and taken to the EL-DE House, where Officers Fink and Manthey started their usual lines of questioning.

"Who are your leaders?"

"Who's been writing graffiti on the walls?"

These were familiar questions and Fritz knew to give the same old answers. But then they surprised him with a new one:

"So, where do you have your gun?" Fink asked.

"Me? What? I don't have a gun, where would I have gotten that?" Fritz responded, trying to mask his uncertainty of whether the officers actually knew anything about the guns.

"Who was involved in the shooting a few days ago? I know that you all were there! Out with it, otherwise we can do this differently."

"I don't have a gun, and I wasn't at this shootout that you're talking about." Deny, deny, deny—Fritz hadn't forgotten what his mom's friend had told him.

"You will all be brought to a camp, especially made for the Edelweiss Pirates. That will be the last chance for you and your friends to become a proper part of society," Fink said and sent Fritz away.

Another night in the Gestapo prison. The uncertainty of what was going to happen next descended like a fog. They could send him back to Brauweiler and try to get more information about what was going on in Ehrenfeld. If the Gestapo actually knew Fritz had a gun or associated with people who had illegal weapons, they could probably have charges brought against him for treason. He could be executed. Or they could just beat him and beat him and beat him until he gave up more information. Or they could send him to a work reeducation camp, a military service camp, or a concentration camp.

During that September in 1944, Fritz turned seventeen. There would be no presents.

Part Five
Fall 1944

"The Nazis are everywhere, and the raids and arrests just keep happening."

Cologne, August 1944

The fall of the Nazi regime seems more imminent than ever. In June 1944, US troops land in Normandy, France, during the invasion known as D-Day, and by mid-August, you hear that Paris is liberated. But that doesn't mean the war is over. German soldiers die as the Allied troops move closer to the border and the Westwall, and now your friends—guys as young as fourteen— are shipped out to build trenches or man guns. In the fall of 1944, around 400,000 young men are sent to this brutal work, and all young men over sixteen across Germany are supposed to register so they can be drafted.

But the end of the war can't come soon enough. In Cologne, it's hard to say that a city even still exists. Standing on the Hohenzollern Bridge, you see only destruction: collapsed shells of houses and rubble in the streets, and the smell of smoke lingers in the air. Ninety-nine percent of structures are destroyed. The Cathedral still stands, but bombs have destroyed the stained-glass windows.

Many people have left, but some still live in the ruins. On the east side of the bridge is the Messe, a convention hall the Nazis have turned into a forced-labor camp. Here and at other sites around the city, approximately 45,000 foreign workers are still slaving for the Nazi war machine. Beneath the rubble, people live illegally. Between three thousand and four thousand deserters from the army are hiding in Cologne, along with Jews who escaped deportation and forced laborers who escaped camps and prisons. After bomb attacks, gas, power, and telephone lines are cut off, and transportation through the city is almost impossible.

Food supplies are dwindling and work hours are getting longer. Money is nearly worthless; it's guns and butter that have real value. The black market grows, and even grocers pretend that goods are stolen so they can sell them on the black market instead.

This wasteland is becoming lawless. Guns go missing. Bombs go missing. People disappear underground; people fight back. The Gestapo becomes ever more vigilant, and even if they know that Germany will lose the war, they won't go down without a fight, without trying to establish law and order in a ruined city.

45 — Jean

Like Fritz, Jean and his friends had no interest in registering to serve on the Westwall, no matter how bad things were in Cologne. They still hung out at Manderscheider Square, the little open space tucked away in the Sülz neighborhood where they liked to meet. The square was smaller than a city block and surrounded by apartment buildings. People knew they were there, but few seemed to care.

One day, they heard footsteps smacking across the cobblestone street that surrounded the square. A troop of Hitler Youth approached, the brown mass that Jean and his friends were well acquainted with. Before they could run away, they were surrounded and escorted to the school next to the square. The HY were planning on making them register for service on the Westwall, whether they wanted to or not.

The apartment buildings were packed tightly around the square, and a neighbor had seen what happened. Earlier in the war, no one in the surrounding neighborhood would have risked looking twice at a HY patrol hassling some kids. But things were changing as the war entered its last year. The neighbor told Jean's aunt, who told Fän's grandmother, and the information quickly trickled from one woman to another in the neighborhood. Sülz wasn't as notoriously Communist as Ehrenfeld, but these women were fed up with the Nazis and fed up with the war. After they heard that their boys had been taken, about eight women approached the school, where a Hitler Youth stood outside with a gun. They said they wanted to get in. He said no. He didn't want to let them in. They weren't okay with that answer.

They started screaming, "We'll pull down your pants and spank your bare bottom if you don't leave this post!"

One of them ripped the gun from the Hitler Youth, and they

all stormed into the office where Jean and the others were about to be forced to register. The room broke into a chorus of the women's voices, complaining and chastising the Hitler Youth leader.

"You dragged our boys here as if they were criminals, when our men bled to death in Stalingrad for Führer, people, and country! That's outrageous!" Jean heard one woman say.

The screaming and shouting worked. Jean and the others were allowed to leave the room without registering. He had believed that the hate for the Nazis was strong and getting stronger, and these women just proved that. He also saw that the passion of being anti-Nazi could manifest into action against the cowardice of the desk-jockey bureaucrat Nazis like the ones forcing young people to register to fight and die.

Jean, Fän, and the other Sülz Edelweiss Pirates realized they needed to come up with a plan to hide from the Nazis. They wanted to build a cabin on a small island in a man-made reservoir near Beethoven Park called Decksteiner Weiher or Lidosee.* The area surrounding Lidosee felt isolated and bigger than it actually was. The park was fields and paths and woods, and even contained an old Prussian fort. Many of Jean's friends had been living illegally in garden huts around the city and others had been amassing weapons and planning actions against the Nazis. The idea of building a secret Pirate hideout on an island wasn't as crazy as it might sound.

Since they couldn't get guns like Fritz, Barthel, and Bubbes had, Jean and his friends started figuring out how they could make weapons. One of their friends worked as a technician printing photographs and had access to chemicals. The guys discovered they could mix explosive black powder to make their own firecrackers. They filled bottles with calcium carbide and added water, creating

---

* Jean calls the reservoir Decksteiner Weiher in his memoir, but the Gestapo refers to the area as Lidosee.

a reaction that let off gas and made the bottles explode. They even built catapults capable of launching big rocks.

Then they saw some younger kids playing with a detonator. Fän knew that when buildings had been bombed but didn't collapse fully, men would use detonators and explosives to collapse the buildings in a controlled manner so they didn't fall unexpectedly and injure more people. One of their friends followed the kids, and saw that an explosive device was still left in the basement of the building where the kids found the detonator. They broke the window, and one of their smallest friends climbed through to retrieve it.

The next time Jean and his friends saw Barthel, Bubbes, and the Ehrenfeld Pirates, they told them about what they'd been up to. Barthel and Bubbes told Jean and Fän they knew someone who would be interested in the explosive, a man named Hans Steinbrück, whom they called Bomben-Hans. Jean and Fritz were both friends with Barthel and Bomben-Hans, and Jean's and Fritz's lives would be changed by this friendship, but during the fall of 1944, Jean and Fritz never met.

Barthel told Jean and Fän to bring the detonator to Schönstein Street No. 7 in Ehrenfeld.

Jean and Fän walked along the street under the train tracks. The fact that the elevated train tracks and the Ehrenfeld train station were still standing was almost a miracle. Bombings and fires had consumed much of the surrounding block. Structures that were still standing—you couldn't really call them buildings—were missing roofs and walls, just shells that were ready to collapse in a plume of smoke at any minute.

At Schönstein Street No. 7, there was still a door, so Jean and Fän went up to it and tapped out a special secret knock. The door opened. They made their way through the damaged building to the small first-floor apartment of Cilly, Bomben-Hans's girlfriend.

From inside the apartment, a string went through a large hole in the wall to the apartment building next door. Jean and Fän followed the string, continued down some broken stairs to a heavy metal door that looked like it was from an air-raid shelter. They knocked again and climbed down into the basement, where the string ended at a small bell.

Jean and Fän learned that Cilly would pull on the string in her apartment to let the people in the basement know if there was danger coming. That was important, because down there was where the really illegal stuff happened. The hideout looked like a gangster lair from a movie. There was a training area with punching bags so they could stay fit. In one room, there were bunk beds taken from an air-raid shelter, where some deserters and escaped prisoners slept during the day so they could go out on raids at night. There were piles of Nazi uniforms. There were spoils of their heists: food, guns, and an enormous amount of butter. Jean and Fän learned that Bomben-Hans was the mastermind behind all of this.

Hans "Bomben-Hans" Steinbrück was twenty-three, and his reputation impressed the younger Pirates. Much like Meik Jovy, he was a daredevil role model. He could do anything: plumbing, bricklaying, electrical work, fixing cars. The Ehrenfeld Pirates wanted to be around him, and they were quite willing to listen to crazy stories about his life, stories that seemed to mix reality and fiction, truth with exaggeration. He had escaped from the Buchenwald concentration camp. He told the Pirates he'd ended up in Buchenwald after applying for a job at the Gestapo and then lying to a landlady that he worked at the Gestapo.* Fourteen days later, he was arrested, put in a police prison, and transferred to Buchenwald. Bomben-Hans never mentioned why he applied to a job at the Gestapo. In October 1942, he was transferred to the Messe in one of the first groups of prisoners brought there.

---

* Although this statement comes from Jean's Gestapo interrogation, I have not seen it validated anywhere else.

He'd spent a year there, sleeping on mattresses filled with wood shavings, crowded with multiple people in each bed. His head was shaved and he wore a striped uniform—clothing taken from the prisoners who had been gassed at the death camp Auschwitz. Bomben-Hans wasn't afraid of telling Jean, Fän, and the other Pirates the horrors he'd seen.

While at the Messe, Bomben-Hans said he had volunteered for the bomb squad, a group that had the job of digging out unexploded Allied bombs and then defusing them or blowing them up. Bomben-Hans would be assigned to an SS officer along with three other prisoners, and they would go find a bomb. A first, everyone would dig with shovels. As more of the bomb was revealed, he had to dig with a smaller shovel, and then finally just his hands. The prisoners would switch between digging and resting every two hours so that no one would get too tired, and everyone would stay sharp for the dangerous work.

The work was hell, demanding patience and unfaltering nerves. One wrong move might cause the bomb to explode. Bomben-Hans volunteered for this knowing how dangerous it was. Maybe he was a daredevil and liked the action, maybe he wanted to get the double ration of soup that the prisoners received for risking their lives, or maybe he wanted to learn more about bombs. In any case, Hans Steinbrück got the nickname Bomben-Hans. "I've defused nine hundred and ninety-nine bombs, but it's the thousandth one that I'm scared of," he told visitors to the basement.

Bomben-Hans also claimed that his bomb-defusing talent gave him the right to come and go from the camp as he pleased, which may or may not have been true. After a year in the Messe camp, Bomben-Hans decided to escape. He never told anyone how exactly he escaped but he did have a complicated story of arrests and escapes that included a trip to Berlin, more time in Buchenwald, and then finally his present stint in Cologne.

Cäcilie "Cilly" Serve had been living at Schönstein Street No. 7

since 1943, and met Bomben-Hans either through another prisoner named Hans Debus or when Bomben-Hans worked in Ehrenfeld as a prisoner.[*]

In early 1944, Bomben-Hans met Büb and Wolfgang Schwarz, who were living illegally with their aunt Gustel Spitzley in the same building as Cilly. Gustel had been arrested and sent to a concentration camp in 1933 for bringing Socialist newspapers from Aachen, on the French border, to Cologne. Gustel and Bomben-Hans talked about their time in the camps and told stories, stories that made an impression on the Pirates. Wolfgang said that Hans had shown them pieces of skin that had come from camp prisoners, that Hans said were being made into lampshades, although other people remember just hearing the story of the skin and not actually seeing the pieces.

By the time Jean and Fän went to go see Bomben-Hans at Schönstein Street No. 7, the building was a hideaway for anyone who wanted to live illegally. There was Bomben-Hans, Büb, and Wolfgang, but also an eighteen-year-old half-Jewish woman named Ruth Kramer, her mother, Friedel, and a Jewish man named Paul Urbat. Like the Schwarzes, they escaped deportation. Cilly hid them in her apartment, but they didn't always know what was going on in the basement.

Shortly before he met Jean and Fän, Bomben-Hans had started burglarizing grocery stores and food reserves with guys named Black Peter and Josef "Jupp" Moll. They stole butter, margarine, sugar, cheese, and any other food they could get. Jean understood it as a Robin Hood situation. He'd seen Nazis who had tobacco, cognac, and butter, but the normal workers? They could hardly eat, and alcohol, tobacco, and butter were luxuries. Bomben-Hans was stealing from the rich to feed his friends.

---

[*] Bomben-Hans says in his Gestapo interrogation that he got to know Cilly through working in the neighborhood, while Wolfgang Schwarz says Hans Debus ("Blonden Hans") introduced them. Bomben-Hans may not have mentioned Blonden Hans to avoid getting him in trouble.

Barthel and the other Ehrenfeld Pirates also loved Bomben-Hans. They were awed by the stories he told about his time defusing bombs, and his time traveling the world as a sailor. They were young men without fathers, without authority figures they respected. They were already against the Nazis, and they were willing to do what Bomben-Hans suggested. So when he wanted weapons to do real harm to the Nazis, Barthel, Büb, and Bubbes brought over Jean and Fän and their detonator.

During one visit in the basement of Schönstein Street, Bomben-Hans had handed Fän a gun. Jean had no idea how to use it and likely neither did Fän.

On the way home, as Fän and Jean were walking through the Green Belt park, Fän fired the gun in the air. They were both shocked, maybe because they didn't realize how real the gun was.

When Fän's grandma saw the weapon, she yelled that he had to return it immediately. She said if someone found out, they'd be in real trouble.

They knew she was right, that the gun was illegal. They also knew that Bomben-Hans had a basement full of handguns, machine guns, ammunition, explosives. They knew that the group in Ehrenfeld wanted to do something with those weapons.

In the end, the boys from Sülz thought the whole thing was a little too dangerous. They only went back to Schönstein Street a few more times that September.

Jean had been on his way to the pharmacy to get medicine for Fän's grandmother when a Hitler Youth patrol caught up with him again. He was brought back to the school at Manderscheider Square, and this time there weren't any neighborhood women to come to his defense. He was registered and told to show up the following day at the train station, ready to be shipped to the Westwall to dig trenches. Jean thought it would have been easy to escape, but somehow he thought an interesting adventure might await him at the Westwall. Jean brought Fän's grandmother her medicine, and Fän agreed to go with him to the Westwall the next day.

At some point, another guy from the neighborhood also agreed to go with them, but his shoes were in bad shape. Jean and Fän knew that Bomben-Hans had clothes in the basement, so they went back to the apartment where Cilly and Bomben-Hans lived to see if they could get a pair of shoes.

When they got to the building, Jean knew immediately that something was wrong.[*] A police officer was out front, apparently standing guard. They knew that a man in uniform standing outside a building full of illegal people and weapons was bad, but before they could get away, the guard saw them. The only way to save themselves was to show that they had papers saying they were supposed to go to the Westwall. Fän showed the officer the papers, and they explained that they'd just come to say goodbye to Cilly. Apparently, that was enough, and the policeman let them go.

Jean's luck still hadn't run out.

---

[*] This whole story would have to have occured on exactly September 29, since Cilly Serve was brought to Brauweiler on October 1. Jean's papers say that he was ordered to show up at the Westbahnhof on September 9 to go to the Westwall. He could have waited or the date on his paper could be wrong. The date would make sense if he was only at the Westwall for a few days and then returned and was arrested shortly thereafter, like he says. The arrest record says Jean was detained on October 8.

Memorandum Regarding Shooting in Ehrenfeld

29TH OF SEPTEMBER 1944

On September 28, 1944 around 11:00 p.m., the local party official of the National Socialist Democratic Worker's Party Soentgen was shot by an unknown man at the corner of Venloer Street and the Ehrenfeld-Belt. The investigation was taken over by the Gestapo during the same night.

Criminal Upper Secretary Trierweiler made the following statement:

On September 28, 1944, Soentgen was biking on Venloer Street in the direction of Bickendorf. He was on his way home. The witness, the train constable Kraus, who at the time was at the intersection of the two streets, said that at the stated time, a bang was audible, and shortly thereafter, another shot followed. At the same time, he saw a bicyclist (it was Soentgen), who was riding in the direction of Bickendorf. Directly after him, a second man rode past, and at a fast speed, turned onto the Ehrenfeld-Belt. Train constable Kraus then heard someone yell loudly, "I'm injured!" The eyewitness tried to follow the second bike, but was unable to reach him. Then Kraus went back to the injured person, and only then realized that it was a party member in uniform. With the help of a car he flagged down, Soentgen was taken to the Franziskus-Hospital, where he died in the early morning hours of September 29 after an operation.

The eyewitness Kraus couldn't give a description of the suspect because it was so dark.

During the night, Kraus told the police, the district and ward leadership of the NSDAP what happened.

Signed,

Criminal Secretary Hilbert

Excerpt from Weekly Report Regarding Opposition

SEPTEMBER 24–30, 1944

G) Anonymous Inflammatory Writings

In the early morning hours of September 29, 1944, inflammatory flyers of unknown origins were found scattered on a Cologne bridge and the steps of a streetcar, with the following message:

"Workers and Soldiers

No hours for the war

Do not go to the front

Fight with us for peace

For freedom

For the people's front

Against the Nazis!

Committee of the People's Front."

The writing on the inflammatory flyer was done with rubber stamps on white blotting paper. Investigations to find the perpetrators have begun. Other or similar inflammatory flyers have not been found or distributed.

H) Opposition and Reaction

1. Oppositional Youth

The handling of operations against so-called Edelweiss Pirates have to be postponed due to the present important events. A large number of the youth are currently at the Westwall, and therefore the activities of the E.P. have markedly diminished.

IV. Planned Actions

B) Opposition from Youth

The search for so-called Edelweiss Pirates must at this time be restricted, given other efforts that are more important to the war.

Report Regarding Schönstein Street No. 7

SEPTEMBER 29, 1944

On Friday, the 29th of September, Staff Sergeant Line did an identity check in Cologne-Ehrenfeld. In doing this, a man, whose name is not known, made him aware that a deserter was being housed in Schönstein Street No. 7. Staff Sergeant Line and three members of the Army patrol went to investigate this house. As the house door was opened for him and he saw down the long hallway of the house, he saw that out of the back part of the house, a man came into sight and then quickly disappeared. With the man, who was called Hans, a second man also escaped the house. They are probably both deserters, whose names have not been determined.

These persons were staying in the apartment of Ms. Cäcilie Serve, born 4-17-1919 in Cologne Ehrenfeld, located in the back house of the apartment at no. 7.

No. 7 and houses in the area are so badly bombed that you cannot see from the street that someone lives in the back apartment. The apartment of Serve was put under observation watch by the army patrol starting at 8:00 p.m. on September 29, 1944.

During a search of no. 7, the basement, and the bombed-out houses next to it on September 30, 1944 by the army patrol, an extensive cache of weapons and other materials was found. In the apartment of Ms. Serve, a machine gun was found. . . .

Memorandum Regarding Involvement of Schink and Reinberger in Shooting

2ND OF OCTOBER 1944

Criminal Upper Secretary Mischauck—Criminal Office of Ehrenfeld—shares verbally that he has received trusted information that a Bubi (nickname) R E I N B E R G E R had been heard saying that he received 1500 Reichmarks for shooting someone. In this matter Barthel (Bartholomäus) S C H I N K is said to have been involved and perhaps a third person.

They are in the age range of 17–18 years old. Details still unknown. Should the situation arise, CUS Mischauck is ready to name the source.

Signed,

Criminal Secretary Hilbert

Statement Regarding Explosives Theft at Fort X

SECRET STATE POLICE

COLOGNE OFFICE

3RD OF OCTOBER, 1944

Captain Blohm appeared and offered the following statement:

On 10-3-44, around 5:45 a.m., the following occurred at Fort X on Neusser Wall:

A Security Service Officer shot at a civilian, who was trying to get close to the explosives storage. This civilian then ran into the shelter and woke Senior Lance Corporal Ritter. Senior Lance Corporal Ritter confirmed with the Security Service Officer that he knew this civilian, Hans Steinbrück, also known as Bomben-Hans.

The Security Officer then said that he (Steinbrück) was fine and didn't need to be apprehended. After that, Bomben-Hans disappeared.

It was subsequently determined that the truck he had parked in the Fort had been loaded with two 250 kg bombs and an unexploded Allied bomb. The truck was already equipped with a rope for towing. The truck also had a detonator that had been stolen from the Commander of the Bomb Unit's car.

The Security officer noticed the civilian, since a car was backing up into the fort. According to statements from the officer, 7 to 8 men were participating in this action. The security officer was interviewed early this morning by the appropriate section.

Signed,

Captain Blohm

Memorandum Regarding Arrests in Blücher Park

THE 4TH OF OCTOBER 1944

In the course of further investigations and interrogations, a shelter in the area of Blücher Park has become known, which was surrounded and overtaken. In the house, the following young men were found, then arrested and transferred to Brauweiler:

1) SCHINK, Barthel, born 11-25-1927
   Cologne-Ehrenfeld, Keppler St. 33
2) RHEINBERGER, Franz, born 2-22-1927
   Cologne-Ehrenfeld, Licht St. 59
3) KLUTH, Julius, born 4-14-1928
   Cologne-Bickendorf, Alpiner St. 28

A loaded and unsecured FN-self-loading pistol, 6.35mm caliber, was found on number 3, Kluth, which was in a holster around his waist that he slept with. Further, at the location a briefcase was found with papers and cash belonging to the deserter Adolf Schütz. When asked, Kluth said that around 5 a.m., Schütz left the garden house and left the briefcase in his care. Accompanying Schütz were Bomben-Hans and Hans Balzer. They left early in the morning to commit a theft. They had with them a Mercedes wagon, a Hanomag wagon, and a DKW wagon.

These statements were confirmed by number 1, Schink. When asked, Schink further explained that the night before, a Hans Müller and Günther Schwarz, and a Gustav Bermel were there. Schink further explained that except for Schaeven [a Pirate Barthel named in his confession but who may have not been present at all], everyone was in possession of guns and ready to fire.

The apartments of the named people were surrounded and searched. Arrested were:

1) Johann Müller, born 1-29-18 in Cologne
>> Living in Cologne-Ehrenfeld
>> Leyendecker St. 13

2) Mrs. Johann Müller, Katharina, née Lersch,
>> born 5-18-1894,
>> Same apartment

3) Gustav Bermel, born 8-11-1927 in Cologne
>> Living in Cologne-Ehrenfeld
>> Melatengürtel 86

Bermel was arrested at the printer Roth & Son.

In the apartment of Müller, a spyglass (binoculars) were found, taken, and secured. Nothing else was found.

The arrest of further individuals must take place.

The above listed were detained and brought to Brauweiler.

Signed,

Criminal Secretary [Josef] Hoegen

Memorandum Regarding Weapons Cache at Lidosee

10TH OF OCTOBER, 1944

From the accused Schink, it has been ascertained that the
island is in Lidosee, in the Stadtwald. Schink was taken to
the island today using a boat, where the cache of weapons was
supposed to be. In the last few days, the place has been hit by
an air raid, so that the weapons cache can no longer be found.
Further searching and digging on the island did not lead to
any discoveries. Schink, was further questioned at the place,
and explained that the weapons cache was created by a group of
young men, that included Edelweiss Pirates, who were from Sülz.
The leader of this group was a Fän, who lives Daunerstr. 20.

It is clear that this means worker Ferdinand Steingass,
who lives with his grandmother Mrs. Schmitz. Further
information from Schink showed that Fän was in direct contact
with Bomben-Hans . . .

Signed,

Hoegen

The military duty Jean and Fän reported to was poorly organized and haphazard. They were in a group of two hundred guys staying in a big dance hall about an hour east of Cologne near the French border. The hall didn't have beds, just straw spread out on the floor. They were supposed to have brought their own bedding but no one had told them that. They were supposed to get new shoes but had only received wooden shoes, so the kids had thrown them into a pile as a protest.

The Hitler Youth leaders were in charge, but this wasn't like Hitler Youth training, where everything was organized and people knew where they were supposed to be and what they were supposed to be doing. Much like Jean and Fän, most of the young guys here didn't seem to have an interest in actually fighting. A rumor was going around the hall that Allied troops had been pushed back, and had left corned beef and other food behind when they retreated. Jean and Fän decided to walk to the front line to see what was going on; they thought no one at the makeshift barrack would miss them. When they arrived, though, the food wasn't there, and the front was more dangerous than they realized.

They went back to camp and pretended to be sick when they were supposed to work, so they ended up hanging around the first aid station. Not long after they arrived, they decided that they were bored and wanted to go back to Cologne. And so they simply left in the middle of the night, slept in a barn, and the next day, got a ride back to Cologne.[*]

❁ ❁ ❁

---

[*] Fän remembered that they hailed down two soldiers in a Chevy, while Jean remembered that they told a Hitler Youth who was directing traffic that they were on leave and he flagged down a car for them.

Something had happened at home while they were gone.* A few days after they got back, Jean went to Fän's apartment to make plans for the weekend. But when Jean rang the doorbell, the door flew open. A man he didn't know towered over him. He pulled Jean into the apartment and asked where Ferdi Steingass was. Jean paused, thinking about what he should say. The man suddenly hit Jean in the face so hard that he flew backward into the cupboard, smashing the glass window. Fän's aunt and grandma were in the kitchen and started crying and screaming.

The man—Gestapo Commissar Josef Schiffer—forced Jean to sit on the sofa, to wait for Fän to come back.

Jean was bleeding from the wound on the back of his head. He asked if he could have a glass of water. This was allowed. Schiffer also sat on the sofa and started nodding off now and again. The thought crossed Jean's mind that he could throw the water in Schiffer's face and run out of the apartment. But he couldn't bring himself to do it. So they—the Gestapo officer and the fifteen-year-old Edelweiss Pirate—just sat on the couch together for an hour.

Later in the afternoon two more men came. One was short, with greasy hair that stuck to his head and a foul expression. The other seemed to be in charge. They marched Jean out of the apartment, guns pressed against his back. Jean's father had put up a fight when he was dragged out of the apartment, but so much had changed in the last eight years. Jean had done illegal things, and the Gestapo

---

* The story of what had happened while they were gone and what happened next is tainted by memory, brutality, and trauma. Jean and Fän tell slightly different stories. What happened while they were gone is based on the records the Gestapo kept, which are biased by the brutality they used to gather information and their ideas of what the real story was. Jean says this occured on Tuesday, October 10, in his memoir, but the International Tracing Service records say that Jean was taken in on Sunday, October 8, and Ferdinand Steingass was arrested on October 10. The Gestapo records say Ferdinand was arrested first, and then Jean. The Gestapo memorandum from October 10 reads: "It was clear that this meant worker Ferdinand Steingass, who lives with his grandmother Mrs. Schmitz. Further information from Schink showed that Fän was in direct contact with Bomben-Hans, and Fän was arrested in the apartment of Mrs. Schmitz. Around 6:00 p.m. he was arrested and brought in. Later, a friend of Steingass, the locksmith apprentice Jean Jülich, who has been staying in the apartment, showed up. Under suspicion, he was also arrested and brought to Brauweiler."

was so angry and frustrated, they would have been willing to shoot him on the way out of the apartment if he'd taken a wrong step. They would have told his family he was killed while trying to escape. The officers dragged Jean out to Manderscheider Square, which was right at the end of Fän's street, placed him in a car, and took him to the EL-DE House.

Unlike Fritz and Gertrud, Jean wasn't immediately brought to the basement. The Gestapo had a different interrogation technique in mind for Jean. First, they brought him to a room and told him to stand against the wall next to a metal bed. In the room were two female stenographers. SS officers came in and out of the room, their boots clacking on the ground. Then, all of a sudden, an SS man walked in and grabbed one of the women and started kissing her on the bed. Jean thought they looked like they were going to have sex. He couldn't watch; he was so embarrassed. He looked down at the ground. When he looked up again, the woman was almost undressed and the officer was groping her. Jean thought they had forgotten he was there. Finally, the man ordered Jean to turn around and face the wall.

Much like Gertrud, Jean's knowledge of sex was incomplete at best. Jean's family was Catholic and no matter what the Nazis thought about the Edelweiss Pirates' morality and sexuality, he had never seen anything like what was happening in front of him. He hadn't even shared a tent with a girl when he was out camping.

Another SS man came into the room and took Jean to the door at the top of the basement stairs. When a Gestapo guard appeared, the SS man closed the door and darkness enveloped Jean.

"So, you're innocent, huh," the Gestapo man asked Jean.

Jean's eyes adjusted to the dark as they walked down the stairs.

"I don't know what I am supposed to have done," Jean replied.

With that, the Gestapo man kicked Jean, and his falling body slammed into the metal-edged stairs.

When he stopped tumbling, all he could do was lie on the cold

Stairs to the basement cells at the EL-DE House, 2017.

cement floor of the basement. He thought he'd broken something. His head hurt and his body hurt, but he was afraid of what was coming next. He didn't know the exact reason he had been arrested, and he didn't know what the Gestapo knew.

Jean had managed to prop himself up on the wall in the hallway of the basement. His eyes had adjusted to the dark, and a few feet away, he could see another prisoner with darker splotches on his face. The splotches were blood, and the man was standing over a sink, trying to clean his wounds. The man looked over at Jean, then down at the ground, and then at him again, trying to let a smile of courage blossom on his face. He was clearly in so much pain that the attempt at a smile ended with a grimace of suffering.

After his arrest in September 1944, Fritz Theilen was loaded on a train and taken south, and was finally unloaded from the train in the village of Ellern. There, in the middle of nowhere, the Nazis had built a work camp for boys ages thirteen to seventeen who had been deemed "difficult to teach," who were against the Nazi ideology, or who had deserted their posts on the Westwall. Other arrivals had been met with the greeting, "Everyone off, here you are in the land of Edelweiss Pirates!" and they didn't mean that in a good way. The Gestapo officer said to Fritz that this was his last chance to work hard and behave, and he might be able to just go home after three months of "reeducation." Reeducation was bullshit; this place was a forced labor camp and children were the forced laborers.

When Fritz got off the train, he walked five minutes from the train station to the barracks. The camp wasn't even really a camp,

Barracks at Ellern, 1946.

just some cabins between the road and the woods. And Ellern was more like a collection of houses than a town, but there was a furniture factory, and that's where Fritz was supposed to work.

Fritz had thought the days working at the Ford-Werke with the forced laborers had been hard. Ellern was harder. He woke up at 5:00 a.m. and was allowed to wash only his face. The prisoners could only take a shower or bath when absolutely necessary, so everyone had lice and each barrack had a pot of cream that was supposed to prevent scabies. They'd spend an hour working on the buildings in the camp, go to their assigned jobs at 6:30 a.m., and then work for ten hours, minus a thirty-minute break in the middle of the day. At 5:00 p.m. they were back in the camp to work on the barracks or watch a propaganda film about how great the Third Reich was. The food was meager: bread and soup, and margarine if they were lucky.

One night, Fritz was lying in bed, part of a three-tiered metal bunk that had been taken from an air-raid shelter. When the camp started getting really crowded, two prisoners would have to sleep on each tier, cramming almost a hundred guys together in the space of trailer. The barracks weren't as uncomfortable as Brauweiler, but the stench of bodies pressed in together and the smell of unwashed sweat on unwashed prison uniforms was always present. Blankets would rustle and the beds would creak as everyone tried to get comfortable and forget about their hunger and the nagging itch of lice bites. Fritz was exhausted every day, which helped him get some sleep.

When everyone had finally passed out, the door to the barracks slammed open. A gust of autumn air and the smell of the woods rushed in, along with the Holy Ghost. He wasn't the biblical Holy Ghost, just a former Hitler Youth who was also at the camp for having done something wrong. But because he was a former HY leader, he got to be the supervisor at the chair factory.

The Holy Ghost turned on the light, making sure to wake everyone up. The floor echoed beneath his stomping feet as he walked over to his victim. They'd seen him do this before. He'd sneak out chair legs from the factory, and in the middle of the night, he'd barge into one of the barracks.

He moved fast, and soon he was standing next to the victim's bed. Fritz didn't even need to be able to see it to know what was going on. The sound of wood, smacking against a body without any fat, the rattling of the bunk bed as the victim tried to wriggle away, the gasps of breath and grunts coming from the victim, who probably knew better than to scream and be punished for waking the guards up. And then the Holy Ghost disappeared.

The next morning at roll call, the victim would be standing in a line with all the other guys. By September, there were about one hundred prisoners, and later in the fall Fritz estimated that there were two hundred. Rows upon rows of gray prison uniforms, guys with their heads shaved, being inspected by the camp leader. The Holy Ghost's victim had bruises, a black eye, or an open wound. The camp leader had no sympathy.

"What happened to you? Why do you look like that?" he would yell.

"Last night I was beaten."

"What? Are you trying to say that you were hit? The German state is providing money so that you can come here and be rehabilitated, and you're still complaining? Here, order rules, my darling. Come see me after work."

"Yessir!"

The guards clearly weren't interested in punishing the former Hitler Youth leader, even if he was at the camp as a prisoner. Fritz and the others decided if they wanted something done about this guy, they'd have to do it themselves. The former Edelweiss Pirates at the camp stuck together and stuck up for one another, even if it put them in more danger.

The next night, they watched the door, and when it swung open, all the guys ambushed the Holy Ghost and started beating on him instead. They must have known they'd get caught, but they had to stop this jerk, no matter the cost.

The next day, Fritz's barrack had to do two hours of punishment exercises at the end of the workday. Punishment exercises were meant to be physically grueling. They might be forced to crawl over harvested grain fields without shirts on so that the cut ends of the dry stalks scraped against their bodies. Or they'd have to march with a pack filled with bricks. One woman from the town remembered seeing the boys with gray prison uniforms, wooden shoes, and shaved heads running for hours through a field. The most ludicrous punishment was the Sisyphean task of sweeping the forest dirt roads clean.

48 — Jean

The door closed behind Jean with metal crashing that made his skin crawl. Jean didn't know how long he had been kept in the EL-DE House basement, but when he was brought back upstairs, they made him get in a car and took him to Brauweiler in the middle of the night. His cell was on the first floor in the same building where the Gestapo took all the Pirates, including Fritz and Gertrud. He climbed onto a table and looked outside. He could see the prison yard and that he was close to the entrance. Inside the cell, the bed was folded up against the wall. He undid the latches and the edge of the metal bed fell and struck his shins. He didn't need more pain at this moment. He sat down and took an inventory of his new home.

He saw a bucket with a tin lid near the door. He made the mistake of opening it up and found a stinking mass inside. He wiped his hands, lay down on the bed, and fell asleep.

The first night at Brauweiler didn't reveal to Jean why he was there. The following day seemed to stretch forever. Jean just waited and waited for something to happen. He had nothing to read, nothing to do. As the day went on, he started learning the rhythm of the prison.

First, two orderlies would stand outside of his door and yell, "Bucket! Bucket!" and he'd hand over his shit bucket. He'd also get a cup of water for washing, a hand towel, and a breakfast of coffee substitute and a slice of dark bread.

He could watch people coming and going from his window, and after breakfast, he heard more doors opening and closing, voices talking. Like Fritz, Jean realized he could hear almost anything in the cell block. He heard crying, screaming, and normal voices between. Then the building was quiet. Then a door would close, a door would open, and the crying and screaming would start again.

For lunch and dinner, he ate watery soup.

That night, something finally happened. He looked out the window and heard faint voices. He realized his friends were talking to one another through the windows. He heard Barthel and Bubbes, and called out to them.

Jean asked them how long they'd been there, and they said they'd already been questioned a few times. And then they told Jean the bizarre chain of events that had brought them all to Brauweiler.

Barthel and Bubbes probably told Jean what they could about the events of the last ten days, starting right around the time when Jean left for the Westwall. The whole thing centered on Bomben-Hans and the people who had been hanging out in the basement at

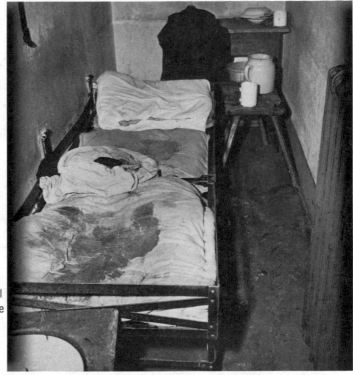

Gestapo prison cell at Brauweiler where a female inmate died after the Gestapo beat her, March 6, 1945.

Schonstein Street No. 7, where Jean and Fän had visited earlier in the fall. A guy that Jean didn't know—Roland Lorent, an unstable deserter whose family had been killed in a bombing—shot a Nazi, and that's when the Gestapo started to get serious about the thefts and illegal people living in Ehrenfeld.

Men in uniforms showed up outside Cilly Serve's apartment, and on the afternoon of October 1, Bomben-Hans wanted everyone to meet up to try to get her out of there. Jean knew some of the people involved, like Barthel, Bubbes, and Büb, but there were other Pirates and older guys he didn't know too.

Bomben-Hans was determined to get guns and ammunition for some kind of raid to rescue Cilly. These kind of crazy ideas were the reason that Jean and Fän had stopped hanging out with Bomben-Hans's crew, although when Barthel was interrogated by the Gestapo, he blamed most of the failed plan on the deserter they didn't really know. The stories the Gestapo got about the actual rescue operation were all different: who was in what car and who had what gun and who had shot whom kept changing. The Pirates might not have known the truth, or they might have been trying to hide the truth.

The basic facts seem likely to be as follows: Barthel, Bubbes, Büb, Bomben-Hans, and the others drove to Cilly's house in two cars, and it wasn't long before everyone was shooting in every direction. They couldn't free Cilly because there were too many guards. They managed to escape back to a garden hut in Blücherpark. The quiet meeting spot of the Pirates was now the target of a Gestapo manhunt. At some point, the deserter who started it all and another guy disappeared, and instead of lying low, Bomben-Hans came up with the even crazier idea. He wanted to blow up the EL-DE House and the railroads. He said it would end the war.

From his time in bomb squad, he knew that they could get explosives and detonators from a Prussian fort in the Green Belt. Bomben-Hans managed to get into the fort and get the explosives into a car before someone raised the alarm. That alarm caused Barthel, Bubbes, and Büb to run back to Blücherpark. When Bomben-Hans got there, he was pissed that they'd run away. Bomben-Hans and Büb left the next morning, but the Gestapo found Barthel and Bubbes in the garden hut on October 4 and brought them to Brauweiler. Barthel was interrogated soon after he'd arrived.

Barthel also explained why Fän and Jean had been arrested. He had lied about their involvement. Barthel told Jean that the Gestapo wanted to know where the Edelweiss Pirates had been hiding weapons. He either didn't say anything or said that they didn't have a secret stash of weapons, which was true. The interrogators must not have accepted that answer. Other sources had admitted to the Gestapo that Barthel had been involved in illegal activities so now they wanted more from him, and they were willing to do anything to get Barthel to tell the whole truth, or at least the truth they wanted to hear.*

Barthel told Jean that the interrogators had beaten him badly during the interrogation. One of the men who was known for his brutality was Gestapo Officer Joseph Hoegen, a short man with greasy dark hair who seemed to take sadistic pleasure in trying to get answers out of the young people taken to Brauweiler. His interrogation techniques included laying Barthel with his belly on the seat of a chair, placing a cord around his neck and a gag in his mouth so he couldn't scream, and then beating him with chair legs or rubber clubs until he couldn't feel or think or say anything.

Even if a prisoner couldn't answer any more questions, it didn't stop the Gestapo from continuing the interrogation. When one prisoner fainted, they threw water on her to keep her awake so they could beat her more. One young forced laborer who falsely confessed to knowing Bomben-Hans committed suicide in her cell rather than face interrogation again. Another prisoner died from an infection in the sores that developed where handcuffs had cut into his wrists. They left the handcuffs on for days, telling the prisoners to eat like dogs. They left them on so long the cuffs started digging into the prisoner's wrists. Then they ripped them off, leaving behind open wounds. Hoegen smacked another prisoner across the face with keys.

Barthel admitted to Jean that the interrogation broke him. He'd told the Gestapo that there was a camp with munitions and weapons in Lidosee. They had, in fact, camped out on the island, but there weren't any weapons. That was a lie. Barthel probably thought that he could say this to stop the beating, and that the lack of physical evidence would supersede his confession. The Gestapo would go out to the island and see that no bunker full

---

* The War Crimes Unit report of the conditions at Brauweiler under Commissar Kütter gives brutal details of how the Gestapo questioned and obtained confessions and statements from prisoners.

of weapons existed, and then Barthel would be able to retract his statement. A lie would save him now; reality would save him later.

But that's not how confessions work. The Gestapo really thought they would find weapons, so they took Barthel out to the island and demanded that he point out the bunker. They dug around and didn't find any weapons. But they believed weapons had been stored there; the island had been hit during a bomb strike and the Gestapo said the area was too destroyed to tell if any weapons had ever been there. They beat Barthel for more answers, but he couldn't figure out enough lies to make them stop.

"I can't describe what happened to me afterward. After what they did, I was brought back unconscious to my cell," Barthel told Jean.

Barthel hadn't meant to turn Fän and Jean in. He probably felt he had to tell the interrogators what he thought they wanted to hear, what the interrogators were prompting him to say. Even a false confession can be rich with details, descriptions, and motivations, which can make them seem true, even if they are not.[*] Officer Hoegen and the others wanted to know the names of the other Pirates in the Ehrenfeld Group—others that might know more about the weapons—and they beat Barthel again to get the answers.

Barthel was forced to give details about the camp, saying that he went out on the island twice. In reality, Fän and Jean had only talked about building a cabin on the island. They didn't know how to get weapons, and when they had gotten a gun from Bomben-Hans, they'd given it back immediately. Barthel said there was a hole with weapons, covered in branches and dirt, and he gave

---

[*] For more on false and forced confessions and innocence, see Saul M. Kassin, "Why Confessions Trump Innocence," *American Psychologist* 67, no. 6 (2012): 431–45; Richard A. Leo, Steven A. Drizin, Peter J. Neufeld, Bradley R. Hall, and Amy Vatne, "Bringing Reliability Back in: False Confessions and Legal Safeguards in the Twenty-First Century," *Wisconsin Law Review* (2006): 102–58; and Sara C. Appleby, Lisa E. Hasel, and Saul M. Kassin, "Police-induced Confessions: An Empirical Analysis of their Content and Impact," *Psychology, Crime & Law* 19, no. 2 (February 2013): 111–28.

descriptions of what types of weapons were down there. Then, he said Fän was the leader.

"All of my bones hurt and that's why I named you and Fän," Barthel told Jean. "I knew what would happen to you, but I was at the end. I hope that you realize that I didn't have another choice.

"Please forgive me," he added quietly.

Jean had noticed how much more serious Barthel became when he recounted everything. He was no longer the smiling, fun-loving guy who wanted to get along with everyone and make people laugh. He was changed.

Gestapo Report on the Cologne-Ehrenfeld Terror Group

OCTOBER 5, 1944

In the course of further investigations, 46 more people were arrested who had a close connection with the terrorist group. They were involved in the burglaries, weapons smuggling, and sale of stolen goods. In total 156 arrests have been made.

According to the previous investigation, in addition to the murders, they have committed about 50 burglaries during the night, and were in possession of weapons ready to fire.

49 — Jean

Jean could see through the windows of his cell the day that Fän was brought into the prison.

A few days later, Bomben-Hans was brought in too. He was limping. He'd been shot while escaping arrest, only to be found later.

Hans Balzer, the Pirate from Ehrenfeld they knew as Lang, was never brought in. He was shot in the head trying to escape arrest.

The open corridor of the Gestapo prison at Brauweiler, March 1945.

Another day, two men came to Jean's cell door.

"I'm cutting your hair," the man with the razor said. "How do you want it? Where should the part go?"

"Decently short, military style," Jean answered. All of the prisoners had their hair cut short.

Two minutes later, Jean looked down as the men left the cell. Around his feet was all his hair. He peered into the little piece of glass on the cabinet by the window. He almost didn't recognize the person reflected back at him. His cheeks were sunken in, and his hair—his long, beautiful hair—was gone.

He grabbed a brush and dustpan, and swept the brown clippings to the side.

Jean spoke through the windows to his friends. They told funny stories and jokes. He made up a poem. He could even talk to Fän, even though he was on another side of the building, one floor up. The fact that they could hear the screams from the interrogation room on the first floor also meant they could sort of talk, or at least communicate, with one another.

They had whistles they'd used as Edelweiss Pirates to communicate with one another when they didn't want to talk. One night, Jean heard a whistle and then the yell, "G1, seven men!" The Gestapo had left the building for the night, and they were counting on the idea that the guards wouldn't care about random yelling.

Jean decoded the message: "Our group, we are seven guys."

Then Fän yelled the code names of another five members of their group. Those five were all at the Westwall, so even if Fän said the names out loud or in an interrogation, the Gestapo wouldn't be able to get to them. The Gestapo always demanded that the Edelweiss Pirates give the names of others, so that they could make sure to arrest everyone in a group. Going back to the beginning of the war, bündische youth groups would give the names of friends who were already in the military, since they knew the Gestapo couldn't arrest them, and they'd try to avoid giving names that could harm other friends.

Fän also communicated that he had been interrogated.

Excerpts from the Statement of Ferdinand Steingass

OCTOBER 30, 1944

On further questioning, I deny decidedly to have created a
cache of weapons on the island in Lidosee in the City Forest,
or that I brought any weapons there. When Schink [Barthel]
makes this statement, he is lying. In connection with this, I
must admit that a few days ago, as I was standing together with
him in the hallway of the prison, he explained and suggested
that it would be best if I admit to the existence of the camp on
the island during questioning and interrogation, otherwise
I would be beaten. I quickly responded to Schink that I would
not admit to this crime, since it would not be the truth.

OCTOBER 31, 1944

When presented and questioned again, in regards to the
statements made by Barthel Schink, and asked to tell the truth:

In my first statement, I did not tell the whole truth and
therefore I would like to correct my statements accordingly.

I also admit that during a visit to Stamm Street [the
apartment of Else Salm], Schink and Rheinberger [Bubbes]
heard a discussion about the creation of a cache of weapons on
the island in Lido-See. I made the plan and the drawings for the
camp, but the idea came from Else Salm, as well as from Schink
and Rheinberger. As they said, it would become too dangerous at
Schönstein Street. My suggestion was only to build a camp. The
idea to bring weapons there came from Salm, who said she would
get guns and made the suggestion that we keep in contact with
the Schönstein Street [group]. When Schink said that this idea
came from me, he must be thinking of this discussion.

50 — Jean

A few days after Fän had told Jean he'd been interrogated, Jean's cell door opened.

Jean walked down the hall to another cell. Inside was a table with a typewriter, two chairs, and the man who'd arrested him, Officer Schiffer. Jean felt lucky that Schiffer seemed tired and like he just wanted to get this questioning over with.

Jean sat down on the other side of the table from Schiffer and answered the first questions: name; parents' names; schooling; membership in the Hitler Youth. He knew to lie about details of his past to protect his family. He knew saying his father was a Communist would have meant harsher treatment or deportation to a concentration camp.

He knew to deny as much as possible about his involvement with the Edelweiss Pirates. He claimed that about six months ago he created an organization with Fän and they called the members "boy scouts;" he insisted they had nothing to do with the Edelweiss Pirates. He gave the names that Fän had told him to. He claimed he knew nothing about Bomben-Hans creating an armed terrorist group that was committing robberies and murders, and he knew nothing about the crimes and previous actions of people there.

Then Jean admitted that he had been at Else Salm's apartment when Fän, Barthel, and Bubbes discussed the creation of the cabin and weapons storage on the island in the reservoir. Was this the truth or a lie? Had Barthel and Fän told him that he should just admit to it happening or he would be beaten? Fän was protective of Jean. He'd told the Gestapo to leave him alone, that he didn't know anything. To the Gestapo, Jean only mentioned the creation of the camp in passing, like it was a silly idea someone had one time, not the serious plot that was cooked up in Else's apartment.

On the other hand, Jean might not have said anything at all about it. If Officer Schiffer was tired and simply wanted to be done with the interrogation, he could have written whatever he wanted on the Gestapo interrogation report and forced Jean to sign the paper. Jean's only other choice would have been another beating.

51 — Fritz

The plan for escape from Ellern started formulating in Fritz's mind when he was doing telephone duty for the camp leader. He had collapsed one day at work from a combination of exhaustion and a lung infection, and he was now the personal assistant of the camp leader. This meant cleaning the leader's room, answering the phone, and running errands in the nearby town of Simmern. He'd take the train to Simmern, and had a travel certificate and train tickets, but he hadn't thought about using those to escape. He was in the middle of nowhere, no one in the town would trust him since they'd been told all of the boys in the camp were serious criminals, and he was wearing a very conspicuous prisoner's uniform. But that day on telephone duty, something changed. He traced the camp leader's signature. He had the best chance he'd ever have to escape—he just needed help from his friend Hugo.

November 5, that would be the day. First, they'd thought about leaving around the Christmas holidays since more people would be traveling, but Fritz had heard that an electric fence was going to be installed at the camp in December. The camp was open; the guards figured no one would run into the woods and no one in town would help an escapee. Fritz also heard that some other prisoners were planning an escape, and he knew everyone remaining would be more closely watched as soon as someone tried leaving. Fritz had stared at the train timetable when he was in Simmern, memorizing when they would be able to sneak on a train.

On November 4, he was alone in the camp leader's office. He was supposed to be answering the phone and taking messages. He had been doing this for a while, so he knew how the day went, but he was nervous. This was chance number one to get caught.

He sat down at the camp leader's typewriter and slowly typed out the travel certificates he and Hugo would need. No one could travel without the proper documents. He took some blank forms and pressed official stamps onto the papers. Then, he lifted the heavy black typewriter and hid the papers underneath. His heart was racing, but he tried to act calm.

By the time the camp leader came back, Fritz was sitting back at his telephone.

When the camp leader finally left for the day, Fritz felt the weight that had been pressing down on his chest evaporate, at least temporarily.

He cleaned up, like he was supposed to, and then cracked the window just a little bit so he could open it from the outside and retrieve the travel documents. He grabbed the key to the clothes closet, locked up the office, and brought the office key to the camp leader, who said, "Good. Everything's in order. You can go."

The pressure in Fritz's chest had shifted to a nervous excitement. He was sure it was going to work. He and Hugo got in bed, and waited for midnight.

Then, they climbed out of bed and snuck out into the dark night.

Fritz and his friend Hugo left the camp in Ellern in the middle of the night. The wind howled and the rain poured down as they walked through the woods from Ellern to Simmern, which although only about six miles away took them three hours. Fritz had on a stolen military uniform and Hugo had on civilian clothes, both outfits stolen from the clothes closet at the camp. Their cover story was that they were going to Cologne to get more young men for the camp. They hoped no one would see their shaved heads.

Just like the escape itself, luck played a big role in getting Fritz back to the city. A man in uniform questioned why Fritz and Hugo hadn't received rations for their trip. This was the second big chance to get caught. But when the officer wanted to call the camp to verify their story, the camp's phone connection wasn't working and the officer trusted them. Fritz and Hugo ended up getting three days' rations for the way home. No one questioned their passes, even though at seventy-five pounds, Fritz must have been swimming in the stolen uniform and looked more like a prisoner than an officer.

They arrived in Cologne in the middle of the day on November 7. Fritz couldn't imagine the city looking worse than it had when he was taken to Ellern. But as he walked back to Ehrenfeld, there hardly seemed to be a building left standing, none of the streetcars were running, and the city had lost gas, water, and electricity in some parts. But he was here; he was free.

Fritz and Hugo decided to meet back up at the Körner Street bunker once they'd gotten clothes from their apartments.

Fritz asked a couple of guys he knew in the bunker about how things had gone since he'd been away. At home, neighbors had told him that the Gestapo kept coming around looking for him. He wasn't sure if that was because he'd escaped the camp, or if there was something else going on.

"The Nazis are everywhere, and the raids and arrests just keep happening," one of the guys told Fritz and Hugo.

"Two weeks ago, they publicly hanged Russians and foreign workers on Hütten Street. There was something going on here in

Ehrenfeld, police and Gestapo everywhere, the whole area blocked off, but yeah, I guess you guys know that."

They didn't know that. They had no idea what had happened since they left, other than that some guys who'd shown up at the camp in Ellern had said things were getting worse.

"And where are the others?" Fritz asked. After his arrest and night in the EL-DE House, he had no idea what had happened to the rest of the Ehrenfeld Edelweiss Pirates.

"We don't really know. Bubbes, Barthel, and Büb were all arrested about three weeks ago. They're in Brauweiler, and it doesn't look so good for them, I'm guessing it won't be easy for them to get out."

Fritz never said whether he was told what specifically had happened with his friends while he was at the camp, but he knew that they had all had guns, that at least Barthel had fired a gun at Nazis, and that they were deep into illegal activities. Fritz never met Bomben-Hans and had no idea how much deeper into illegal activities his friends were. Fritz knew that what he'd done was enough to get him sent to Brauweiler again and that the Gestapo was looking for him.

"Shit, we have to move on, otherwise we'll end up in there too," Fritz said to Hugo.

52 — Jean

They had to stand with their noses pressed against the cold cement wall. Someone hit their heads from behind so their noses smashed into the wall. The Gestapo men seemed to take pleasure from making the prisoners hurt.

Fän and Jean saw each other against the wall, waiting to go into the interrogation room. Jean could tell by the look in Fän's eyes that they were thinking the same thing: *Man, you look shitty.*

Fän had been the animated one, always imitating how people talked and gesticulating. Jean was the musician, the one who loved to sing. They had been adventurous together. With ready smiles and hair that flopped down over their faces, they'd probably imagined themselves handsome young men. Now, they looked like hollow outlines of who they used to be. Vibrant beings had been replaced with gray skin, sunken eyes, cheekbones piercing their faces, shaved heads.

Fän was taken into the interrogation room first. Jean heard the whacks against his friend's flesh.

Leave him alone, you pigs! Jean wanted to yell. But he couldn't. His turn would come too.

Fän came out, and the next guy went in. Next to Jean stood Black Peter, who had been helping Bomben-Hans with break-ins for months. He claimed in his interrogation that he ended his connections when everything got more political. That probably wasn't true. He'd already escaped being a forced laborer once and had been arrested for possession of weapons and theft in the early 1930s.

"Everyone who is here, everyone, everyone, is going to be killed," Black Peter told Jean.

One night after that, around ten o'clock, when the Gestapo had left, Black Peter started making noise in his cell. Banging, yelling, stomping, going crazy. One of the guards went over to see what was happening. As the guard opened the door, Peter hit him and made a run for the door. That was as far as he got. He was handcuffed and brought back to his cell.

Jean thought Black Peter's escape attempt had been crazy and desperate. The entrance had a gate, an iron door, and a wooden door, and then there was a wall that surrounded the whole prison building. Jean thought Black Peter never had a chance to make it out, and he was probably brutally beaten afterward. Jean didn't know that someone else had managed to escape. Else Salm slipped out the window, went over the bars, climbed the wall, and got out, all before she could deny any accusations of creating a weapons cache on Lidosee.

Everyone suffered the consequences of Black Peter's escape attempt and Else Salm's escape. At night, they had to strip and give the guards their clothes, as a way either to make sure they wouldn't run out into the cold night or just to make them as uncomfortable as possible. Jean lay naked in his bed with a thin blanket, teeth chattering, praying for morning to come so he could have clothes again.

A few days after Peter's escape attempt, all the prisoners had to go out into the yard, "to be made softer," as one of the Gestapo men told Jean. They lined up in rows, skinny bodies in oversized uniforms, malnourished from a diet of bread, fake coffee, and watery soup, broken and worn from beating after beating. Now they were forced to do physical exercises for which they had no energy.

Run, jump, lie down; up, down, up, down, jump up, march, march, march, run, jump, down, up, down, up, jump, march, march.

Some of the older men collapsed.

Jean cut his hand on a rock in the path. Pain shot up his arm as he pressed his body down to the ground, and a red spot remained when he got up again. The next time he went down, he dropped down onto the lawn instead of the gravel path. That didn't escape Officer Kütter's notice.

"The lawn is too good for you," Kütter said as he pushed Jean's small body back onto the path with his leather boot. "Besides, soon you'll be under the grass anyway," he added.

Jean got back up.

Run, jump, lie down; up, down, up, down, jump up, march, march, march, run, jump, down, up, down, up, jump, march, march.

He had no sense of time; he didn't know how long they were tortured like that. Finally, they were led back to their cells.

Inside Jean's cell, the words came back to him.

Soon you'll be under the grass anyway.

And then there were the words that Peter said: *Everyone, everyone, is going to be killed.*

Something grabbed the air from his lungs, his eyes sucked backward into his head, his body filled with fear. If he was going to die here, then why be tortured another day?

He looked to the ceiling. The lightbulb hung from a cloth cable. He could climb up there, tie a knot, and hang himself. Then it would all be over.

He gasped for breath, sucking his stomach in. He was crying. Was there really no hope? He was sobbing. The black rope beckoned.

Jean's eyes flickered open. He'd passed out from exhaustion and awoken in his cell. The black rope was still hanging above him.

"No," he told himself. Maybe he could survive.

53 — Fritz

Fritz's life seemed to be a roller coaster with hills of luck and freedom, and dales of capture and imprisonment. He left Cologne after the news in the bunker that all of his friends had been arrested. He knew he wasn't safe staying with anyone in the area. He went south on the trains to try to find his mom and brother, who were in a town near the border of Switzerland. His fake papers had worked until he was south of Koblenz on the Rhine River. Then his luck ran out. He didn't have the right travel papers and his shaved head gave him away. From there, he was transported hundreds of kilometers east to a sub-camp of Dachau. They traveled the whole night; this was the farthest he'd ever been from home. He knew about concentration camps, but he'd never heard of Dachau before.

Then he was brought to another camp, probably farther to the east. All the prisoners were Austrian, Czech, or Yugoslavian. Something about the place made him question reality, like this was a bad dream and he couldn't quite figure out what was going on.

He'd lied about what his name was and where he'd escaped from, so it really was like a dream, where you know you are yourself but something is just a little bit different, so you're not yourself at all. Fritz did remember that the work was hard and that the food was terrible.

He hadn't been there a month when some Austrian prisoners persuaded him to escape with them. They hopped on a train, got shot at, and jumped off the train as it was pulling into the woods. The Austrians left Fritz, and he decided to go back to Bonn, to his aunt. He left Cologne because it was too dangerous, but was inextricably pulled back. He got food and a Hitler Youth uniform from a farmer and hitched a ride back to Bonn. Almost as soon as he got there, he realized he couldn't stay, and with money his aunt gave him, he went back south, and finally made it to the house where his mother and brother were staying.

They were thrilled to see him again. They hadn't expected to see him before the war was over, and maybe privately his mother feared she'd never see him again. Fritz finally felt safe. He was home now, even if home was hundreds of miles away from Ehrenfeld. He slept in a bed, in a house, for the first time in months.

There was a loud knocking at the door. He had slept a whole night, but he wasn't really safe anywhere. His mother had let the camp in Ellern know that she had moved. Fritz could be found wherever he went. There was a policeman at the door, looking for Fritz.

"You are under arrest," he said. "I have an arrest warrant, don't make any trouble, or I'll have to use this weapon." He must have been convinced that Fritz had a weapon.

"He definitely doesn't have a weapon, you don't have to wave that thing around," Fritz's mother said, and the policeman put his gun away.

"How old are you?" the policeman then asked.

"My son is seventeen years old. Can't he at least eat breakfast with us?"

Fritz was allowed to eat breakfast, and then the policeman brought him to the station. Fritz wasn't sure what to say. He had told a lot of lies; he'd denied doing things he knew could get him in trouble. He had not seen the worst of the Nazis, but had experienced beatings, starvation, and slave labor. Maybe he finally wanted to tell the truth because the lies were becoming too much, or maybe he was tired of being on the run and the stress that caused him.

Whatever his reasons, he told them the truth: about being an Edelweiss Pirate, about being against the Nazis, about how he hadn't ever been found guilty of anything criminal. At the end, he didn't think that the officers believed him. They didn't seem upset or angry like the Cologne Gestapo he'd clashed with so many times before. They seemed calm.

Then they left the room and started talking to each other. Fritz couldn't hear what they were saying, but the discussion was intense.

The feeling swelled over him like a tidal wave. He'd made a mistake. Why had he told the truth? Never admit to anything. That had kept him alive for years. The danger was present and he thought about escape. He could escape again; he'd done it so many times now. Prison was more tiring than lies. He couldn't go back. This time, he might actually die from being overworked.

They came back in the room.

The policeman who'd arrested Fritz started talking. His tone was gentle, and Fritz already couldn't believe what he was hearing. Usually at this stage, there would be more yelling, more anger. Instead, his words were something Fritz had never heard before.

"You are still so young and you've suffered enough for your membership in the Edelweiss Pirates, as you told us. We want to believe you. We're not going to turn you in to the Gestapo, since the war won't last much longer. You can go home. Thank the local party leader, since we should be sending you back to Ellern."

The last year and everything that Fritz had gone through was unreal, but this was the moment he couldn't believe. This wasn't how the Nazis were supposed to act. They weren't supposed to show him mercy.

Then the local party leader said something that made it all clear. He told Fritz he thought the war would be over soon, and that the Nazis would be punished for their actions. The local party leader could help Fritz now, and Fritz could help him later. The idea was hard for Fritz to comprehend. The Nazis had all been so terrible to him, everyone from the foreman at the Ford factory to the Hitler Youth on the streets to the guards in Ellern. Why should he help any Nazi at all? But after a year of arrests, imprisonment, beatings, living underground, and being on the run, Fritz wouldn't put himself back into the hands of the Gestapo if he could help it. What was one more lie to the Nazis at this point? He agreed to support a statement about the local party leader's mercy after the war.

The war was almost over, and the even the Nazis could feel it. For Fritz, that meant he could be free. But not all the Nazis were ready to be merciful.

54 — Jean

Once a week, the prisoners at Brauweiler got a butter ration.

In early November, Fän asked Jean through the window of his cell if he'd gotten the butter.

Jean said he had.

Fän had heard that some people on the other side of the walkway hadn't gotten any.

Every day, Jean got a clean towel; every prisoner did.

He heard Barthel and Bubbes whispering that they didn't get new towels.

Barthel said his case must have been closed. They'd stopped the interrogations.

New prisoners arrived and were interrogated.

Barthel thought he was being transferred to a concentration camp. They'd heard of concentration camps, although they didn't know about the extermination of Jews, Roma, Sinti, homosexuals, Jehovah's Witnesses, and other "undesirable" people at those camps.

Gestapo Order, Brauweiler

6TH OF NOV. 1944

Subject: Execution of thirteen Germans, as perpetrators and members of the terrorist group in Cologne-Ehrenfeld.

The following specified 13 Germans are handed over for execution on November 7, 1944:

1) Hans S T E I N B R Ü C K
2) Peter H Ü P P E L E R
3) Roland Cornelius L O R E N T
4) Josef M O L L
5) Johann M Ü L L E R
6) Bartolomäus S C H I N K
7) Franz R H E I N B E R G E R
8) Wilhelm K R A T Z
9) Gustav B E R M E L
10) Johann K R A U S E N
11) Adolf S C H Ü T Z
12) Heinz K R A T I N A
13) Günther S C H W A R Z

55 — Jean

Jean looked out his window. The yard was still obscured by darkness. He could make out a group of prisoners, chained together, making their way from the building across the yard. They were loaded into a truck.

Jean knew that Barthel and Bubbes were in the group, because he got two new neighbors, but none of the prisoners in Brauweiler knew what was about to happen with those thirteen prisoners when they left that morning.

Part Six
1944–1945

"I don't believe it, it's impossible."

November 10, 1944

In front of you, the arches above the car-repair garages hold up the train tracks. To the right is the tunnel that goes under the tracks, toward the city center and the Cathedral. How has this not been bombed yet? Everything else looks like ruins. People crowd around, and behind you is Schönstein Street No. 7, the house that hid Communists, Jews, deserters. This is the heart of Ehrenfeld, and everyone in the neighborhood has been told to come down here to the train station.

The area is full of Nazis, in uniform and in plain clothes. A truck pulls up. A short man with dark, shaved hair gets out. He looks like he was once stout, but is now skinny. He's only wearing socks, no shoes. "It's Bomben-Hans," someone whispers. Twelve more follow. Their faces are sunken, and it's hard to tell how old they are, but it's a mix of young and old.

They march forward toward a wooden structure. The Gestapo erected the gallows for a hanging a couple weeks ago, and they left it up. Last time, it was forced laborers, POWs, and other non-Germans, whose execution didn't require approval from the head of the SS, Heinrich Himmler. Hangings aren't supposed to happen in public like this, but the Nazis are desperate and want to show any resistance in this neighborhood what will happen if they continue.

A younger guy with high cheekbones and a big chin walks forward, with an officer on each side of him. He spots someone in the front row, and his eyes lock in on a teenage boy. The boy looks back, but the prisoner must know that he doesn't look like himself. His head is shaved; his body is weak and thin; his cheeks aren't chubby and rounded; his skin has no glow. He doesn't say anything; he just stares. Finally, the boy in the crowd realizes he is looking at his older brother. But why doesn't the prisoner yell something at him? Why is he just staring?

Thirteen-year-old Adi Schink came down to the hanging probably because everyone was told to come and because this is a rare moment when you might actually know what happened to a loved one. Adi hadn't expected to see his brother, Barthel Schink.

The prisoners, five teenagers and eight adults, line up parallel to the gallows. The whole structure is probably only twelve feet high, and thirteen ropes with nooses hang from the top beam. Each person stands at the bottom of a wooden plank that leads up to the platform of the structure, although it isn't really a platform, just a board that is two and a half feet off the ground.

An SS officer in uniform on top of a truck reads the judgment through a loudspeaker. None of the prisoners say anything. No one yells or screams or pleads. The foreigners who had been hanged yelled anti-Nazi slogans and "Stalin lives!" before they were killed. Later, Adi and others in the neighborhood will start rumors that the Germans must have been drugged, and that was why they hadn't said anything, that's why Barthel didn't say anything to his brother.

An officer comes up and grabs Adi by the hair.

"Just look there, you little Communist pig," the man growls. "You could also be standing there."

Barthel and the others walk up the planks and stand on the board. The officers pull down the ropes over their shaved heads and skull-like faces. In a normal hanging, the force of the drop between the surface the condemned is standing on and the end of the rope breaks the person's neck, resulting in immediate paralysis and death. That drop is usually four to six feet. This drop is less than three feet, so the nooses tighten around the necks of the prisoners and they strangle to death. Instead of an instant death, strangling by hanging can take as long as twenty minutes.

Some of the nooses are also too long, especially for the taller men. The taller men's feet reach the ground and their feet start kicking as they try to regain their footing. An officer grabs one man and pulls him downward, so that his neck is pulled against the noose harder, another ties a rope around a prisoner's legs and pulls down that way.

The bodies of Barthel Schink, Franz "Bubbes" Rheinberger, Günther "Büb" Schwarz, Hans "Bomben-Hans" Steinbrück, "Black" Peter Hüppeler, Roland Lorent, Josef "Jupp" Moll, Johann "Little Hans" Müller, Wilhelm Kratz, Gustav Bermel, Johann Krausen, Adolf "Dolfes" Schütz, and Heinz Kratina are left hanging all day.

Later in the afternoon, Barthel's mother comes back to see the bodies. She doesn't recognize her son.

The bodies hang there until the evening, when they are loaded in a trash truck and taken to the Westfriedhof Cemetery and buried in unmarked graves in a special section called the Gestapo Field.

Photographs of the hanging of foreign nationals in Ehrenfeld on October 25, 1944. A little over two weeks later, the "Ehrenfeld Group," including six Edelweiss Pirates, was executed on the same gallows on November 10, 1944.

Jean found out from new prisoners what had happened in Ehrenfeld: his friends had been taken from Brauweiler and publicly hanged. Immediately after he found out, Jean thought that he was next.

Soon you'll be under the grass!

After November turned into December and he still hadn't been taken away, he started waiting for the Allied troops to show up. He hadn't heard what was going on with the war, but he knew that it had to be over soon.

On February 10, 1945, the prisoners were transferred from Brauweiler to the Siegburg prison on the east side of the Rhine. As American troops approached, the Nazis retreated.

Siegburg was better than Brauweiler in a way. Jean and Fän were together in a cell now, and at least they had real human contact again. They sang songs and played air guitar to pass the time. But the conditions were horrible, worse than Brauweiler. Everyone had typhoid fever or typhus, diseases transmitted through bedbugs, lice, and unsanitary conditions. Fän got sick, and Jean took care of him. Fän didn't think he would have lived if it hadn't been for Jean.

They knew that the Americans were coming, but they kept being transported farther and farther east. They ended up at a youth prison north of Frankfurt.

57 — Gertrud

Gertrud's mother looked out at the hills stretching before them from the farm at the base of the Alps mountain range. It was March 1945, and they had been at the farm for almost two years. Gertrud had finished her teenage years on this farm. She would turn twenty-one in a few months and it seemed likely her mother would survive her second world war. Gertrud thought her mom still looked good, given everything they had been through over the last thirteen years—her father's arrest and death, her arrest, fleeing Cologne.

"There's something over there," Gertrud's mother yelled. "What is that?"

The farmer came out, and said he would get his binoculars, which he usually used when a cow escaped.

"It's a tank." The statement made Gertrud uneasy. "Hopefully not a German one," he added.

Gertrud's mom turned to her, her eyes not glinting in the sunlight, but full of fear. "Hide in the basement, in the potato box," she said.

"I'm not getting in the potato box," Gertrud replied. "I'm not a little kid anymore."

"No, but you are a pretty young woman. And since we don't know who is coming—into the basement with you."

"Then you have to come too. You're pretty too."

Her mom looked irritated. After everything they had been through, Gertrud thought she could handle whatever was coming next. Her mom shrugged, and Gertrud stayed by her side.

The tank got closer, and they could see that four or five more were following behind. They were French tanks. They were the Allies; the Nazi line was crumbling. They were going to be free, really free.

"The Americans! The Americans are there! I see an American tank," yelled one of Jean's cellmates.

Another prisoner sat on the floor, waved his hand, and said, "I don't believe it, it's impossible."

Jean couldn't believe it either. He closed his eyes and said to himself, "I don't believe it, I don't believe it, it can't be."

But the tank was there, outside the prison wall. They all knew the difference between American and German tanks.

He didn't know what to feel. He didn't know what to think.

"What do I do now?" he asked himself.

Another prisoner explained who they were in English to an

Destruction of Cologne, 1945.

American soldier, and the door opened. They were free. Or at least, they weren't locked in anymore. They didn't really have anywhere to go.

Jean could go over to the building where Fän was, except he wasn't allowed in. Jean had ended up with the political prisoners, and Fän was with the criminal youth in the sick ward. Some Edelweiss Pirates would remain in jail long after the Americans arrived because they were called criminals rather than political prisoners.

Even when Jean had the chance to go back to Cologne in May 1945, he couldn't imagine going back without Fän. Jean went back to the prison and looked for Fän. He couldn't find him anywhere.

Finally, a man told him that Fän had gotten better with medicine from the Americans and he was working in the kitchen.

Jean found him. They laughed and talked the whole night. Then they biked back to where the transports were and took a bus back to Cologne.

59 — Fritz

Fritz took a long time to recover from the malnourishment and hard labor in the town of Pfronten with his mother, but he did recover. The Americans had finally arrived and he made his way back to Cologne. But when he got there, the city was a wasteland. Almost everything was gone, but somehow the Theilens' apartment was still standing. Fritz had a place to live.

After a few days at home, he found Hugo, with whom he'd

escaped from the camp in Ellern. Hugo was the one who told Fritz about everything that had happened in the fall, how the Gestapo had arrested so many people and brought them to Brauweiler, and how his friends Barthel Schink, Bubbes Rheinberger, and Büb Schwarz had been hanged in the street, right there in the middle of their neighborhood. Fritz's arrest was both unlucky and lucky; he had been through hell, but he was still alive.

They wanted to hang out with the Edelweiss Pirates that were coming back to the city, but the Allied troops that were occupying the city wouldn't allow it. Pro-Nazi youth groups had been committing acts of sabotage against the Allies, and so, all youth groups were banned.

The Edelweiss Pirates were seen as a criminal band by many Germans, and many of Fritz's friends didn't want to be in the group or never talked about having been members.

For many Pirates, the end of the war was the beginning of years of silence.

Part Seven

1945–2019

"We were against the Nazis. Isn't that enough?"

Cologne, Winter 2000

The year is 2000, and you are standing on the new Hohenzollern Bridge. Fifty-five years have passed since the end of World War II, and Cologne is no longer a site of destruction and devastation. The bridge from fifty-five years ago survived countless Allied bombs only to be blown up by the Nazis as the Allied troops advanced into Germany in the spring of 1945. In the years following the war, the bridge was rebuilt as a railroad and pedestrian bridge. Look to the south and you'll see a road that leads to the city of Bonn. This is the year that the seat of government has moved back to Berlin from Bonn. From 1949 to 1990, Germany was two countries: the German Democratic Republic, or East Germany, first occupied by the Soviet Union and ruled by a party that evolved from the KPD and SPD, and the Federal Republic of Germany, or West Germany, first occupied by the United States, England, and France. Konrad Adenauer, who was once mayor of Cologne and who had also been held in the Gestapo prison at Brauweiler, was the first chancellor of West Germany. In 1990, Germany was reunified, but for nine years, the seat of government remained in the west, here in the Rhine Valley.

To the east of the bridge, the Messe building, the place where Bomben-Hans and thousands of others slowly starved as prisoners and forced laborers, still stands. The exhibit halls are now some of the busiest in Europe, hosting expos and conventions for the world's biggest industries, including the largest food industry trade show in the world.

Look to the west, and you'll see that the stained-glass windows of the Cathedral have been replaced and that tourists once again flock to see the magnificent church. It took four years after the end of the war for the official Karneval celebrations to start again, but now Cologne has become known for them, and people come from all over Germany and the world to see the floats, parades, and parties. The train station was rebuilt, and this year, it will transform into a more modern station, with shops and restaurants, and only a small fraction of the architecture of the old train station will remain. The city used the opportunity of destruction to build underground garages, new hotels, and office buildings in the Innenstadt. Cologne is now a prosperous, modern European city.

Cathedral, bridge, and train station, 2017.

Mucki walked along Appellhof Place in the Innenstadt as the January cold bit at her nose and cheeks. The city had changed, and Mucki had changed too. She was now seventy-five years old, and officially Gertrud Koch. Her husband and friends still called her Mucki, though.

She stepped up to the door of the large beige building. Above the door, the glass was painted in gold with the letters EL DE. She walked inside. She was there to see an exhibit called *Against the Brown Tide: Portraits of the Men and Women of Cologne's Resistance*. The EL-DE House had transformed too. Right after the war, as one of the only buildings left standing, it had just been a city office building. Then, in 1988, it became home to the National Socialist Documentation Center, a place to research and document the Nazi era in Cologne. In 1997, a museum opened in the former Gestapo offices.

Gertrud's portrait wasn't on the wall at the *Against the Brown Tide* exhibit. She hadn't told anyone outside her friends and family that she too had resisted the Nazis. Few people wanted to know about her Edelweiss Group, the Edelweiss Pirates, the Navajos, or the other youth resistance groups. In fact, these groups had never been officially recognized as part of the resistance against the Nazis. People said they weren't really against the Nazis; they were just kids who didn't like being controlled by the Hitler Youth.

The postwar West German government had used the forced confessions taken by the Gestapo to prove that the Edelweiss Pirates had committed illegal activities—activities like stealing weapons and writing graffiti. Since 1945, many of the Germans who knew anything about the Pirates considered them little better than common criminals, and even foreign press after the war got the story about the Edelweiss Pirates wrong, claiming they were terrorizing displaced persons and refugees. In 1946, a headline in the *Washington Post* read, "British Break up German Gang of Anti-Nazi Youths," calling the Pirates "young hooligans" without higher morals. But something at this moment so many years later must have made Gertrud feel comfortable enough to tell her story. Maybe someone would now see that what she did was resistance.

She told the museum docent that she had been arrested by the Gestapo and once sat in a cell in this very building. The docent knew how significant this was and called the museum director, Dr. Werner Jung, who immediately scheduled an oral history interview with Gertrud. Someone finally wanted to hear her story.

61 — Fritz

Fritz Theilen knew exactly why people didn't want to know about his experiences as an Edelweiss Pirate. People claimed the Pirates were criminals who stole and shot people. His friends who had been Edelweiss Pirates didn't want to say they were involved in the group. Fritz believed that the Gestapo propaganda against the Pirates was stronger than the truth. And while the Gestapo had tortured and killed children, the perpetrators hadn't really been held accountable for the full impact of their actions during the war.

But Fritz Theilen remained the same person who'd defecated in a Hitler Youth leader's briefcase, defiant as ever and happy to call himself an Edelweiss Pirate. In the mid-1970s, he finally connected with Jean Jülich, who was also ready to denounce their mischaracterization.

62 — Jean

One of the things Jean had always loved the most about being an Edelweiss Pirate was singing and playing music with his friends. In the years after the war, he organized festivities for Karneval and opened a bar that became famous in Cologne's music scene. During those years, he didn't tell anyone about his life as an Edelweiss Pirate because no one seemed to care. That changed in the late 1970s, when a magazine article told the story of Barthel Schink and how, even though he was murdered by the Nazis, he was still considered a criminal.

In February 1984, Jean received a letter. Yad Vashem, Israel's official memorial to the victims and heroes of the Holocaust, wanted to honor him "for the bravery and human kindness you showed in risking your life in order to save Jews during the Holocaust." Such honorees are called "The Righteous Among the Nations." Meik Jovy was also being honored as a non-Jewish person who helped save the lives of Jewish people during the war, but he had died that January. In April, Jean flew to Israel with Barthel Schink's sister Caroline, Günther "Büb" Schwarz's brother Wolfgang, a historian named Matthias von Hellfeld, and Anneliese Knoop-Graf, a member of the White Rose resistance group from Munich. During the ceremony, they were led into the dark stone Memorial Hall of Yad Vashem. Jean couldn't understand the ceremony in Hebrew, but he

Mucki, Fritz, and Jean outside the EL-DE House, 2003.

recognized names of death camps and of his friends. He couldn't hold his tears back as he thought of his friends who had been murdered by the Nazis.

In 2004, Gertrud's interview, along with those of Jean, Fritz, Wolfgang, and others, became the basis for an exhibit at the National Socialist Documentation Center called *Von Navajos und Edelweißpiraten—Unangepasstes Jugendverhalten in Köln 1933–1945*, which translates as "Of Navajos and Edelweiss Pirates: Nonconformist Youth Behavior in Cologne from 1933 to 1945." "Nonconformist." Even here, in the place that was supposed to function as collective memory about what had happened in Cologne, they were still not recognized as a true resistance movement.

When I first started learning about these young people, the fact that they weren't seen as resisters shocked me. How could they not be considered resistance? Part of this is linguistic. "Resistance" has so many definitions. In German, the word *unangepasst*, used to describe the various Edelweiss groups, translates as "nonconformist," but the word also literally means "not" (*un*) "fitting in" (*anpassen*). Ironically, the word *unangepasst* can also mean "maladjusted" in the same pejorative sense we associate with that word in English.

One of the first researchers into the Edelweiss Pirates, Detlev Peukert, created a framework of dissident behavior in the Third Reich. He classified private criticism of a small part of the system as nonconformist behavior. He knew that all the Edelweiss Pirates weren't the same, and that some people had engaged with "open protest and political resistance," but because the group as a whole didn't subscribe "to an explicit political doctrine," they were simply putting their "youth-based subculture against the National Socialist call for integration." He argues they were maybe a little more than unangepasst, but without concrete values or a clear political stance, they're not resistance. They're basically punk kids.

In German, the word *Widerstand* means "resistance," and it has a very specific meaning. Peukert explained that Widerstand must be public or political actions, and those actions must be against a system as a whole. Scholars argue that because the Edelweiss Pirates and other related youth resistance groups in the Rhine Valley were a loose group without leadership, without a clear political goal, and without complaints about the Third Reich as a whole, they were not Widerstand.

The Edelweiss Pirates numbered in the hundreds, maybe the

thousands, and the group as a whole can't fit into Peukert's binary classification of "resistance" or "nonconformist." There were those who were nonconformist; they may have simply wanted to be left alone to sing their songs. But there were also those—like Gertrud, Jean, and Fritz—who were part of the resistance. They didn't approve of any part of the Nazi state and took conscious, public action against it, both in words and in deeds.

As nuanced as the German language is, perhaps it doesn't do justice to this youth group. When *Widerstand* is broken into *wider* and *stand*, the words mean "standing in opposition." Even when you simply dress differently, you are standing in opposition. And sometimes, that's the only form a young person's resistance can take.

The messages the Pirates managed to print on leaflets or paint on walls and trains may not have amounted to a sophisticated political ideology, but to discount the loud and clear "no" of a group of young people with everything to lose is to misunderstand both youth and resistance.

The other reason that the Edelweiss Pirates were not considered resistance is tied up with the question of who has the right to write history. When I was working on this book, I realized that, for many people in Germany and the United States, youth resistance against Nazi Germany has become synonymous with the White Rose. Led by siblings Hans and Sophie Scholl, the White Rose distributed material condemning the Nazis in 1942 and the beginning of 1943. The well-organized group was made up of university students and connected to a network of resistance groups. They were young people who had graduated from high school, then attended university, and were from the upper-middle class. The arguments in their pamphlets were based on philosophy and Christian ideas. Any condemnation of the Nazis was an incredible risk, and members of the White Rose paid the highest price for their resistance. On February 22, 1943, Hans and Sophie Scholl were executed by guillotine in Stadelheim Prison in Munich.

In middle school, I did a project on Sophie Scholl. I pictured a young woman to admire, a woman throwing down anti-Nazi flyers at the university in Munich, doing what she believed in, even if it meant dying in a fight for justice. As a twelve- or thirteen-year-old, I didn't realize how much history can be controlled. But that control is why I'd never heard of the Edelweiss Pirates, about Mucki, who took very similar actions at an age even closer to mine when I did that project.

After 1945, Germany fell victim to the Cold War. The country was split in two, and Cologne and Munich both became part of West Germany, occupied by the western Allies, whereas East Germany was occupied by the Soviet Union and ruled by the Communist Party. After the horrors of Fascism, England, France, and the United States wanted to build a German democracy in their image. They wanted political parties that were in the

Memorial in Ehrenfeld, 2017.

center-right, and Socialist and Communist ideas were to be actively opposed. In telling the story of the war that had just ended, the Allies wanted to showcase a resistance that opposed Nazism from a center-right position; this was where the White Rose fell. In short, they were the image of good Germans: their arguments were thoughtful; they held the same goals as the Western Allies; and they could be trusted. The Edelweiss Pirates were clearly leftists—Communists and Socialists—even if most of them were too young to fully understand political parties. They were working-class, and many of their parents had been Communists and Socialists and sympathetic to the Soviet Union, the new enemy of the western Allies. As the aftermath of World War II turned into the Cold War, any resistance from the left wasn't going to be publicly venerated by the West. It wasn't even going to be a part of public history.

But around Cologne, a small grassroots movement started forming in the late 1960s. It wanted to see the Edelweiss Pirates recognized as a resistance movement. A man named Walter Kuchta wanted to recognize that the Nazis had hanged resisters outside the train station in Ehrenfeld. Kuchta was one of the founders of the Union of Persecutees of the Nazi Regime in Cologne and had also been imprisoned by the Nazis. In February 1969, he stood on a corner on Schönstein Street in a concentration camp uniform with images of the hangings and a sign that read:

10TH NOVEMBER 1944
13 YOUNG PEOPLE FROM COLOGNE
WERE PUBLICLY HANGED
AT THIS EXACT SPOT BY
THE GESTAPO AND SS.
WHO RECOGNIZES THE MURDERERS
IN THE PHOTOS?
DO YOU KNOW THEIR NAMES?

Walter Kuchta in Ehrenfeld, February 1969.

On November 10, 1970—thirty-two years to the day after Kristallnacht and twenty-six years after the thirteen in the Ehrenfeld group were hanged—Kuchta placed a wreath at the site of the hanging, the beginning of the memorial to the Edelweiss Pirates. He raised money to have a plaque placed at the site in 1972, a plaque that was updated in 1986.

In the late 1970s, filmmaker Dietrich Schubert interviewed Jean and Fritz, who had never met during their time as Edelweiss Pirates, but who had since met and become friends. They were asked to talk at schools, and slowly some Germans began to know the Pirates' story. The wreath-laying ceremony that Kuchta started grew, and Jean, Fritz, and Wolfgang Schwarz went to Schönstein Street every year on November 10 to remember their friends.

In 1978, a magazine article told the story of their friend Barthel and how he had been murdered by the Nazis, but was still considered a criminal. Already in 1952, Barthel's sister Caroline had tried to prove that her brother was a political victim of the Nazis. In a discussion in 1979 commemorating the attempt on Hitler's life on July 20, 1944, Caroline said, "I want [my brother] to be vindicated and that . . . it cannot be said that Barthel is a criminal. Barthel is not a criminal, he was a child, and one shouldn't forget that." But the West German government used Barthel's forced confessions to prove he stole food and shot at men in uniform, acts that were not politically motivated, they claimed.

In 1984, the same year Jean was invited by the Israeli government to be honored by Yad Vasham, Fritz Theilen published his first memoir about his time as a Navajo and Edelweiss Pirate.

Edelweiss members, as they were called by the German government, were finally recognized as a resistance movement in Germany in 2005, and the permanent exhibit at the German Resistance Memorial Center in Berlin, opened in 2014, now has a small section on the Edelweiss Pirates and youth resistance around Cologne.

The street outside the train station was renamed Bartholomäus Schink Street, and a privately funded memorial to the Edelweiss Pirates inaugurated in 2010 recognizes not only those who were hanged, but all the young people who resisted the Nazis in Cologne.

This story focuses on what happened to Fritz, Jean, Gertrud, and the young people that they knew because they eventually told their stories in memoirs and interviews and became vocal about their experiences during the war. I couldn't even include every part of their stories in this book, let alone all of the stories of all of the Edelweiss Pirates and bündische youth—at one point the Gestapo estimated that there were thousands of dissident youth in the Rhine area—both because the book would be too long and because the narratives of their experiences were never told. There are always more stories to be told, if we take the time to listen. Let us not forget the people who fight against Fascism, then and now.

EL-DE House entrance, 2017.

A NOTE ON "THE NAVAJOS"

History is nuanced, and often both sides in a conflict will invoke the same names, people, and ideas for their own purposes. The Edelweiss Pirates belong to a large web of German youth movements, which started with the Wandervogel, or Wandering Birds, around 1900. They were essentially back-to-nature hippies before that was a concept in the United States. They wanted to enjoy nature, hike, camp, and sing songs. One splinter of these movements became the Bündische Jugend of the 1920s and early 1930s, groups of youth who were against the strict morality and self-aggrandizement of older generations. These groups inspired the Edelweiss Pirates and other groups in the Rhine Valley during the Third Reich.

One bündisch-inspired group called themselves the Navajos. This name stemmed from the back-to-nature romanticism of the post-industrialization of the late 1800s—the same movement that birthed the Wandervogel—and the work of German author Karl May. Starting in 1887, May wrote stories in a young people's magazine romanticizing the American West. The magazine serials featured a fictional Apache chief called Winnetou and his adventures serving his "blood brother," a white man called Old Shatterhand. May presented German audiences with what he claimed were real stories, even though he never traveled farther west than New York State in his lifetime. Instead, he served up simplistic stereotypes of American Indians: faithful; close to nature; and, though oppressed, still willing to fight for what they believe. His stories lumped together distinct Native cultures and contained few (if any) specific facts about actual Apache tribes or people.

One of the more common stereotypes in May's work is the idea that Native Americans exist to "serve European American cultures." Winnetou serves as sidekick of Old Shatterhand, and the heroes of the story are white with German characteristics while the Native American, African American, and Mexican characters are shown with "racial inferiority." His Native American characters are also connected to a larger myth of the "Noble Savage." This motif began appearing in American literature in the 1700s, which often portrayed American Indian characters as uncorrupted—as "innocent children of nature," a stereotypical description placed on indigenous people around the world since at least the early 1800s. These stereotypes appealed to Germans when May was writing. They saw themselves as "fellow underdogs . . . in a brotherhood with Indigenous peoples." May reflected typical German characteristics like longing for the outdoors and distant places and a sense of being oppressed in his stereotypes of the Native Americans in his stories. Outdoor romanticism was also at a high point in response to industrialization. This appropriation and distortion of the history and lives of Native Americans came to be what many Germans understood as reality.

May turned the serials into a series of novels, which soon became bestsellers. The names Winnetou and Old Shatterhand were as ubiquitous in Germany as Harry Potter and Hermione Granger are today. And just like the Harry Potter books, people could—and did—read into May's books what they wanted. For the young Germans living in the shadow of World War I, the stereotypes of the American Indians likely inspired the name of the bündische group the Navajos (although we don't know for sure). They had grown up reading Karl May's books, and in the face of oppression, they could connect with all the stereotypes that May had injected into his books. While they didn't dress up like Native Americans, even using the name "Navajo" perpetuated the stereotypes of Karl May's novels, whether the young Germans understood that or not.

When the Edelweiss Pirates wrote "Heil Navajos" graffiti or sang a song that referenced Navajos, like "Under the Mexican Sun," they were likely responding both to the earlier bündische groups and Karl May's work. Their bündische and Wandervogel predecessors were groups the Pirates could look up to: they didn't follow Nazi orders, and they didn't want to join the Hitler Youth. The Pirates may have also seen the stereotyped ideal of May's Navajo people in their actions: fighting for what they believed in and enjoying nature, friendships, and communal living.

When a story and characters are universally understood, they provide opportunities for people to find meaning that speaks to them. For example, while some want to ban the Harry Potter books because of the presence of witchcraft, other readers see the books as stories about fighting Fascism, and still other critics have pointed out undertones of white supremacy. While the Navajos and Edelweiss Pirates were likely inspired by Winnetou and the Karl May novels and used them accordingly, so was Adolf Hitler. He was a fan of the stories (like most every German), had copies of the series printed for troops at the front, and was rumored to have suggested his generals take lessons from Winnetou.

However, pointing out stereotypes and a legacy of appropriation are not simply ways of interpreting an existing text. When J. K. Rowling released "History of Magic in North America" in 2016, Native Americans saw her using the same stereotypes about their cultures that Karl May used more than one hundred years earlier. Critics rightly saw dangerous and harmful trivializations of Native traditions and beliefs. And while the Pirates and bündische youth used "Indian" stereotypes as symbols of resistance to the Nazis, that doesn't make their use of these symbols or of a name like "Navajo" less harmful.

Both the Nazis and the bündische youth groups—and many other Germans—perpetuated these stereotypes, known today as "Indianthusiasm." Germans haven't lost their obsession with Winnetou and Old Shatterhand, and since the end of World War II, various media forms have retold the stories—still completely stereotyped—including a live-action drama that is still performed during the summers in Radebeul, Germany (home of the Karl May Museum) and a 2016 feature film called *Winnetou: Die letzte Kampf* (*The Last Battle*).

Acknowledgments

This book wouldn't exist without the help of so many people. The first person I have to thank is Pete, my partner and the person who first told me about the Pirates. I'm glad I listened to you and trusted that there was a book in an anecdote about rebel kids fighting Nazis. Thank you for your relentless encouragement.

My parents provided emotional and practical support in the creation of this work. I thank you both for encouraging me to learn German in high school, sending me to Germany in college many times, and helping me with translations in the book. Mom, thanks for coming with me to Germany and tracking down leads. I couldn't have reported this book without you.

I am indebted to librarians, researchers, and archivists, past and present, who want to preserve and share the story of the Holocaust, Third Reich, and the Edelweiss Pirates. Vincent Slatt and the other librarians at the United States Holocaust Memorial Museum helped me early on with finding published materials relating to the Pirates and Cologne during the Third Reich. Astrid Sürth at the Nazi Documentation Center Cologne assisted me with going through published and unpublished materials at their library. The staff helped me in getting so many of the wonderful images of the Pirates in the book. Dr. Sabine Eibl and the staff of the Landesarchiv Nordrhein-Westfalen provided access and help with the Gestapo files. I reached out to Peter Trinogga of Cologne's chapter of the VVN/BdA to find out more about Walter Kuchta, and he was kind enough to share Kuchta's archive with me, and his own thoughts about the so-called Cologne Controversy and the legacy of the Pirates. Peter's walking tour of Ehrenfeld brought the neighborhood alive for me. At Brauweiler, Herbert Schartmann was kind enough to give me a private tour of the remaining cells in the women's prison building and tell the larger history of the Abbey. Thank you to Heinz and Hella Horeis for offering a place to stay near Ellern and being local guides when I was trying to track down Fritz's time at the camp.

Thank you to Dr. Lisa Michelle King for providing feedback on "A Note on 'the Navajos'" and offering insights about Indianthusiasm. I encourage anyone interested in the subject to read her work.

Thank you also to Richard Leo, Steven Drizin, and Saul Kassin for sharing insights and helping me better understand confessions and forced confessions, and the psychology of young people who have been imprisoned.

Thank you to Andrew Karre, for seeing my vision for this book. I knew the first time we spoke that you understood what I was trying to do, and you've made this book better than I could have imagined. I've learned so much from working with you.

Thank you to my whole team at Penguin for their tireless work behind the scenes. Julie Strauss-Gabel, Melissa Faulner, Anna Booth, Natalie Vielkind, Rosanne Lauer, Rob Farren, Kate Renner, Tessa Meischeid, Maggie Edkins, and Kristin Boyle—I'm so grateful for all you've done for my book.

I would also like to thank the mentors and faculty of the Goucher MFA program in Creative Nonfiction. Without all of you, I wouldn't know how to write a book. My writing friends Rachel Dickinson, Cate Hodorowicz (and her daughters, Ella and Quinn), Neda Semnani, Memsy Price, Stephanie Gorton-Murphy, and Jen Adler encouraged this project and helped me along the way.

Thank you to my friend Laura Paul for reading an early, early draft of my manuscript and offering feedback. Thanks to Benjamin, Matney, and Thomas for being such supportive family, and Sidney for making me smile no matter what. And thank you to countless friends and family for just being excited to read my first book.

SOURCE NOTES

PROLOGUE

"Teen-age Lads Tell of Anti-Nazi 'Pirates.'": *New York Times*, May 9, 1945, 11.

Mucki stepped out of her apartment . . . : Koch. The chapters about Gertrud are taken from her memoir unless otherwise noted.

Jean had first noticed . . . : Jülich. The chapters about Jean are taken from his memoir unless otherwise noted.

The fact that Fritz . . . : Theilen. The chapters about Fritz are taken from his memoir unless otherwise noted.

Kids weren't supposed . . . : Peukert, *Inside Nazi Germany*, 154.

They didn't have a leader . . . : *"Erlebte Geschichte,"* Jülich interview.

Ferdinand was outspoken and gregarious . . . : *"Erlebte Geschichte,"* Steingass interview.

PART ONE

For about thirty years . . . : Walker, chapter one.

The Rhine Valley is . . . : Billstein, Dings, Kugler, and Levis, 1.

In 1929, the Great Depression . . . : Kershaw, 404.

But the three other parties . . . : Hamilton, 129–155.

But even though both left-leaning parties . . . : Administration of the German Bundestag, Research Section WD 1, "The political parties in the Weimar Republic," accessed May 18, 2018, created 2006, bundestag.de/blob/189776/01b7ea57531a60126da86e2d5c5dbb78 /parties_weimar_republic-data.pdf.

In the summer of 1932 . . . : Kershaw, 368.

On the street . . . : Kershaw, 404.

And on the Cathedral . . . : Rheindorf, *Köln im Dritten Reich, Part 1.*

Students didn't talk . . . : *"Erlebte Geschichte,"* Koch interview.

"All right, go home": *"Erlebte Geschichte,"* Koch interview.

When young Jean's father . . . : Kuchta, VVN-BdA Archive, 5. (Page numbers refer to my scans of the documents since the original pages were unnumbered.)

When the officers . . . : Kuchta, VVN-BdA Archive, 5.

He had thought the Hitler Youth . . . : Heberer, 14.

They were unorganized . . . : Walker, chapter two.

"Remember what your father said?": *"Erlebte Geschichte,"* Koch interview.

These were all businesses . . . : *"Erlebte Geschichte,"* Theilen interview.

PART TWO

"Our aims: I am determined to solve the question of Danzig": "War on Poland Begun, Hitler Tells Nation," *Chicago Daily Tribune,* September 1, 1939.

In Cologne, an electricity flows . . . : Rheindorf, *Köln im Dritten Reich, Part 1.*

The Nazis wanted everyone to celebrate . . . : "War on Poland Begun, Hitler Tells Nation."

Report from the Justice Press Office of Düsseldorf, August 8, 1937: Klönne, *Jugend im Dritten Reich,* 209.

Report of the Gestapo, Düsseldorf, December 10, 1937: Heberer, 254.

Provincial Administration Letter, April 23, 1940: Daners and Wißkirchen, *Die Arbeitsanstalt Brauweiler,* 249.

"Yes, under the Mexican sun": Dittmar, 28.

"Under the Mexican Sun" was a bündische song . . . : Daners, 241.

Guidelines for the Hitler Youth Patrol Duty: Dittmar, 20.

Fritz knew these exercises . . . : *"Erlebte Geschichte,"* Theilen interview.

The Wandervogel—literally Wandering Birds—was the first bündische youth group . . . : Walker, chapter two.

By the 1920s, there were . . . : Steck, np.

The group known as *Deutsche Jungenschaft vom 1.11.1929* . . . : Klönne, *Jugend im Dritten Reich,* 199.

They made sure to ban bündische groups . . . : Steck, np.

They weren't going to let a curfew stop them . . . : Klönne, *Jugend im Dritten Reich*, 234.

To the Secret State Police [Gestapo] Office, Düsseldorf: Peukert, *Edelweisspiraten*, 116–117.

Jean couldn't believe . . . : "*Erlebte Geschichte*," Steingass interview.

The Ford factory was built . . . : Billstein, et al., 1.

Jean was in the first bunker of the house . . . : "*Erlebte Geschichte*," Jülich interview.

First, Jean heard . . . : "*Erlebte Geschichte*," Jülich interview.

Memorandum of the Reich Youth Leadership: Klönne, *Jugend im Dritten Reich*, 250.

PART THREE

In 1938, hundreds of Jews from Cologne . . . : Daners, 190.

The day after the 1,000-bomber raid . . . : "*Erlebte Geschichte*," Jülich interview.

We have to do something . . . : "*Erlebte Geschichte*," Koch interview.

He could talk to girls too . . . : "*Erlebte Geschichte*," Steingass interview.

. . . their conversations were never interrupted . . . : "*Erlebte Geschichte*," Jülich interview.

They didn't make it that far. . . . : Deutscher Kunstverlag, 118, 125.

"Forests and pines swim in the morning fog": Daners and Wißkirchen, *Die Arbeitsanstalt Brauweiler*, 241.

Just as they reached the top of a hill . . . : Peukert, *Edelweisspiraten*. Another Pirate arrested said that these were HJ-Streifendienst, or Hitler Youth Patrol Force, they came across during their hike. If that's the case, then they probably wouldn't have been arrested, just cited and fined.

"To the subjugated German youth!": Helmers and Kenkmann, 225.

Someone had brought a little keg . . . : Landesarchiv Nordrhein-Westfalen, Ger. Rep. 112 nr. 18704, 147. Mucki says in her memoir they didn't have beer; Lolli (Käthe Thelen) says they did in her interrogation statement taken at Brauweiler.

The song brought back reality . . . : Landesarchiv Nordrhein-Westfalen, Ger. Rep. 112 nr. 18704, 147.

No one resisted, and no one panicked . . . : Huiskes, 18.

The men stomped around . . . : Landesarchiv Nordrhein-Westfalen, Ger. Rep. 112 nr. 18704, 147.

That was part of the power of the Gestapo . . . : Stackhouse, 89.

The basement was dark . . . : Huiskes, 58.

"Excerpt from the Arrest Reports, December 1942": Landesarchiv Nordrhein-Westfalen, Ger. Rep. 112 Nr. 18705, 8–9.

"Excerpts from the Interrogation Report of Käthe Thelen": Landesarchiv Nordrhein-Westfalen, Ger. Rep. 112 nr. 18704, 147–148.

But the principal didn't . . . : *"Erlebte Geschichte,"* Steingass interview.

These were the types . . . : Stackhouse, 80.

Some Edelweiss Pirates in the area . . . : Kenkmann, 150.

Others stuck them . . . : *"Erlebte Geschichte,"* Schwarz interview.

In July 1943 . . . : Klönne, *Jugend im Dritten Reich,* 277.

That same year . . . : Von Hellfeld, *Edelweisspiraten in Köln,* 61. Matthias von Hellfeld writes in his history of the Pirates that the year was 1940; Jean Jülich was under the impression that it was 1939. Michel Jovy was arrested 1939 and sentenced 1940.

These two were well-known in Cologne . . . *"Erlebte Geschichte,"* Steingass interview.

Not just the physical bodies . . . : *"Erlebte Geschichte,"* Theilen interview.

PART FOUR

The Nazis increase fortifications . . . : Chambers, "Germans Fight to Save Hidden Nazi Bunkers," Reuters, September 11, 2007.

Forced laborers and concentration camp prisoners . . . : Rheindorf, *Köln im Dritten Reich, Part 1.*

"Report of the Public Prosecutor on Activities of the Edelweiss Pirates in November, 1943": Peukert, *Edelweisspiraten*, 52.

He also had to go back to work at Ford . . . : Billstein, et al., 1. The authors add, "Very few of the former forced laborers have ever received compensation in any form for their labor or their suffering." This also occurred in other factories small and large, but not sure that's relevant, given Fritz knew about the Ford experience.

It seemed like everywhere . . . : Billstein, et al., 6, 9, 181, 195.

After they'd dropped the parts in . . . : Billstein, et al., 195.

Fritz was panicked . . . : *"Erlebte Geschichte,"* Theilen interview.

Hans had to go join the military: Billstein, et al., 197.

One of the memories . . . : Seibert, 28. Today, some say that Barthel witnessed the beating, while others say that would have been impossible since the incident occurred inside the barber's home.

"Dad! Dad, help Spiro!": Von Hellfeld, *Edelweisspiraten in Köln*, 13.

"I can't help him. If I helped him, they'd smash me and kill me too.": Kühn, 84.

He had died . . . : Kühn, 81.

Just like the day had been beautiful . . . : "Bomber Command: Royal Air Force Bomber Command 60th Anniversary." The National Archives, United Kingdom. Archived July 6, 2007, accessed online. A large bombing raid occurred on the night of April 20, concentrated mostly in the western and northern parts of the city, with almost 1,000 buildings damaged, according to the RAF.

And after the assassination attempt . . . : *"Erlebte Geschichte,"* Jülich interview.

Büb and his maternal aunt . . . : Schubert, *Nachforschungen über die Edelweißpiraten*.

And when he . . . : *"Erlebte Geschichte,"* Schwarz interview.

Both Büb and Wolfgang . . . : Schubert, *Nachforschungen über die Edelweißpiraten*.

Wolfgang was more withdrawn . . . : *"Erlebte Geschichte,"* Schwarz interview.

PART FIVE

In the fall of 1944 . . . : Rusinek, "Desintegration," 283.

But the end of the war . . . : Von Hellfeld, *Edelweisspiraten in Köln*, 31.

Here and at other sites . . . : Rusinek, "Desintegration," 274.

Beneath the rubble . . . : Rüther, *Köln im Zweiten Weltkrieg*, 425.

Food supplies . . . : Rüther, "Senkrecht stehen bleiben," 96.

Then they saw some younger kids . . . : *"Erlebte Geschichte,"* Steingass interview.

Jean and Fän learned . . . : *"Erlebte Geschichte,"* Jülich interview.

Hans "Bomben-Hans" Steinbrück . . . : *"Erlebte Geschichte,"* Schwarz and Steingass interviews.

Fourteen days later . . . : Landesarchiv Nordrhein-Westfalen, Ger. Rep. 248 Nr. 64II, 323–340.

In October 1942, he was transferred . . . : International Tracing Service records, accessed at the US Holocaust Memorial Museum.

His head was shaved . . . : Fings, 77.

The prisoners would switch . . . : Fings, 110.

In any case, Hans Steinbrück . . . : Landesarchiv Nordrhein-Westfalen, Ger. Rep. 248 Nr. 64II, 323.

"I've defused nine hundred and ninety-nine bombs, but it's the thousandth one that I'm scared of": Schubert, *Nachforschungen über die Edelweißpiraten.*

Bomben-Hans also claimed . . . : Landesarchiv Nordrhein-Westfalen, Ger. Rep. 248 Nr. 64II, 323–340.

He never told anyone how . . . : Landesarchiv Nordrhein-Westfalen, Ger. Rep. 248 Nr. 64II, 323–340. Hans Steinbrück ITS records.

Gustel had been arrested . . . : Schwarz, *"Erlebte Geschichte."*

Wolfgang said that Hans . . . : Schwarz, *"Erlebte Geschichte."*

There was Bomben-Hans, Büb, and Wolfgang, . . ." : Seibert, 18–19.

Like the Schwarzes . . . : Schubert, *Nachforschungen über die Edelweißpiraten.*

Shortly before he met Jean and Fän . . . : *"Erlebte Geschichte,"* Jülich interview.

Barthel and the other Ehrenfeld Pirates . . . : *"Erlebte Geschichte,"* Schwarz.

When Fän's grandma . . . : *"Erlebte Geschichte,"* Jülich interview.

The only way to save themselves . . . : Kuchta, VVN-BdA Archive, statement by Jean Jülich.

Fän showed the officer . . . : *"Erlebte Geschichte,"* Jülich interview.

"Memorandum Regarding Shooting in Ehrenfeld": Landesarchiv Nordrhein-Westfalen, Ger. Rep. 248 nr. 63, 126.

"Report Regarding Schönstein Street No. 7": Landesarchiv Nordrhein-Westfalen, RW0034 00008, 13.

"Memorandum Regarding Involvement of Schink and Reinberger in Shooting": Landesarchiv Nordrhein-Westfalen, Ger. Rep. 248 nr. 63, 139.

"Statement Regarding Explosives Theft at Fort X": Landesarchiv Nordrhein-Westfalen, Ger. Rep. 248 Nr. 64 I, 205–206.

"Memorandum Regarding Arrests in Blücher Park": Landesarchiv Nordrhein-Westfalen, Ger. Rep. 248 Nr. 64 I, 221.

"Memorandum Regarding Weapons Cache at Lidosee": Landesarchiv Nordrhein-Westfalen, Ger. Rep. 248 Nr. 64 I, 228.

After his arrest in September 1944 . . . : Diether, 55.

Fritz had thought . . . : Diether, 56.

The guards clearly weren't interested . . . : *"Erlebte Geschichte,"* Theilen interview.

The most ludicrous punishment . . . : Diether, 59.

Then they ripped them off . . . : Landesarchiv Nordrhein-Westfalen, Ger. Rep. 231 Nr. 289.

Barthel was forced to give details . . . : Landesarchiv Nordrhein-Westfalen, Ger. Rep. 248 Nr. 64 I, 433.

"Report on the Cologne-Ehrenfeld Terror Group": Landesarchiv Nordrhein-Westfalen, RW0034 00008, 69.

Hans Balzer, the Pirate from Ehrenfeld they knew as Lang . . . : Goeb, *Die Verlorene Ehre des Bartholomäus Schink*, 35; Daners and Wißkirchen, *Was in Brauweiler geschah*, 106.

Excerpts from the Statement of Ferdinand Steingass . . . : Landesarchiv Nordrhein-Westfalen, Ger. Rep. 248 Nr. 64II, 502–502v.

October 31, 1944: Landesarchiv Nordrhein-Westfalen, Ger. Rep. 248 Nr. 64II, 514–514v.

Jean sat down on the other side . . . : *"Erlebte Geschichte,"* Jülich interview.

He knew to deny as much as possible . . . : Landesarchiv Nordrhein-Westfalen, Ger. Rep. 248 Nr. 64II, 527.

Then Jean admitted . . . : Landesarchiv Nordrhein-Westfalen, Ger. Rep. 248 Nr. 64II, 527v.

They had to stand with their noses . . . : *"Erlebte Geschichte,"* Steingass interview.

The Gestapo men seemed . . . : *"Erlebte Geschichte,"* Jülich interview.

Fän came out . . . : Landesarchiv Nordrhein-Westfalen, Ger. Rep. 248 Nr. 64 I, 269.

He'd already escaped being a forced laborer . . . : Von Hellfeld, *Edelweisspiraten in Köln*, 25.

Else Salm slipped out the window . . . : Seibert, 423–424.

Barthel thought he was being transferred . . . : *"Erlebte Geschichte,"* Jülich interview.

Execution of thirteen Germans . . . : Landesarchiv Nordrhein-Westfalen, Ger. Rep. 248 Nr. 65I, 697.

PART SIX

"It's Bomben-Hans": Goeb, *Die Verlorene Ehre des Bartholomäus Schink*, 49.

"Just look there, you little Communist pig": Kühn, 86.

Some of the nooses are also too long . . . : Schubert, *Widerstand und Verfolgung in Köln 1933–1945*.

An officer comes up and grabs . . . : Daners and Wißkirchen, *Die*

Arbeitsanstalt Brauweiler, 319.

. . . another ties a rope . . . : Schubert, *Widerstand und Verfolgung in Köln 1933–1945.*

Later in the afternoon . . . : Goeb, *Die Verlorene Ehre des Bartholomäus Schink,* 49.

Fän didn't think he would have lived if it hadn't been for Jean . . . : *"Erlebte Geschichte,"* Steingass interview.

"I don't believe it, I don't believe it, it can't be": *"Erlebte Geschichte,"* Jülich interview.

PART SEVEN

In 1946, a headline in the *Washington Post* read . . . "British Break up German Gang of Anti-Nazi Youths": *Washington Post,* April 14, 1946, M2.

One of the first researchers into the Edelweiss Pirates . . . : Peukert, *Inside Nazi Germany,* 164–165.

"I want [my brother] to be vindicated and that . . . it cannot be said that Barthel is a criminal. Barthel is not a criminal, he was a child, and one shouldn't forget that": Kuchta, VVN-Bda Archive, 103.

A NOTE ON "THE NAVAJOS"

"serve European American cultures . . . ": King, 28.

Winnetou serves as sidekick . . . : Von Feilitzsch, 180.

"fellow underdogs . . . in a brotherhood with Indigenous peoples": King, 30.

May reflected typical German . . . : Von Feilitzsch, 173.

while some want to ban the Harry Potter . . . : Brinks, "Cloaking White Supremacy."

BIBLIOGRAPHY

ARTICLES, BOOKS, AND FILM

Appleby, Sara C., Lisa E. Hasel and Saul M. Kassin. "Police-induced Confessions: An Empirical Analysis of Their Content and Impact." *Psychology, Crime & Law* 19, no. 2 (February 2013): 111–128.

Baird, Jay W. "From Berlin to Neubabelsberg: Nazi Film Propaganda and Hitler Youth Quex." *Journal of Contemporary History* 18, no. 3, Historians and Movies: The State of the Art: Part 1 (July 1983): 495–515.

Bettelheim, Bruno. "The Problem of Generations." *Daedalus* 91, no. 1, Youth: Change and Challenge (Winter 1962): 68–96.

Biddiscombe, Perry. "The Enemy of our Enemy: A View of the Edelweiss Pirates from the British and American Archives." *Journal of Contemporary History* 30, no. 1 (January 1995): 37–63.

Billstein, Reinhold, Karola Dings, Anita Kugler, and Nicholas Levis. *Working for the Enemy: Ford, General Motors and Forced Labor in Germany during the Second World War.* New York: Berghahn Books, 2004.

Bönisch, Georg. "Widerstand aus der Gosse." *Der Spiegel.* November 7, 2005 (No. 45).

Breivogel, Wilfried, ed. *Piraten, Swings, und Junge Garde: Jugendwiderstand im Nationalsozialismus.* Bonn: Dietz, 1991.

Brinks, Melissa. "Cloaking White Supremacy: Harry Potter's Legacy of Blood Purity," *Bitch,* November 6, 2017: bitchmedia.org/article /cloaking-white-supremacy/harry-potters-legacy-blood-purity.

Brodsky, Patricia P. "The Hidden War: Working Class Resistance During the Third Reich and the Postwar Suppression of Its History." *Nature, Society, and Thought* 11, no. 2 (1998): 170–185.

Brooklyn Daily Eagle. "Uncle Ray: White Flower Emblem of 'Edelweiss Pirates.'" April 6, 1945, 8.

Buscher, Paulus. *Cliquen und Banden von Widerstandsschmarotzern.* Burg Waldeck: Dokumentation, 1987.

Chambers, Madeline. "Germans Fight to Save Hidden Nazi Bunkers." Reuters. September 11, 2007. Accessed online at reuters.com/article /us-germany-bunkers/germans-fight-to-save-hidden-nazi-bunkers -idUSL2992082320070912.

Chicago Daily Tribune. "War on Poland Begun, Hitler Tells Nation." September 1, 1939, 1.

Corbach, Dieter. *Departure: 6.00 a.m. Messe Köln-Deutz: Deportations 1938–1945.* Cologne: Scriba, 1999.

Daners, Hermann. *'Ab nach Brauweiler . . . !' Nutzung der Abtei Brauweiler als Arbeitsanstalt, Gestapogefängnis, Landeskrankenhaus . . .* Pullheim: Verein für Geschichte und Heimatkunde, 1996.

Daners, Hermann and Josef Wißkirchen. *Die Arbeitsanstalt Brauweiler bei Köln in nationalsozialistischer Zeit.* Essen: Klartext, 2013.

Daners, Hermann and Josef Wißkirchen. *Was in Brauweiler geschah: Die NS-Zeit und ihre Folgen in der Rheinischen Provinzial-Arbeitsanstalt: Dokumentation.* Vienna: Verein für Geschichte, 2006.

Deutscher Kunstverlag. *Schloss Drachenburg: Historistische Burgenromantik am Rhein.* Berlin: Deutscher Kunstverlag, 2010.

Diether, Dieter. "Das 'Wehrertüchtigungs-Bewährungslager' in Ellern." *Rhein-Hunsrück-Kalender,* 1994, 55–60.

Dittmar, Simone. *'Wir wollen frei von Hitler sein:' Jugendwiderstand im Dritten Reich am Beispiel von der Kölner Edelweißpiraten.* Frankfurt am Main: Peter Lang, 2010.

Evans, Richard J. *The Third Reich in Power.* New York: Penguin, 2006.

Felinska, Kamila and Projektgruppe "Messelager" et al. *Zwangsarbeit bei Ford.* Köln: Betrieb Rode-Stankowski, 1996.

Fings, Karola. *Messelager Köln: Ein KZ-Außenlager im Zentrum der Stadt.* Köln: Emons, 1996.

Gedenkstätte Buchenwald. *Buchenwald Concentration Camp: 1937–1945, A guide to the Permanent Historical Collection.* Göttingen: Wallstein, 2004.

Goeb, Alexander. *Die Verlorene Ehre des Bartholomäus Schink: Jugendwiderstand im NS-Staat und der Umgang mit den Verfolgten von 1945 bis heute: Die Kölner Edelweisspiraten.* Frankfurt am Main: Brandes & Apfel, 2016.

Goeb, Alexander. "Keine Ehrung für die Ermordeten: Fünf 'Edelweißpiraten' im Kölner Rathaus ausgezeichnet—Interviews." *Neue Rheinische Zeitung.* April 20, 2011, http://www.nrhz.de/flyer /beitrag.php?id=16407.

Hamilton, Richard F. *Who Voted for Hitler?* New Jersey: Princeton, 1982.

Heberer, Patricia. *Children During the Holocaust.* Lanham: AltaMira, 2015.

Helmers, Gerrit and Alfons Kenkmann. *'Wenn die Messer blitzen und die Nazis flitzen...": Die Widerstand von Arbeiterjugendcliquen und -banden in der Weimarer Republik und im 'Dritten Reich.'* Lippstadt: Leimeier, 1984.

Huiskes, Manfred. *Die Wandinschriften des Kölner Gestapogefängnisses im El-De-Haus 1943–1945.* Köln: Böhlau, 1983.

Jahnke, Karl Heinz. *Jugend unter der NS-Diktatur 1933–1945: Eine Dokumentation.* Rostock: Ingo Koch, 2003.

Johnson, Eric A. and Karl-Heinz Reuband. *What We Knew: Terror, Mass Murder, and Everyday Life in Nazi Germany, an Oral History.* Cambridge: Basic Books, 2005.

Jovy, Michael. *Jugendbewegung und Nationalsozialismus: Zusammenhänge und Gegensätze Versuch einer Klärung.* Lit: Munster, 1984.

Jülich, Jean. *Kohldampf, Knast un Kamelle: Ein Edelweißpirate erzählt sein Leben.* Cologne: Kiepenheuer & Witsch, 2003.

Kassin, Saul M. "Why Confessions Trump Innocence." *American Psychologist* 67, no. 6, (2012): 431–445, https://doi.org/10.1037 /a0028212.

Kenkmann, Alfons. "Navajos, Kittelbach und Edelweißpiraten: Jugendliche Dissidenten im 'Dritten Reich.'" In *Piraten, Swings, und Junge Garde: Jugendwiderstand im Nationalsozialismus*, edited by Wilfried Breyvogel. Bonn: Dietz, 1991.

Kershaw, Ian. *Hitler: 1889–1936 Hubris.* New York: W.W. Norton, 2000.

King, Lisa Michelle. "Revisiting Winnetou: The Karl May Museum, Cultural Appropriation, and Indigenous Self-Representation," *Studies in American Indian Literatures* 28, no. 2 (Summer 2016): 25–55.

Klönne, Arno. *Jugend im Dritten Reich: die Hitler-Jugend und ihre Gegner.* Köln: Papyrossa, 2014.

Klönne, Arno. *Jugendliche Opposition im 'Dritten Reich.'* Thüringen: Erfurt Landeszentrale für politische Bildung, 2016.

Koch, Gertrud. *Edelweiss: Meine Jugend als Widerstandskämpferin.* Hamburg: Rowohlt Tacschenbuch Verlag, 2006.

Kühn, Heinz. *Es Gab Nicht Nur den 20. Juli ... Dokumente aus einer Sendereihe u.a. Heinz Kühn zum Widerstand im Dritten Reich.* Wuppertal: Jugenddeinst-Verlang, 1980.

Lange, Sascha. *Meuten, Swings und Edelweißpiraten: Jugendkultur und Opposition im Nationalsozialismus.* Mainz: Ventil, 2015.

Leo, Richard A., Peter J. Neufeld, Steven A. Drizin, and Andrew E. Taslitz. "Promoting Accuracy in the Use of Confession Evidence: an Argument for Pretrial Reliability Assessments to Prevent Wrongful Convictions." *Temple Law Review* 85, no. 4 (Summer 2013): 759–836.

Leo, Richard A., Steven A. Drizin, Peter J. Neufeld, Bradley R. Hall, and Amy Vatner. "Bringing Reliability Back in: False Confessions and Legal Safeguards in the Twenty-First Century." *Wisconsin Law Review,* 2006: 479–539.

Lukaßen, Dirk. *'Menschenschinder vor dem Richter:' Kölner Gestapo und Nachkriegsjustiz: Der 'Hofgen-Prozess' vor dem Kölner Schwurgericht im Jahr 1949 und seine Rezeption in den lokalen Tageszeitungen.* Siegburg: Rheinlandia, 2006.

McDonough, Frank. *Opposition and Resistance in Nazi Germany.* Cambridge: Cambridge University Press, 2001.

Neugebauer, Manuela. *Der Weg in das Jugenschutzlager Moringen: eine entwicklungspolitische Analyse nationalsozialistischer Jugendpolitik.* Mönchengladbach: Forum-Verlag Godesberg, 1997.

Neumann, Andreas. *Gegen den braunen Storm: Kölner WiderstandskämpferInnen heute in Portraits der Abeiterfotographie Köln: Ausstellung von NS-Dokumentationszentrum und Arbeiterfotographie Köln in der Alten Wache des Kölnischen Stadtmuseums, Zeughausstrasse 1-3, 14. März bis 12. Mai 1991.* Köln: NS-Dokumentationszentrum der Stadt Köln, 1991.

Neunzig, Anne. *Staatsjugenorganisationen - ein Traum der Herrschenden: Hitlerjugend/Bund Deutscher Mädchen und Freie Deutsche Jugend im Vergleich.* Leipzig: Engelsdörfer, 2014.

New York Times. "Teen-age Lads Tell of Anti-Nazi 'Pirates.'" May 9, 1945, 11.

Peukert, Detlev. *Edelweisspiraten: Protestbewegungen jugendlicher Arbeiter im Dritten Reich: eine Dokumentation.* Cologne: Bund-Verlag, 1980.

Peukert, Detlev. *Inside Nazi Germany: Conformity, Opposition and Racism in Everyday Life.* Translated by Richard Deveson. New Haven: Yale University, 1987.

Rheindorf, Hermann, dir. *Köln im Dritten Reich, Part 1: Köln 1930–1933 Der Weg in die NS-Diktatur.* April 2, 2015, Cologne: KölnProgramm, accessed online.

Rusinek, Bernd A. "Desintegration und gesteigerter Zwang. Die Chaotisierung der Lebensverhältnisse in den Großstädten 1944/45 und der Mythos der Ehrenfelder Gruppe." In *Piraten, Swings, und Junge Garde: Jugendwiderstand im Nationalsozialismus,* edited by Wilfried Breyvogel. Bonn: Dietz, 1991.

Rusinek, Bernd A. *Gesellschaft in der Katastrophe: Terror, Illegalität, Widerstand—Köln 1944/45.* Essen: Klartext-Verlag, 1989.

Rüther, Martin. *Köln im Zweiten Weltkrieg: Alltag und Erfahrungen zwischen 1939 und 1945.* Cologne: Emons, 2005.

Rüther, Martin. *"Senkrecht stehen bleiben:" Wolfgang Ritzer und die Edelweißpiraten. Unangepasstes Jugendverhalten im Nationalsozialismus und dessen späte Verarbeitung.* Cologne: Emons, 2015.

Schubert, Dietrich, dir. *Nachforschungen über die Edelweißpiraten.* 1980; SchubertFilm. DVD. http://www.schubertfilm.de/dvds /edelweisspiraten/.

Schubert, Dietrich, dir. *Widerstand und Verfolgung in Koln 1933–1945.* 1976; West Germany: SchubertFilm. DVD. http://www.schubertfilm .de/dvds/widerstand/.

Seibert, Winfried. *Die Kölner Kontroverse: Legenden und Fakten um die NS-Verbrechen in Köln-Ehrenfeld.* Essen: Klartext, 2014.

Stackhouse, J. Ryan. "Gestapo Interrogations." In *Interrogation in War and Conflict: a comparative and interdisciplinary analysis,* edited by

Christopher Andrew and Simona Tobia. New York: Routledge, 2014, 75–92.

Steck, Carla. "Edelweißpiraten—Widerstandskämpfer oder Kriminelle?" München: GRIN Verlag, 2000. https://www.grin.com/document /101974.

Strauch, Dietmar. *Ihr Mut war grenzenlos: Widerstand im Dritten Reich.* Weinheim Basel: Belty / Gelberg, 2006.

Theilen, Fritz. *Edelweißpiraten.* Hermann-Josef Emons Verlag: Köln, 2003.

Von Feilitzsch, Heribert. "Karl May: The 'Wild West' as seen in Germany," *Journal of Popular Culture* 27, no. 3 (Winter 1993): 173–190.

Von Hellfeld, Matthias. *Edelweisspiraten in Köln: Jugendrebellion gegen das 3. Reich.* Köln: Pahl-Rugenstein Verlag, 1981.

Wachsmann, Nikolaus. *KL: A History of the Nazi Concentration Camps.* Farrar, Straus and Giroux: New York, 2015.

Walker, Lawrence D. *Hitler Youth and Catholic Youth, 1933-1936: A study in Totalitarian Conquest.* Washington: The Catholic University of America Press, 1970.

Washington Post. "British Break up German Gang of Anti-Nazi Youths." April 14, 1946, M2.

UNPUBLISHED MATERIALS AND ARCHIVES:

"Erlebte Geschichte," video archive of interviews with Fredericke Greven, Jean Jülich, Gertrud Koch, Fritz Prediger, Wolfgang Schwarz, Ferdinand Steingass, and Fritz Theilen. Nazi Documentation Center Cologne. http://www.eg.nsdok.de/.

Hans Steinbrück, Buchenwald, 1.1.5/01010503 oS/ITS Digital Archive, Bad Arolsen.

International Tracing Service Archives, Collection: Sub-collection 1.1.5: Buchenwald Concentration Camp, ITS Digital Archive, Bad Arolsen; Sub-collection 1.2.2: Prisons (accessed at the United States Holocaust Memorial Museum); Sub-collection 1.2.3: Gestapo (accessed at the United States Holocaust Memorial Museum).

Kuchta, Walter. Personal archive of the former president of the Vereinigung der Verfolgten des Naziregimes—Bund der

Antifaschistinnen und Antifaschisten, Cologne. Now belongs to the VVN-BdA.

Landesarchiv Nordrhein-Westfalen, Collections: RW0034 00008, RW0034 00010, RW0034 00016, RW0034 00021, RW0034 00024, Ger. Rep. 248 nr. 54, Ger. Rep. 248 nr. 65II, Ger. Rep. 248 nr. 63, Ger. Rep. 112 nr. 18704, Ger. Rep. 231 Nr. 289, Ger. Rep. 248 Nr. 64 I, Ger. Rep. 248 Nr. 64II.

Von Hellfeld, Matthias. *Edelweisspiraten sind Treu*. Schauspiel Köln (Hrsg.). Self-published, 1980.

PHOTO CREDITS

p. 6: Retrieved from the Library of Congress Prints and Photographs Division

pp. 22, 25, 34, 41, 53, 55, 56, 62, 64, 71, 73, 74, 98, 99, 102, 105, 143, 176, 183, 186, 214: © NS-Documentation Center of the City of Cologne

pp. 39, 99, 115, 147, 213, 257, 265, 268: © K. R. Gaddy

pp. 50, 93, 95, 110, 139: © Landesarchivs Nordrhein-Westfalen (LAV NRW)

pp. 129, 225: © United States Holocaust Memorial Museum, courtesy of National Archives and Records Administration, College Park

p. 219: © United States Holocaust Memorial Museum, courtesy of Solomon Bogard

pp. 247, 266: © VVN-BdA Archive, from prints at the (LAV NRW)

p. 250: © National Archives photo no. 111-SC-206174

p. 261: © ZIK Images, a divison of XTRASYSTEM GmbH

INDEX

Page numbers in italics indicate photos.

firefighting brigade, 89–90
flyer distribution, 127, 132–34, 138–40
Hitler Youth experiences, 35–37, 60–62, 77–78, 151
honesty with the police in return for safety, 237–38
interrogation by the Gestapo, 144–49, 170–72, 187–88
involvement with the Edelweiss Pirates, 10–11, 82, 155, 167–69, 184–88, 259–60
military training, 164–65
sabotage of Nazi equipment, 162–63, 165–66
Thelen, Käthe ("Lolli"), 103, 105–08, 124–25
Theresienstadt camp-ghetto, 86
Treaty of Versailles, 14–15, 47

U
"Under the Mexican Sun" (song), 52–53
Urbat, Paul, 199

W
Waltraud (Gertrud Kühlem's friend), 29, 32–33
Wandervogel ("Wandering Birds"), 14, 35–36, 62, *62*, 271
weapons used by the Edelweiss Pirates, 179–80, 181, 195–96, 206, 219–20
"We March Along the Rhine and Ruhr" (song), 112
Westdeutscher Beobachter (Nazi newspaper), 24
the White Rose (Die Weisse Rose), 263–64, 265
Winnetou (fictional Apache chief), 271–74
World War I
economic instability following, 15, 17

political instability following, 15–17
World War II
German losses, 132, 159
liberation by France, 249
liberation by the Allies, 249–52
Normandy invasion, 180, 182, 192
public opinion about the Nazi Party towards the end of the war, 238

Y
Yad Vashem's honoring of those who helped save Jews during WWII, 260–61
youth groups. *See also* Hitler Youth
Bündische Jugend, 14
League of German Girls (LGG), 35, 54, 58–59
Wandervogel ("Wandering Birds"), 14, 35–36, 62, *62*, 271
Youth Prison Friedersdorf, 50